# THE LIFE OF CHRIST
# IN STEREO

# THE LIFE OF CHRIST IN STEREO

## THE FOUR GOSPELS COMBINED AS ONE

BY JOHNSTON M. CHENEY

EDITED BY STANLEY A. ELLISEN, Th.D.
*Chairman of the Division of Biblical Studies*
*Western Conservative Baptist Seminary*

FOREWORD BY EARL D. RADMACHER, M.A., Th.D.
*President and Professor of Systematic Theology*
*Western Conservative Baptist Seminary*

WESTERN BAPTIST SEMINARY PRESS
Portland, Oregon

Library of Congress Catalog Card Number:    No. 74-84672

First Edition, 1969
Second Edition, 1971
Third Printing, 1973

*Printed in the United States of America*

# FOREWORD

The earthly life of Jesus Christ stands unique in human history as the pattern life for all believers. The Apostle Peter states: "For even hereunto were ye called, because Christ also suffered for us, leaving us an example that ye should follow his steps" (I Peter 2:21). The Apostle John, emphasizing the same point, says: "He that saith he abideth in him ought himself also so to walk, even as he walked" (I John 2:6). In like manner, the writer of Hebrews exhorts us to look away unto Jesus "the author and finisher of our faith" (Hebrews 12:2).

Why is it that the Epistles time and again direct our attention back to the Gospels? The answer is simple, but tremendously important. They alone contain the account of the only perfect life ever lived. People need a pattern, especially in the maturing years. A pattern makes abstract thought concrete. The pattern life of Christ was meant to be a guide for all believers in Christ to follow closely; for, you see, as we spend time beholding the glory of the Lord, we "are changed into the same image from glory to glory, even as by the Spirit of the Lord" (II Corinthians 3:18). As we concentrate on the Person of Christ, we find ourselves being metamorphosed, transfigured, changed into the likeness of Christ. Just as the crawling worm is metamorphosed into a beautiful swallow-tail butterfly, so the Holy Spirit works on us by means of the life of Christ "until Christ be formed in you" (Gal. 3:19).

It is distressing to me, therefore, to find so little attention given to an intensive study of the life of Christ. An outstanding seminary professor confessed in class one day, "When I had finished seminary, I read through the Gospels and was embarrassed. I could not put them together. I found a lot in the Epistles to preach, and so I preached there. It was very embarrassing one day when one of my deacons came to me and asked why—if there was any special reason—I had very seldom preached from the Gospels. Frankly, I had no answer except that I just didn't know enough about the Gospels to preach on them. I couldn't fit the Gospels into one whole system. But, the Gospels have now become one of the major emphases in my teaching."

As I move around among the churches, I find a great emphasis upon the death of Christ, but very little on the life of Christ. I also find much emphasis on the past tense of salvation—salvation from the *penalty* of sin—but little emphasis on the present tense of salvation—daily salvation from the *power* of sin. I believe there is a significant connection in these observations. The *death* of Christ relates primarily to the penalty of sin, but it is the *life* of Christ that is basic to daily salvation from the power of sin—both the efficacy of His resurrection life and the unique pattern of His incarnate life so clearly taught in such verses as I Peter 2:21, I John 2:6, Hebrews 12:2, II Corinthians 3:18, and Philippians 2:5. The death of Christ is primarily a *birth* message, whereas the life of Christ is a *growth* message. Today's churches are witnessing some new births, but very little genuine growth, thus, evangelization apart from disciplization. There is a great need for messages geared to maturation. Lambs need to become sheep and, thus, capable of reproduction of more lambs. There is no better way to move into maturity in Christ than to give careful study to the life of Christ.

I believe that Johnston Cheney has, under God, brought to the fore what may prove to be one of the most significant tools of the century for bringing about a renewed emphasis on the life of Christ. This unique compilation of the Gospels was not merely an exercise in mental gymnastics for him; it was rather, the blending of mind and heart in a serious attempt to find a reconciliation of the apparent discrepancies in Scripture which had caused him, in college days, to surrender his faith in the supernatural authority of the Scriptures.

After working intensively on this compilation of the life of Christ for more than twenty years, almost memorizing the Gospels in the original language, Johnston Cheney went to see his Saviour "face to face" within a few days after completing his work.

Just before the Lord received him home, he wrote the following testimony:

As a boy, I expected to become a minister like my Dad. _____College had a pre-ministerial course in which I specialized in English, the humanities, public speaking and Greek, as well as three years of Bible. During my time in college, I lost my faith in the supernatural authority of the Scriptures, and abandoned preparation for the ministry, after which the first World War took me.

After the war, I got established in my faith again under the ministry of Dr. W. B. Hinson and became a deacon in the East Side Baptist Church of Portland, Oregon. I took fresh interest in the Scriptures because of this renewed faith, did some teaching of adult Bible classes through the years, memorized some ninety favorite chapters, joined the Gideons and became their local president, and found places of other usefulness in Melrose Baptist Church of Oakland, California. All the time I had a feeling that somehow I was to prepare a book some day based on the Scriptures and especially to prove their real character.

It took a serious bout with tuberculosis to bring this about. The TB was far advanced, complicated by bronchial TB as well as pulmonary. I decided that, as a job I could do in bed, I would make a scrapbook of the Scriptures. It was in the course of this operation that I discovered by pure accident, humanly speaking, that the three accounts of Jesus' baptism, for example, could be made into one account for my scrapbook purposes and without losing anything.

This was found to apply to every part of the Story, but remained only a sick-bed hobby until the discovery of the four-year length of Jesus' ministry and how this removed insuperable difficulties, and then how the four accounts of Peter's denials form one to demonstrate that one Author had to plan the Gospels. From that time until now, it has been a matter of ever-new discoveries, which though made by a layman, seem to prove a challenge to theologians.

The statement that this work proved "a challenge to theologians" found reality with me three years ago when I first met "Jack" Cheney. I shall never forget how impressed I was by this man's keen ability in the Greek of the Gospels, how challenged I was by the potential of this compilation, and how thrilled I was to become aware of the many solutions it offered to problems in Gospel studies. From that day to this, the challenge and thrill have continued to increase.

Space does not allow us to tell of all the wonderful provisions God has made for this work, in both its production and its promotion. One such provision was that of a deeply interested specialist in the life of Christ, Dr. Stanley A. Ellisen, who was equally challenged by the work and has laboured side by side with Mr. Cheney for the past three years. His editorial work has been an invaluable asset to the work because of some ten years of specializing in the area in classroom presentation, study in the land of the Saviour's sojourn, and an unpublished interpretive work on the life of Christ.

A final provision has been the generous contributions of Ralph G. Cheney of Seattle, Washington, brother of the author, and of W. H. Bueermann, M.D., Portland, Oregon. These provisions are gratefully acknowledged, for without them this work could not have become a reality.

I sincerely trust that the results of Johnston Cheney's labors will be as thrilling to those who read them as they have been to Dr. Ellisen and me, who have worked so closely with him in the years of preparation of the manuscript. The more we pore over this thrilling harmony of the Gospels, the more we are impressed with the most exciting life that was ever lived. What amazing potential is to be found here for the metamorphosis of II Corinthians 3:18!

Earl D. Radmacher

Portland, Oregon

# PREFACE

One of the purposes of this book is to display the fact that the four Gospels agree together in all their details and reveal the guiding hand of an unseen Author. In many circles today, scholarly and otherwise, it is commonly held that, "the life of Jesus cannot be reconstructed in biographical form; . . . the comforting figure of the Sunday School color cards is gone." These folk contend that the four Gospels can no longer be regarded as history because, "In detail and many important points, the Gospels do not agree." On the contrary, this minute combination displays the fact that they agree so completely and minutely that they fit together into a single, coherent story, without the addition or omission of a single detail.

Combining the Gospels is certainly not new, Tatian's *Diatessaron* in the second century being one of the first such attempts. But this combination is an attempt to interweave the four Gospels in such a way as to incorporate all the details into a single chronological story, without repeating any parts. In so doing, the Gospels fold together like the pieces of a stupendous jigsaw puzzle. The combination effect is both stereophonic and stereoscopic.

In pursuing this work, it was early discovered that such a combination, to be successful, must follow the Greek text very closely, rendering it in the best English idiom. While over twenty translations and versions were constantly consulted, we have sought to preserve the beauty of the "King James" version, testing each rendering by the original. The process has involved much labor, prayer, years of research, consultation, and presenting of papers before scholarly societies. But the effort has been intensely rewarding and gratifying because of the ever-unfolding consistency of the four Gospels and the ever-heightening evidence of a divine Hand Who guided the four Evangelists.

As the compiler of this work, I would eagerly commend its reading to all men, for it is not my work, but the matchless composition of a divine Author concerning the most peerless and enthralling Personality of the ages. The reader is urged to observe how smoothly the story unfolds and how seeming discrepancies or inconsistencies simply melt away. But beyond this apologetic evidence, the reader is invited to become enraptured in the Story itself as it transports him into the full-dimensioned setting of the life and ministry of our Lord. To follow His footsteps and feel His heart-throb as He walked with men and blessed the race by His brief redemptive visit is an unspeakable joy and adventure. If this work serves to bring others into the fellowship and joy of His divine Life and presence, the labors will be eternally rewarding for all.

Johnston M. Cheney

Oakland, California

\* \* \* \* \*

## EXPLANATION OF SYMBOLS

Raised numerals    [1]Matthew;   [2]Mark;   [3]Luke;   [4]John.

Raised letters    Explanatory Footnotes

Brackets, [   ]    Passages included in TEXTUS RECEPTUS, but not in the most ancient texts extant today.

Italics    Used to express emphasis in the Grk., Old Testament quotes, and phrases or statements of special significance.

# PREFACE TO THE REVISED EDITION

In sending forth this revised edition the publishers gratefully acknowledge the warm reception given the initial edition of this work. This most gratifying response has come from many parts of the Christian church, both at home and abroad, suggesting to us the urgent need for such a work on the life of Christ in all parts of the Christian world. For this interest we are humbly thankful and sincerely hope that this edition may further stimulate interest in the Person and ministry of Jesus Christ.

In this second edition, however, a quite extensive revision of the auxiliary materials has been undertaken to further increase the usefulness of the volume. One such change, suggested by many readers, is the incorporation of the first appendix as part of the preface so that the purpose of the work may be thoroughly understood before one begins the reading of the combined Gospel story. The following paragraphs constitute that explanation which we herewith submit that all may be fully aware of:

## The Purpose of This Harmony

THE LIFE OF CHRIST IN STEREO is a meticulous combination of the four Gospels which seeks to bring into stereoscopic relief the four dimensional portrayal of Christ and His ministry. It presents a composite portrait of the One Who is the Central Personality of history, tracing the events of His ministry in chronological order, without omission of the smallest detail.

The question may be raised as to whether it is legitimate to combine that which God has separated. If God had wanted the Gospels combined into one story, would He not have provided such a presentation through an inspired writer? And is not the fact that church history knows of no such minute combination of the Gospels an evidence of the illegitimacy of initiating such a harmony at this time?

In view of such questions that may arise, the compiler and publishers of this Gospel harmony desire to make clear the purpose and allied objectives of this work. The portrayal here given does not pretend to be another Gospel; nor does it presume to take the place of any of the four Gospels. Its purpose is rather that of a companion-piece to the four Gospels, seeking to precipitate their individual features and relate them to each other. By combining the complete story, this harmony serves the purpose of providing an historical and grammatical background for the study of any one of the four Gospels. It has the effect of driving the Bible student back to the Gospels themselves with a larger and more discerning perspective. And with this perspective, the distinctive features of each book are enhanced, making both the omissions and the points of emphasis to stand out.

This harmony is in reality another "Life of Christ," distinctive in that it utilizes *all* the details of the inspired records and *only* materials of the inspired records. It furthermore uses the phraseology that the Spirit of God chose to employ in its most exact expression. To deny the propriety of so arranging the materials of the four Gospels would constitute a challenge also to other Scripture arrangements such as that of systematic theology. Theology itself is a logical organization of the truths of God and His relations with men. THE LIFE OF CHRIST IN STEREO is such an arrangement, but it uses the materials of the Gospel texts alone, admitting no extraneous editorial comments into the story.

It is believed that such a precise four-dimensional presentation of the Gospels can have immeasurable significance in the study of this the heart of the Scriptures. As A. T. Robertson once said, "The whole is infinitely richer than the picture given by any one of the Four Gospels." The whole is always greater than the sum of the parts. In combining the four accounts into a composite whole, a stereo confrontation with the Central Personality of history is achieved, and all the recorded details of His story are brought into sharp focus. The utility of this arrangement has immense values both for chronological and expositional purposes. The publishers, therefore, feel that this work is so universally significant for every student of the Life of Christ that its publication should constitute something of a milestone, if not a "breakthrough," in the study of the Gospels.

Stanley A. Ellisen

Portland, Oregon

# CONTENTS

FOREWORD

PREFACE

PREFACE TO THE REVISED EDITION

## PART II

## HIS MESSIANIC LABORS BEGIN

## PART III

## THE YEAR OF GREAT PUBLIC FAVOR

**7. KINGDOM PARABLES AND KINGLY POWER** - *Mt.8-13*
*Mk.3-5; Lk.7,8*

**8. ANSWERING JERUSALEM'S LEADERS** - *Mt. 13; Mk. 6; Jn. 5*

**9. THE CLIMAX OF ISRAEL'S ACCLAIM** - *Mt.10,14; Mk.6;*
*Lk. 9; Jn. 6*

PART IV

CRUCIAL REJECTIONS BY ISRAEL

**10. REPUDIATED AT CAPERNAUM** - *Mt. 15; Mk. 7; Jn. 6*

## PART V

## HIS FACE TURNS TO THE CROSS

## PART VII

## THE CONSUMMATION

### 20.  THE HOUR OF THE POWER OF DARKNESS
*Mt. 26,27; Mk. 14,15; Lk. 22,23; Jn. 18,19*

### 21.  RISEN VICTORIOUS - *Mt. 28; Mk. 16; Lk. 24; Jn. 20,21*

# Four Introductions Form One

### 1. *The Biography's Divine Title*
   *(Mk. 1:1)*

The Beginning[a] of the Glad News of
JESUS THE MESSIAH, THE SON OF GOD.

### 2. *Jesus Was GOD'S EXPRESSION in Flesh*
   *(Jn. 1:1-18)*

In the beginning was *the Word.* And the Word was with God, and the Word *was God;* this One was in the beginning with God.

All things were made through him, and without him was not anything made that has been made. In him was life, and the life was the light of men. And the light shone in the darkness, and the darkness extinguished[a] it not.

There came a man sent from God whose name was John; this man came as a witness, to bear witness of the light, that all might believe through him. He was not the light, but came to bear witness of the light. Coming into the world was the true *Light* which shines upon every man.

He was in the world, and the world was made through him, and the world recognized him not; he came to his own creation, and his own people received him not. *But as many as received him, those who put their trust in his name, to them gave he the high estate of being made[b] children of God; who were born, not by means of blood descent, nor of the will of the flesh, nor of the will of man, but of God.*

And the Word became flesh, and sojourned among us—and we beheld[c] *his glory,* glory as of the only begotten of the Father—full of grace and truth.

John bore witness of him and cried out, saying, "*This* was he of whom I said, 'He who is coming after me ranks before me.' For *He was* before me."[d]

And from his fulness have *we* all received, and grace added

1

upon grace. For the law was given through Moses, but *grace and truth came through Jesus Christ.* No one has seen God at any time; the only begotten Son, who is at the bosom[e] of the Father, *He* showed *what God is like.*

### 3. Legally He Was of Israel's Royalty
### (Mt. 1:1-17)

The scroll[a] of the genealogy of Jesus Christ, *the Son of David, the Son of Abraham:*

> Abraham begot Isaac,
> and Isaac Jacob,
> and Jacob Judah and his brothers;
> and Judah Perez and Zerah by Tamar,
> and Perez Hezron,
> and Hezron Ram,
> and Ram Amminadab,
> and Amminadab Nahshon,
> and Nahshon Salmon,
> and Salmon Boaz by Rahab,
> and Boaz Obed by Ruth,
> and Obed Jesse,
> and Jesse David the king.
> And David the king begot Solomon
> by the widow of Uriah;
> and Solomon Rehoboam,
> and Rehoboam Abijah,
> and Abijah Asa,
> and Asa Jehoshaphat,
> and Jehoshaphat Jehoram,
> and Jehoram Uzziah,[b]
> and Uzziah Jotham,
> and Jotham Ahaz,
> and Ahaz Hezekiah,
> and Hezekiah Manasseh,
> and Manasseh Amon,
> and Amon Josiah,
> and Josiah Jechoniah and his brothers

about the time of the exile to Babylon.
And after the exile to Babylon
Jechoniah begot Shealtiel,
and Shealtiel Zerubbabel,
and Zerubbabel Abiud,
and Abiud Eliakim,
and Eliakim Azor,
and Azor Zadok,
and Zadok Achim,
and Achim Eliud,
and Eliud Eleazar,
and Eleazar Matthan,
and Matthan Jacob,
and Jacob Joseph[c]
*the husband of Mary,*
*of whom was born Jesus, who is called Christ.*

So all the generations from Abraham to David are fourteen
generations, and from David until the exile to Babylon fourteen generations, and from the exile to Babylon until the
Christ fourteen[d] generations.

### 4. The Certainty of the Story's Facts
### (Lk. 1:1-4)

Inasmuch as many[a] have taken in hand to set down a record
of the things which have come to fulfillment among us, even
as they who from the beginning were eyewitnesses and minis-
ters of the Word reported them to us, it seemed good to me also, having inquired carefully concerning all things from the
very beginning, to write them in order to you, most excellent
Theophilus, so that you may know *the certainty* of the facts
of which you have been informed.

\* \* \*

*Comment.* The combined accounts display a remarkable unity as
they supplement each other to form a well-ordered introduction for a biography. A proper biography should contain in general four basic factors:
(a) the identity of the one whose life is being reviewed; (b) his importance to the world, or other good reasons why people should read of his
life; (c) evidence that the work was pursued with care and the facts were

derived from reliable sources; and (d) often a dedication is included, though not essential.

Although none of the four Gospels contain all of these main factors (none having as its purpose to present a complete biography), the *combination* does provide these basic features: (a) Mark's introduction, though less than a sentence, serves as a striking title; it identifies the Person to be portrayed, calls His story the Glad *N*ews, and declares His recognized official status. (b) John identifies Him as being one with God and describes His colossal importance to all mankind. On this point, Matthew also identifies Jesus in terms of His Old Testament relationships, declaring His legal right to Israel's throne. (c) Luke submits evidence of the credibility of the facts presented, asserts his careful sifting of the records, and declares his intention of presenting the account in an orderly arrangement. (d) Finally a dedication is also provided by Luke in that his Gospel was specifically written for his worthy friend, Theophilus. Since "Theophilus" means *friend of God,* it would not be far from the mark to say that . . .

"the Gospels are dedicated to *everyone who is enough of a friend of God* to read God's record of His Son."

# PART I.

## THE PERIOD OF PREPARATION

### Chapter 1. The Forerunner's Birth

*5. Zechariah's Prayer Is Answered*
  *(Lk. 1:5-25)*

There was in the days of Herod the king of Judea a priest named Zechariah, of the division of Abijah; and his wife was of the daughters of Aaron, and her name was Elisabeth. And they were both righteous before God, walking in all the commandments and ordinances of the Lord blameless; but they had no child, because Elisabeth was barren, and they were both far along in years.

Now it came to pass that, as he performed his priest's duties before God at the time set for his division, according to the custom of the priestly service his lot was to burn incense when he went into the temple of the Lord. And all the multitude of the people were praying outside at the hour of incense. And there appeared unto him an angel of the Lord, standing at the right side of the altar of incense.

And when Zechariah saw him, he was troubled, and fear fell upon him; but the angel said to him, "Fear not, Zechariah; for your prayer has been heard, and Elisabeth your wife will bear you a son. And you shall call his name John; and you will have joy and gladness, and many will rejoice at his birth. For he will be great in the eyes of the Lord, and shall drink neither wine nor strong drink; and he will be filled with the Holy Spirit even from his mother's womb.

"And many of the children of Israel will he turn to the Lord their God. And he will go before him in the spirit and power of *Elijah,* to *'turn the heart of the fathers to the chil-*

5

dren,"ᵃ and the disobedient to the wisdom of the righteous, *to prepare for the Lord a people made ready for him."*

Then said Zechariah to the angel, "Whereby shall I know this? For I am an *old* man, and *my wife* is far along in years." And the angel answering said to him, *"I am Gabriel,*ᵇ who stand in the presence of God; and I have been sent to speak to you and to bring you these glad tidings. And lo, you shall be dumb and unable to speak till the day when these things shall come to pass; because you did not believe my words, which *will be fulfilled* in their season."

Now the people were waiting for Zechariah, and marveled that he tarried so long in the temple. Then when he came out, he could not speak to them; and they perceived that he had seen a vision in the temple, for he made signs to them and remained speechless.

And it came to pass that, when the days of his service were ended, he departed to his home. And after these days his wife Elisabeth conceived; and she kept in seclusion for five months, saying, "This is how *the Lord* has dealt with me, in the days when he took notice of me to remove my reproach among men."

## 6. Gabriel's Announcement to Mary
### (Lk. 1:26-38)

Then in the sixth month the angel Gabriel was sent from God to a city of Galilee called Nazareth, to a virgin betrothed to a man whose name was Joseph, of the line of David; and the virgin's name was Mary. And the angel came unto her and said, *"Hail, you who are richly blessed! The Lord is with you."*

But on seeing him she was troubled at his greeting, and cast in her mind what this salutation might mean. And the angel said to her, "Fear not, Mary, for you have found favor with God. And behold, you will conceive in your womb and bring forth a son; and you shall call his name *Jesus.* He will be great, and will be called the Son of the Highest. *And the Lord God will give unto him the throne of his father David; he will reign over the house of Jacob forever, and of his Kingdom there shall be no end.*"[a]

Then said Mary to the angel, "How shall this be, since I have known no intimacy with man?" And the angel answered and said to her, *"The Holy Spirit* will come upon you, and the power of the Highest will overshadow you; wherefore also the holy thing born [of you] shall be called *the Son of God.* And behold, your kinswoman Elisabeth, even she in her old age has conceived a son; and this is now the sixth month with her, the woman who was called barren! For with God will *nothing* be impossible."

And Mary said, "Behold the bondmaid of the Lord; be it done to me according to your word." And the angel departed from her.

### 7. Mary and Elisabeth Rejoice
*(Lk. 1:39-56)*

Then in those days Mary arose and with haste went into the hill country, to a city of Judah; and she came into the house of Zechariah and greeted Elisabeth. And it came to pass that when Elisabeth heard the salutation of Mary, the babe leaped in her womb; and Elisabeth was filled with the Holy Spirit, and cried out in a loud voice, saying, *"Blessed* are you among women! And *blessed is the fruit of your womb!* And for what is this permitted me, that the mother of my Lord should come to *me?* For lo, when your greeting sounded in my ears, the babe leaped in my womb for joy. And blessed is she who believed that those things *would be accomplished* which were told her from the Lord."

And Mary said,

"My soul magnifies *the Lord,*[a]
and my spirit has rejoiced in *God my Savior!*
For he has regarded the low estate of his bondmaid;
for behold, from this time forth
all generations will call me blessed;
for the Mighty One has done to me great things,
and holy is His name!

*"And His mercy* is, from age to age,

toward those who reverence him.
He has wrought strength with his arm:
he has scattered those who were proud
in the imaginations of their heart;
he has put down rulers from their thrones
and exalted those of low degree.
He has filled the hungry with good things,
and the rich he has sent away empty.
He has helped *his servant Israel*
in remembrance of the mercy
which he promised to our fathers,
to Abraham and to his seed forever."

And Mary stayed with her about three months,[b] and went back to her home.

## 8. *"His Name Is John"*
### (Lk. 1:57-80)

Now Elisabeth's time came that she should be delivered, and she brought forth a son. And her neighbors and kinsfolk heard how the Lord had shown great mercy toward her, and they rejoiced with her.

And it came to pass that on the eighth day they came to circumcise the child; and they began to call him Zechariah, after the name of his father. But his mother answered and said, "Not so; for he shall be called John." So they said to her, "There is none of your kindred called by this name." And they made signs to his father, how he would have him named.

Then he asked for a writing tablet and wrote, "His name is *John."* And they all marveled; and at once his mouth was opened and his tongue was loosed, and he began to speak, praising God. Then fear came on all who dwelt round about, and all these things were noised abroad through all the hill country of Judea. And all who heard them laid them up in their hearts, saying, "What then will this child be?" And the hand of the Lord was with him.

And his father Zechariah was filled with the Holy Spirit, and spoke in a prophetic utterance,[a] saying,

*"Blessed be the Lord God of Israel!*
For he has regarded and redeemed his people,
and has raised up a Horn of Salvation for us
in the house of his servant David—
even as he promised in ages past
by the mouth of his holy prophets—
that we should be saved from our enemies
and from the hand of all who hate us:
to perform mercy toward our fathers,
and to remember *his holy covenant,*
the oath which he swore to our father Abraham;
to grant unto us that we, without fear,
being saved from the hand of our enemies,
should serve him in holiness and righteousness
in his eyes, all the days of our life.
        "As for you, little one, you will be called
*the prophet of the Highest;*
for you will go before the face of the Lord
to prepare his pathways,
to give knowledge of Salvation to his people
in *the remission of their sins*—
through the heart of mercy of our God,
whereby the *Sunrise* from on high has dawned upon us:
to shine on those who sit in darkness
and in the shadow of death;
to guide our feet into *the way of peace."*

And the little child grew and became strong in spirit, and
was in the wilderness till the day of his appearing unto Israel.

# Chapter 2. Jesus' Infancy and Youth

## 9. *Joseph Is Reassured*
### *(Mt. 1:18-25)*

Now the birth of Jesus Christ was on this wise. When his mother Mary had been betrothed to Joseph, before they came together she was found to be with child—from the Holy Spirit.[a] Then Joseph her betrothed, being a just man and not willing to put her to public shame, was minded to renounce her privately. But while he thought on these things, behold, an angel of the Lord appeared unto him in a dream, saying, "Joseph, son of David, do not fear to take to you Mary as your wife; for that which has been conceived in her is from *the Holy Spirit.* And she will bring forth a Son, and you shall call his name *Jesus;* for he will *save*[b] *his people from their sins.*"

Now all this was done that there might be fulfilled what was spoken by the Lord through the prophet, saying, *"Lo, the virgin shall be with child, and will bring forth a son; and they shall call his name Immanuel,"* which being translated is, *God with us.* So when Joseph was aroused from sleep, he did as the angel of the Lord had bidden him, and took unto him his wife. But he knew her not in intimacy till she had brought forth a son.[c]

## 10. *"A Savior, Christ the Lord!"*
### *(Lk. 2:1-21)*

Then it came to pass in those days that a decree went forth from Caesar Augustus that all the world should be registered. (This first taxing was done when Quirinius[a] was governor of Syria.) And everyone went to be registered, each to his home city. So Joseph also went up from Galilee, out of the city of Nazareth, to Judea, to the city of David called Bethlehem (since he was of the house and lineage of David), to be registered with Mary his betrothed wife, now great with child.[b] And it came to pass that, while they were there, the days were fulfilled for her to be delivered; and she brought forth her first-born son. And she wrapped him in swaddling clothes and laid him in a manger, because there was no room for them in the inn.

Now there were in the same countryside shepherds, dwelling in the field, keeping watch over their flock by night. And lo, an angel of the Lord stood beside them, and the glory of the Lord shone round about them, and they were sorely afraid. But the angel said to them, *"Fear not; for behold, I bring you glad tidings of great joy, which shall be to all the people. For unto you is born this day a Savior, who is Christ the Lord—born in the city of David!* And this will be the sign for you: you will find a babe, wrapped in swaddling clothes, lying in a manger." And suddenly there was with the angel a multitude of the heavenly host, praising God and saying, *"Glory to God in the highest! And on earth peace, good will among men."*[c]

And it came to pass that, when the angels had gone away from them into heaven, the shepherds said to one another, "Let us indeed then go to Bethlehem and *see* this thing which has come to pass, which the Lord made known to us." And they came with haste, and found Mary and Joseph, and the babe lying in a manger. And when they had seen it, they made known to all what had been told them concerning this child.

And all they that heard it marveled at the things which were told them by the shepherds; but Mary kept all these things, and pondered them in her heart. And the shepherds returned, glorifying and praising God for all that they had heard, and had seen just as it was told them. And when eight days had passed for the circumcising of the child, his name *was called* JESUS, as the angel had named him before he was conceived in the womb.

## 11. Simeon and Anna Testify

*(Lk. 2:22-39)*

Now when the days for the purification according to the law of Moses had ended, they brought him up to Jerusalem to present him to the Lord, as it is written in the law of the Lord,

*"Every firstborn male shall be counted set apart for the Lord,"*
and to offer a sacrifice in keeping with the law of the Lord, *"A pair of turtledoves, or two young pigeons."*

And behold, there was a man in Jerusalem named Simeon; and this man was righteous and devout, waiting for the consolation of Israel, and the Holy Spirit was upon him. And the Holy Spirit had revealed to him that he should not see death till he had seen the Lord's Anointed. So, moved by the Spirit, he came into the temple; and when the parents brought in the child Jesus, to do for him in keeping with the custom of the law, then took he him up in his arms and blessed God, and he said,

"Now art thou letting thy bondman depart, O Lord, according to thy word, in peace!
*For my eyes have seen thy Salvation,*
which thou hast prepared in the sight of all peoples,
a Light for revelation to the Gentiles
and a glory to thy people Israel."

And Joseph and the mother of Jesus marveled at the things which were said concerning him. And Simeon blessed them, and said to Mary his mother,

"Behold, this child is appointed for the fall
and the rising again of many in Israel,
and for a sign which will be spoken against—
and a sword will go through *your* own soul also!—
that the thoughts out of many hearts may be revealed."

Then there was Anna, a prophetess, a daughter of Phanuel of the tribe of Asher, who was of a great age, having lived with a husband seven years from her maidenhood and as a widow about eighty-four years;[a] who departed not from the temple, but served with fastings and prayers night and day. And she, coming up at that very hour, gave praise to the Lord, and spoke concerning Jesus to all who were looking for deliverance in Jerusalem.

And when they had performed all the things required in the law of the Lord, they journeyed back into Galilee, to their own city of Nazareth.

## 12. Worshipers Come from the Gentiles

*(Mt. 2:1-12)*

Now after[a] Jesus was born in Bethlehem of Judea in the days of Herod the king, behold, there came Wise Men from the east to Jerusalem, saying, "Where is he that is born *King of the Jews?* For we saw his star in the east and have come to do him homage."

But when Herod the king heard these things, he was troubled, and all Jerusalem with him. And when he had called together all the chief priests and scribes of the people, he asked them in agitation[b] where the Messiah was to be born. And they said to him, "In Bethlehem of Judea; for so it was written through the prophet:

'*And you, Bethlehem, in the land of Judah,*
*are by no means the least among the rulers of Judah;*
*for out of you shall come forth a Ruler*
*who will shepherd my people Israel.*'"

Then Herod, having secretly sent for the Wise Men, asked them carefully what time the star had appeared. And he sent them to Bethlehem, and said, "Go, and search with care for the young child; and when you have found him, bring word back to me, that *I*, too, may come and pay him homage."

So when they had heard the king, they departed. And lo, the star which they had seen in the east went before them, till it came and stood over[c] where the young child was. When they saw the star, they rejoiced with exceedingly great joy. Then, on entering the house, they saw the young child with Mary his mother, and fell down and worshiped him. And opening their treasures, they presented to him gifts: gold, and frankincense, and myrrh. And being warned from God in a dream that they should not return to Herod, they went back into their own country by another way.

## 13. Escape from Herod into Egypt
### (Mt. 2:13-23; Lk. 2:40)

¹Now when they had departed, behold, an angel of the Lord appeared unto Joseph in a dream, saying, "Arise, and take the young child and his mother and flee into Egypt, and stay there until I bring you word; for Herod is about to seek the young child, to destroy him." So he arose, and took the young child and his mother by night and departed into Egypt, and was there until the death of Herod; that there might be fulfilled what was spoken by the Lord through the prophet, saying, *"Out of Egypt have I called my son."*

Then Herod, finding that he had been tricked by the Wise Men, was furiously angry; and he sent forth and slew all the male babes in Bethlehem and in all that countryside, two years old and under, according to the time which he had ascertained from the Wise Men. Then was fulfilled what was spoken by the prophet Jeremiah, when he said,

*"In Ramah a voice was heard,*
*wailing and a great lamentation,*
*Rachel weeping for her children;*
*and she refused to be comforted,*
*because they were no more."*

But when Herod was dead, lo, an angel of the Lord appeared in a dream unto Joseph in Egypt, saying, "Arise, and take the young child and his mother and go into the land of Israel; for they are dead who were seeking the young child's life." And he arose and took the young child and his mother, and came into the land of Israel. But when he heard that Archelaus was reigning in Judea in the place of his father Herod, he was afraid to go thither; and being warned by God in a dream, he withdrew into the region of Galilee. So he came and dwelt inᵃ Nazareth, that there might be fulfilled what was spoken through the prophets, that he should be called a Nazarene.

³And the young child grew and became strong, filled with wisdom; and God's favor rested upon him.

## 14. The Boy Jesus in the Temple

(Lk. 2:41-52)

Now his parents went to Jerusalem every year for the feast of the Passover; and when he was twelve years old, they went up to Jerusalem in accordance with the custom of the feast. But when the days were completed, as they returned, the boy Jesus stayed behind in Jerusalem; and Joseph and his mother did not know of it, so they sought him among their kinsfolk and acquaintances, and when they did not find him, turned back to Jerusalem in their search.

And it came to pass that after three days they found him in the temple—seated in the midst of the rabbis, both listening to them and asking questions, all who heard him being astonished at his understanding and answers. When they saw him, they were amazed; and his mother said to him, "Child, why have you dealt thus with us? Lo, in anguish your father and I have been seeking you." And he said to them, "Why were you seeking me? Did you not know that *I* must be engaged in the things of *my Father?*"

And they did not understand what he said to them; but he went down with them and came into Nazareth, and was subject to them. And his mother treasured all these matters in her heart.[a] And Jesus increased in wisdom and stature, and in favor with God and men.

## Chapter 3. Heralded, Tested, and Approved

### 15. John Preaches in the Wilderness
*(Mt. 3:1-12; Mk. 1:2-8; Lk. 3:1-18)*

[3] Now in the fifteenth year[a] of the reign of Tiberius Caesar, Pontius Pilate being governor of Judea, Herod being the tetrarch of Galilee, his brother Philip tetrarch of Iturea and the region of Trachonitis, and Lysanias tetrarch of Abilene, Annas and Caiaphas being the high priests, the word of God came upon John, the son of Zechariah, in the wilderness. [1] In those days,[b] [2] as it is written in the prophets,

*"Behold, I send my messenger before thy face,*
*who shall prepare thy way before thee,"*

[2] John came [3] into all the region around the Jordan [1] in the wilderness of Judea, [3] preaching a baptism of repentance unto remission of sins, [1] and saying, *"Repent! For the Kingdom of heaven is at hand!"* For this [1] John the Baptist [1] is he that was spoken of [3] in the book of utterances of the prophet Isaiah, saying,

*"The voice of one crying in the wilderness,*
*'Make ready the way of the Lord,*
*make his pathways straight!*
*Every valley shall be filled up,*
*and every mountain and hill be brought low,*
*and crooked paths shall be made straight,*
*and the rough shall be made smooth;*
*and all men will see the Salvation of God.'"*

[1] Now the same John wore raiment made of camel's hair, with a girdle of leather about his loins, and he lived upon locusts and wild honey.

Then went out to him [2] they of Jerusalem [1] and all Judea, and all the region around the Jordan, and on confessing their sins they were baptized by him in the Jordan. But when he saw [3] the crowds—[1] many of the Pharisees and Sadducees—[3] coming out to be baptized by him, he said therefore [1] to them, "You offspring of vipers, who forewarned *you* to flee

16

from *the wrath to come?* Bring forth therefore fruits that belong to *repentance!* And think not to say among yourselves that 'We have *Abraham* as father.' For I say to you, that even from these *stones* God can raise up children unto Abraham! And even now the ax is ready at the root of the trees; every tree therefore that does not bear good fruit is being hewn down and cast into the fire."

[3] So the crowds were asking him, "What then shall we *do?*" And he answering said to them, "He that has two garments, let him share with him who has none; and let him who has food do likewise." And publicans[c] also came to be baptized, and said to him, "Teacher, what shall we *do?*" And he said to them, "Exact no more than is appointed you." And soldiers also were asking, "And what shall *we* do?" And he said to them, "Take no money by violence, nor accuse men falsely; and be content with your wages."

Then with the people in expectation and all debating in their hearts whether John were *the Messiah*[d] or not, John answered them all [2] and proclaimed to them, saying, [1] *"I indeed baptize you in water for repentance;* but [2] coming after me is *One mightier than I,* [1] whose sandals I am not worthy to remove—[2] whose sandal thong I am not fit to stoop down and untie! [3] *He* will baptize you *in the Holy Spirit and in fire;* whose winnowing fan is in his hand, and he will thoroughly clean his threshing floor, and gather his wheat into the granary but burn up the chaff with unquenchable fire." Thus with many various exhortations he was preaching good news to the people.

## 16. Jesus' Baptism and Physical Lineage
### *(Mt. 3:13-17; Mk. 1:9-11; Lk. 3:21-38)*

[1] Then [2] it came to pass in those days, [3] when all the people had been baptized, [2] that *Jesus* came from Nazareth [1] to the Jordan unto John to be baptized by him. Now John would have stopped him, saying, *"I* have need to be baptized *by You,* and are You coming to me?" But Jesus answering said to him, "Grant that it be so now; for it is fitting that we thus should

fulfill all righteousness." Then he yielded, and Jesus [2] was baptized by John in the Jordan.

And coming up immediately out of the water, [3] and praying, [1] behold, [2] he saw the heavens opened [1] [unto him], [3] and the Holy Spirit [1] of God descending [3] upon him in bodily form as a dove, [1] and resting on him; and lo, [2] a Voice came from out of the heavens, [1] saying, [2] "YOU ARE MY BELOVED SON, [1] IN WHOM I HAVE DELIGHTED."

[3] Now Jesus, making his appearance at about age thirty, being a son, as was supposed, of Joseph, *was himself descended from Heli,* [a]

| | | |
|---|---|---|
| son of Matthat, | son of Jeshua, | son of Judah, |
| son of Levi, | son of Eliezer, | son of Jacob, |
| son of Melchi, | son of Jorim, | son of Isaac, |
| son of Jannai, | son of Matthat, | son of Abraham, |
| son of Joseph, | son of Levi, | son of Terah, |
| son of Mattathias, | son of Simeon, | son of Nahor, |
| son of Amos, | son of Judas, | son of Serug, |
| son of Nahum, | son of Joseph, | son of Reu, |
| son of Esli, | son of Jonam, | son of Peleg, |
| son of Naggai, | son of Eliakim, | son of Heber, |
| son of Maath, | son of Melea, | son of Shelah, |
| son of Mattathias, | son of Menna, | son of Cainan, |
| son of Semein, | son of Mattatha, | son of Arphaxad, |
| son of Josech, | son of Nathan, | son of Shem, |
| son of Joda, | son of David, | son of Noah, |
| son of Johanan, | son of Jesse, | son of Lamech, |
| son of Rhesa, | son of Obed, | son of Methuselah, |
| son of Zerubbabel, | son of Boaz, | son of Enoch, |
| son of Shealtiel, | son of Salmon, | son of Jared, |
| son of Neri, | son of Nahshon, | son of Mahalaleel, |
| son of Melchi, | son of Amminadab, | son of Cainan, |
| son of Addi, | son of Admin, | son of Enos, |
| son of Cosam, | son of Aram, | son of Seth, |
| son of Elmadam, | son of Hezron, | son of Adam, [b] |
| son of Er, | son of Perez, | son of God. |

## 17. Tempted in Body, Soul, and Spirit

*(Mt. 4:1-11; Mk. 1:12-13; Lk. 4:1-13)*

[1] Then [3] Jesus, filled with the Holy Spirit, returned from the Jordan; [2] and immediately the Spirit drove him out into the wilderness, where he remained for forty days and was with the wild beasts. [3] And he was led by the Spirit in the wilderness; [1] he was led up to be tested by the Devil.

[3] Now during those days he ate nothing, and when [1] he had fasted forty days and forty nights, he at length became hungry. So the tempter, [2] Satan, [1] came to him and said, "If you are the Son of *God,* command that these stones become loaves of bread." But [3] Jesus answered him, saying, "It is written, *'Man shall not live by bread alone,* [1] *but by every word that proceeds from the mouth of God.'"*

Then the Devil took him into the holy city, [3] Jerusalem, and set him on the pinnacle of the temple, and said to him, "If you are the Son of *God,* cast yourself down from here; for it is written that *'He will command his angels concerning you, that they guard you...',* and, *'Upon their hands they will bear you up, lest you strike your foot against a stone.'"* And Jesus answering said to him, [1] "Again, it is written, *'You shall not tempt the Lord your God.'"*

And again, the Devil [3] led him up [1] on an exceedingly high mountain, [3] and showed him in a moment of time [1] all the kingdoms of the world and the glory of them; and he said to him, "All these things— [3] all this power and their glory—will I give you; for to *me* has it been delivered, and to whomever I will I give it. If therefore you [1] will fall down and make obeisance [3] to *me,* it shall all be yours." Then Jesus answered and said to him, [1] *"Go away,* Satan![a] For it is written, *'You shall worship the Lord your God, and him only shall you serve.'"*

So the Devil, [3] having finished every kind of testing, departed from him for a time; [1] and behold, [2] the angels [1] came and ministered to him.

*18. John Answers the Jews' Committee*
   (Jn. 1:19-34)

And here is the affirmation John made, when the Jews sent priests and Levites from Jerusalem to ask him, "Who are *you?"*—and he confessed, and denied not, but confessed, *"I am not the Messiah."* And they asked him, "What then? Are you *Elijah?"* And he said, "I am not." "Are you *the Prophet?"*[a] And he answered, "No." Then said they to him, "Who *are* you?—that we may give an answer to those who sent us. What do you say of yourself?" He said, "I am *'a voice crying in the wilderness, Make straight the way of the Lord!'* as said the prophet Isaiah."

Now those who had been sent were from among the Pharisees; and they asked him, and said to him, "Why then are you *baptizing,* if you are not the Messiah, nor Elijah, nor the Prophet?" John answered them, saying, *"I* baptize *in water,* but standing among you is One whom you know not; *He* it is who coming after me ranks before me, whose sandal thong I am not fit to untie." These things occurred in Bethabara beyond the Jordan, where John was baptizing.

The next day John saw Jesus coming toward him, and said,
   *"Behold the Lamb of God,*
   *who takes away the sin of the world!*

*"This* is he of whom I said, 'After me is coming a man who ranks before me.' For *He was* before me. And *I* knew him not; but that he might be made known to Israel, for this *I* came *baptizing in water."*

And John made an affirmation, saying, "I saw the Spirit descending out of heaven as a dove, and he abode upon him. And *I* knew him not; but he who sent me to baptize in water, that same One said to me, 'He on whom you see the Spirit descending and remaining, He it is who baptizes *in the Holy Spirit.'* And I have seen and have borne witness, that *this is the Son of God."*

## 19. Jesus Finds the First Three Disciples
*(Jn. 1:35-42)*

Again the next day John was standing with two of his disciples, and gazing at Jesus as he walked, he said, *"Behold the Lamb of God!"* The two disciples heard him speak, and they followed Jesus. Then Jesus turned and saw them following, and said to them, "What are you seeking?" And they said to him, "Rabbi," (which is to say, Teacher) "where are you lodging?" He said to them, "Come and see." They came and saw where he was lodging, and remained with him that day—it was about ten[a] in the morning.

One of the two[b] who heard John speak and followed Jesus was Andrew, Simon Peter's brother. He found first his own brother Simon, and said to him, "We have found *the Messiah!"* (which is translated, *the Christ).* And he brought him to Jesus. And when Jesus had beheld him intently, he said, "You are Simon the son of John? You shall be called *Cephas"* (which is translated, *a Stone).*[c]

## 20. Philip and Nathanael Respond
*(Jn. 1:43-51)*

The next day Jesus purposed to proceed into Galilee, and he found Philip and said to him, *"Follow Me."* Now Philip was of Bethsaida, the city of Andrew and Peter. Philip found Nathanael, and said to him, *"We have found* him of whom Moses in the law, and the prophets also, wrote: *Jesus,* the son of Joseph,[a] from Nazareth." But Nathanael said to him, "Can anything good come out of *Nazareth?"* Philip said to him, "Come and see."

Jesus saw Nathanael coming to him, and said of him, "Behold truly an Israelite in whom there is no deceit!" Nathanael said to him, "How is it that you know *me?"* Jesus answered and said to him, "Before Philip called you—while you were under the fig tree—I saw you." Nathanael answered him and said, "Rabbi, You are *the Son of God!*[b] You are *the King of Israel!"*

Jesus answered and said to him, "Because I said to you that I saw you under the fig tree, do you believe? Greater things than these shall you see!" And he said to him, "Verily, verily, I say to you both, the time is coming when you will see heaven opened, and the angels of God ascending and descending upon *the Son of man.*"

### 21. Jesus' First Miraculous Sign
(Jn. 2:1-12)

Then the third day there was a wedding in Cana of Galilee, and the mother of Jesus was there; and Jesus also and his disciples were invited to the wedding. And when the wine ran short, the mother of Jesus said to him, "They have no wine." Jesus said to her, "Woman, what are you doing to me?[a] My time is not yet here." His mother said to the servants, "Whatever he says to you, do it."

Now there were sitting there six water jars of stone, used for the Jews' rites of purification, holding twenty to thirty gallons each. Jesus said to them, "Fill up the water jars with water." And they filled them up to the brim. Then he said to them, "Draw out some now, and take it to the maitre of the feast." So they took it.

And when the maitre of the feast had tasted the water now made wine, not knowing from where it came (although the servants who had drawn the water knew), the maitre of the feast called the bridegroom and said to him, "Everyone sets forth the good wine first, and when men have drunk freely, then that which is poor; but *you* have kept the good wine until *now!*"

Thus in Cana of Galilee Jesus wrought this beginning of his miraculous signs and manifested his glory; and his disciples believed upon[b] him. After this he went down to Capernaum with his mother and brothers and his disciples, and they stayed there a short while.

\* \* \*

*Comment.*    As the heading designates, the central emphasis of this period was that of preparation. The preparation described is not only that of Jesus, the central Figure involved, but preparation for the message to be presented by Jesus. That message is that Jesus came into the world first of all as the *offered Messiah of Israel.* All segments of the S tory build up to this presentation. The testimonies of Gabriel, Mary, Zechariah, the heavenly host, Joseph, Simeon, Anna, the Wise Men, John the Baptist, Andrew, Philip, and Nathanael all center about that Message. He came as the promised Messiah in fulfillment of Old Testament prophecies.

The Story at this juncture has progressed to the place where Jesus is about to present Himself to the nation in fulfillment of this purpose. Appropriately He will do this at the Passover in Jerusalem, the nation's capital city. He does not come as the Passover Lamb at this point, but as the *Messenger of the Covenant* in fulfillment of the prophecy of Malachi, the last Old Testament prophet. Judgment had to precede blessing as the prophet Malachi had predicted:

*And the Lord whom you seek will come suddenly to his temple, even the Messenger of the Covenant, whom you delight in; behold, he is coming, says the Lord of hosts. But who shall endure the day of his coming, and who shall stand when he appears? For he is like a refiner's fire, and like fullers' soap . . . and he will purify the sons of Levi . . . . (Mal 3:1-3)*

In the following narrative, therefore, Jesus is seen appearing in the temple at Jerusalem, burning with zeal as hot as a refiner's fire, seeking righteousness in the conduct of the temple on the part of the descendants of Levi. Judgment was to begin at the house of God.

# PART II.

## HIS MESSIANIC LABORS BEGIN

### Chapter 4. Jerusalem's Leaders Are Offended

*22. "Take These Things Out!"*

*(Jn. 2:13-22)*

Then the Passover of the Jews drew near, and Jesus journeyed up to Jerusalem; and he found in the temple those who sold oxen and sheep and doves, and the changers of money sitting. And when he had made a scourge of small ropes, he drove them all out of the temple, with the sheep and the oxen; and he dumped out the changers' money and overturned their tables, and said to the sellers of doves, *"Take these things out! Make not my Father's house a place of merchandise!"* And his disciples remembered that it is written, *"Zeal for thy house has consumed me."*

The Jews therefore answered and said to him, "What miraculous *sign*[a] are you showing us, since you are doing these things?" Jesus answered and said to them, *"Destroy this temple, and in three days I will raise it up."* The Jews therefore said, *"Forty-six years* was this temple in building, and will you raise it up in three *days?"* But he was speaking of the temple of his body. So when he had been raised from the dead, his disciples remembered that he had said this to them, and they believed the Scripture and the reply which Jesus had made.

*23. Jesus' Answer to Nicodemus*

*(Jn. 2:23-3:21)*

Now while he was in Jerusalem at the Passover, many believed upon his name when they saw the miraculous signs he was performing. Yet Jesus on his part did not trust himself to them; because he knew all men and needed no witness to tell about man, for He himself knew what was in man.

But there was a man of the Pharisees named Nicodemus, a ruler of the Jews; this man came to Jesus by night, and said to him, "Rabbi, we know that you are a Teacher come from God; for no one can do these miraculous signs which you are doing, except God be with him." Jesus answered and said to him, "Verily, verily, I say to you, *except a man be born again, he cannot see the Kingdom of God."*

Nicodemus said to him, "How can a man be born when he is *old? Can* he enter a second time into his mother's womb, and be born?" Jesus answered, "Verily, verily, I say to you, except a man be born *of water and the Spirit,* he cannot enter the Kingdom of God. That which is born of the flesh is flesh, and that which is born of the Spirit is spirit. Marvel not that I said to you, 'You must all be born *again.'* The wind blows where it will, and you listen to its sound, but know not from where it is coming or where it is going; so it is with everyone who has been *born of the Spirit."*

*"Whoever Believes Upon Him"*

Nicodemus answered and said to him, *"How can these things be?"* Jesus answering said to him, "Are *you* the teacher *of Israel,* yet you do not know these things? Verily, verily, I say to you, we speak what we know, and testify what we have seen—and you people *are not accepting* our witness! If I told you earthly things and you believe not, how will you believe if I tell you heavenly things?

"And no one has ascended into heaven but He who came *down out of* heaven, the Son of man [whose home is in heaven]. And as Moses lifted up the serpent in the wilderness, even so must *the Son of man* be lifted up, that whoever believes upon *Him* should not perish but should have *everlasting* life.[a]

*"For God so loved the world that He gave his only begotten Son, that whoever believes upon Him should not perish but should have everlasting life.*[a]

"For God sent not his Son into the world that he should

condemn the world, but that the world might be saved
through Him. He who believes upon Him is not condemned;
but he who believes not is condemned already, because he has
not believed upon the name of *God's* only begotten *Son.*

"And the condemnation is this, that the Light has come into
the world, but men loved the darkness rather than the Light,
because their deeds were evil. For everyone making a practice
of evil hates the Light and does not come to the Light, lest his
deeds should be disclosed. But he who practices the truth
comes to the Light, that his deeds may be made evident, that
they have been wrought in *God.*"[b]

### 24. John the Baptist's Tribute to Jesus
#### (Jn. 3:22-36)

After these things Jesus went with his disciples into the Judean countryside, where he tarried with them, baptizing. And
John, too, was baptizing, in Aenon near Salim, since the waters were abundant there. And the people kept coming and being baptized, for John had not yet been cast into prison.

Then a question arose between John's disciples and some
Jews concerning purification; and they came up to John, and
said to him, "Rabbi, he who was with you beyond the Jordan,
to whom *you* have borne witness, behold, this man is baptizing and all the people are going to *him.*" John answered and
said, "A man can take nothing except as it be given him from
heaven. You yourselves bear me witness, that I said that *I* am
not the Messiah but was sent to introduce him. The *bridegroom* is he that has the bride. And the friend of the bridegroom, who stands and listens for him, *rejoices* greatly when
he hears the bridegroom's voice. This joy of *mine* therefore is
fulfilled. *He must increase, and I must decrease.*"[a]

He who comes *from above* is over all. A man from the earth
belongs to the earth, and from the earth he speaks; but the
One who comes *from heaven* is over all.

And what he testifies is what he has seen and heard; yet no
one is accepting his testimony! He who has accepted his testimony has set his seal that *God* is true; for he whom God has

sent *speaks God's words.*

For it is not by measure that God gives the Spirit; the Father loves the Son and has given *all things* into his hand. *He who believes upon the Son has everlasting life; but he who obeys not the Son shall not see life, but the wrath of God abides upon him.*

### 25. *Jesus and the Woman at the Well*
*(Mt. 4:12; Lk. 3:19-20; Jn. 4:1-42)*

[3] Now Herod[a] the tetrarch, on being rebuked by John about Herodias, his brother Philip's wife, and all the evil things Herod had done, added yet this above all, that he shut up John in prison. [4] When therefore the Lord knew that the Pharisees had heard that Jesus was winning and baptizing more disciples than John (although Jesus himself was not baptizing, but rather his disciples), [1] and when he heard that John had been arrested, [4] he left Judea and [1] withdrew [4] again into Galilee.

And he needed to pass through Samaria. He came therefore to a city of Samaria called Sychar, near the portion of land which Jacob gave to his son Joseph. Now Jacob's well was there. Jesus therefore, being worn from the journey, sat in weariness by the well. It was about six in the evening.

There came a woman of Samaria to draw water. Jesus said to her, "Give *me* some to drink." For his disciples had gone away into the city to purchase food. Then said the woman of Samaria to him, "How is it that you, a *Jew,* are asking a drink of *me,* a woman of Samaria?" (For the Jews have no dealings with Samaritans.) Jesus answered and said to her, "If you had known the gift of God, and Who he is who says to you, 'Give *me* some to drink,' you would have asked of Him, and He would have given you *living* water."

The woman said to him, "Sir, you have nothing to draw with, and the well is deep; from where then do you have the *living water?* Are *you* greater than our father Jacob, who gave us the well, and drank from it himself, and his sons, and his cattle?" Jesus answered and said to her, "All who drink of this water will thirst again; but anyone who drinks of the water

that *I* will give him shall never thirst again, but the water that I
will give him will become in him a fountain of water springing
up into *everlasting life.*"

The woman said to him, "Sir, give me this water, that I need
not thirst nor have to come here to draw." Jesus said to her,
"Go call your husband, and come back here." The woman answered and said, "I have no husband." Jesus said to her, "Well
did you say, 'I have no husband;' for you have had five hus-
bands, and he whom you have now is not your husband. This
you have spoken truly."

The woman said to him, "I perceive, Sir, that you are a
prophet. Our fathers worshiped on this mountain—and you
*Jews* say that in Jerusalem is the place where men ought to
worship." Jesus said to her, "Woman, believe me, an hour is
coming when neither on this mountain nor in Jerusalem you
will worship the Father. You Samaritans worship what you
know not; *we* worship what we know, for salvation *is* from the
Jews. But an hour is coming, and now is, when the true wor-
shipers shall worship the Father *in spirit and truth.* For it is
also *such* the Father seeks to worship *him.* God is a Spirit, and
they who worship him *must* worship in spirit and truth."

The woman said to him, "I know that *Messiah* is coming,
who is called *Christ;* when *he* comes, he will tell us all things."
Jesus said to her, *"I* who am speaking to you AM HE."[b]

### *"The Fields Are White for Harvest"*

Now upon this his disciples came; and they marveled that he
was talking with a woman, but none of them asked, "What are
you seeking?" or, "Why are you talking with her?" Then the
woman left her water jar, and went back into the city and said
to the men, "Come see a man who told me everything I did!
Would not this be *the Messiah?"* So they went out from the
city and made their way toward him.

Meanwhile his disciples were urging him, "Rabbi, *eat!"* But
he said to them, *"I* have food to eat which you know not of."
The disciples therefore began to say to one another, "No one
brought him anything to eat, did they?" Jesus said to them,

"My food is *to do the will of Him who sent me, and to accomplish His work.* Are not *you* saying that it is yet *four months*[c]
and then the harvest is coming? Lo, I say to you, lift up your
eyes and behold the *fields,* for they are white for harvest already! And he who reaps receives a reward and gathers fruit
unto life everlasting, that both he who sows and he who
reaps may rejoice together. For in this is the saying true, that
'One sows and another reaps.' *I* sent you to reap what *you*
have not labored on; others have labored and *you have entered
into* their labor."

And many of the Samaritans of that city believed upon him
through the word of the woman who testified, "He told me
everything I did!" So when the Samaritans came to where he
was, they besought him to remain with them; and he remained
there two days. And many more believed because of his own
word, and they said to the woman, "No longer do we believe
because of what *you* said; for we have heard for ourselves, and
we know that this is truly [the Messiah,] *the Savior of the
world!"*

## Chapter 5. He Is Welcomed in Galilee

### 26. A Dying Boy Is Healed from Cana
#### (Jn. 4:43-54)

But after the two days he departed from that place; and he
journeyed a ways into Galilee,[a] for even Jesus testified that a
prophet has no honor in his home town. When therefore he arrived in Galilee, the Galileans welcomed him, having seen all
the things which he did in Jerusalem at the feast; for they, too,
had attended the feast. He thus came once more into Cana of
Galilee, where he had made the water wine.

Now there was a certain court officer in Capernaum whose
son was sick. When he heard that Jesus had come from Judea

into Galilee, he journeyed to him and besought him to come
down and restore his son, for he was about to die. Jesus said
therefore to him, "Unless you people see miraculous signs and
wonders, you will not at all believe." The court officer said to
him, "Sir, do come down before my child dies!" Jesus said to
him, "Go—your son *is living.*"

And the man believed the word which Jesus spoke to him,
and went his way. And even while he was on his way down, his
bondservants met him and reported, saying, "Your child is
*alive!*" So he asked them at what hour he began to mend, and
they said to him, "Yesterday at seven in the evening the fever
left him." The father therefore knew that it was at the very
hour when Jesus had said to him, "Your son *is living,*" and he
himself and all his household believed. This is again a second
miraculous sign which Jesus wrought on his return from Judea
into Galilee.

### 27. But Nazareth Is Outraged at Him
#### (Lk. 4:14-30)

So Jesus returned into Galilee in the power of the Spirit;
and a report concerning him went out into all the region round
about, and he began to teach in their synagogues, being praised
by all.

Then[a] came he to Nazareth, where he had been brought up;
and as was his custom, he went into the synagogue on the Sabbath. And he stood up to read, and there was handed him the
book of the prophet Isaiah; and when he had unrolled the
scroll, he found the place where it was written:

> *"The Spirit of the Lord is upon me;*
> *because of this he has anointed me.*[b]
> *To publish glad news to the lowly has he sent me;*
> *to restore those broken in heart;*
> *to proclaim deliverance to the captives,*
> *and recovery of sight to the blind;*
> *to give freedom to the oppressed;*
> *to proclaim the acceptable year of the Lord...",*

and he rolled up the scroll and returned it to the attendant and

sat down. And the eyes of all in the synagogue were fixed upon him. And he began to speak to them: *"Today* has this scripture been fulfilled—*in the things of which you have heard."*
And they all bore him witness and marveled at the words of
grace which proceeded from his mouth.

But they began to say, "Is not this *Joseph's son?"*[c] So he
said to them, "Assuredly you will quote to me this proverb,
*'Physician, heal yourself.* All that we have heard that was done
at Capernaum do here also in your home town.'" And he said,
"Verily I say to you, that no prophet is acceptable in his home
town. And I say to you in truth, there were *many* widows *in
Israel* in the days of Elijah, when heaven was shut up for three
years and six months, with a great famine over all the land;
but to none of them was Elijah sent, but only to a widow
woman in Zarephath of Sidonia. And there were *many* lepers
*in Israel* in the time of Elisha the prophet; but none of them
was cleansed, but only Naaman the Syrian."

Now at hearing these things all in the synagogue were infur-
iated; and they rose up and thrust him out of the city, and led
him up to the brow of the hill on which their city had been
built, to hurl him down headlong. But he, passing through the
midst of them, went his way.

### 28. Giving the Glad News to Capernaum
*(Mt. 4:13-17; Mk. 1:14-15; Lk. 4:31a)*

[1] And leaving Nazareth, [3] he went down and [1] dwelt at Capernaum, [3] a city of Galilee, [1] which is by the sea in the region
of Zebulon and Naphtali; that there might be fulfilled what
was spoken through the prophet Isaiah, saying,
> *"Land of Zebulon and land of Naphtali,*
> *the way to the sea across the Jordan—*
> *Galilee of the Gentiles—*
> *the people who were sitting in darkness*
> *have seen a great Light,*
> *and those dwelling in the land*
> *and in the shadow of death,*
> *on them has a Light arisen."*

From that time Jesus began to preach, [2] proclaiming the gospel of the Kingdom of God, and saying, *"The time is fulfilled, and the Kingdom of God has drawn near. Repent, and believe the Glad News!* [1] For the Kingdom of heaven *is at hand."*[a]

### 29. *"I Will MAKE You Fishermen"*
#### *(Mt. 4:18-22; Mk. 1:16-20)*

[2] Now as he was walking by the Sea of Galilee, he saw Simon [1] called Peter, and Andrew his brother, casting a net into the sea; for they were commercial[a] fishermen. [2] And Jesus said to them, "Come, follow Me, and I will *make* you fishermen—*of men!"* And immediately they left their nets and followed him.

And going on from there, he saw [1] two other brothers, James the son of Zebedee, and John his brother, [2] who were [1] in the boat with their father, mending their nets; [2] and at once he called them. [1] And forthwith they left the boat, and their father [2] Zebedee in the boat with the hired helpers, and went away [1] and followed him.

### 30. *An Unclean Spirit Obeys Him*
#### *(Mk. 1:21,23-28; Lk. 4:31b,33-37)*

[2] Then went they into Capernaum, and at once he went into the synagogue on the Sabbath days and began to teach. And there was in their synagogue a man possessed with a spirit [3] of an unclean demon, and it cried out with a loud voice, saying, *"Let us alone!* What are you doing to us, Jesus, you Nazarene? Have you come to destroy us? I know you, who you are: *the Holy One of God."* But Jesus rebuked it, saying, [2] "Be quiet, and come out of him."

So when the foul spirit [3] had hurled him down in their midst, [2] and had convulsed him and cried out in a shrieking voice, [3] it came out of him, having harmed him not. And they were all amazed, [2] so that they questioned within themselves [3] and spoke to each other, [2] saying, "What is *this?"* "What *new teaching* is this?" [3] *"What an utterance* is this! For with authority and power he commands [2] even the unclean spirits, and they obey him [3] and come out." [2] And immediately his fame spread abroad [3] into every place [2] through all the region of Galilee round about.

## 31. Many Healings and an Extended Tour
### (Mt. 8:14-17;4:23; Mk. 1:29-39; Lk. 4:38-44)

[1] And Jesus [3] arose and left the synagogue, [2] and forthwith he came with James and John into the home of Simon [1] Peter [2] and Andrew. Now Simon's wife's mother lay sick, [3] suffering with a great fever, [2] and at once they told him about her [3] and besought him in her behalf. [2] So he came and [1] saw her, [3] and standing over her he [1] touched her hand and [3] rebuked the fever; and [2] he took her by the hand and raised her up. And immediately the fever left her, [3] and she arose at once and ministered to their needs!

[2] Then with evening [3] and the setting of the sun, all who had any sick with whatever diseases began bringing them to him, [2] and [1] many possessed with demons. [3] And he laid his hands on each of them and healed them, [1] and cast out the spirits with a word; that there might be fulfilled what was spoken through the prophet Isaiah, when he said, *"He took upon himself our infirmities, and removed our diseases."* [2] So all the city gathered at the door. [3] And demons coming out from many cried out and said, "You are [ *the Messiah,* ] *the Son of God!"*[a] But he rebuking them would not let them speak, because they knew that he was the Messiah.

[2] And rising very early, a great while before day, he went out [3] at dawn [2] and betook himself to a secluded place, and there prayed. Then Simon and those with him searched after him; and when they found him, they said to him, "All the people are looking for you." But he said to them, "Let us go on to the other towns nearby, that I may preach there also; it was for this that I came out."

[3] And the crowds *were looking* for him, and came upon him and attempted to stay him from leaving them. But he said to

them, "I *must* preach the Glad News, the Kingdom of God, to the other cities also; *it is for this that I have been sent forth.*"

[1] And Jesus went throughout all Galilee, teaching in their synagogues and preaching the Glad News of the Kingdom, healing every sickness and infirmity among the people, [2] and casting out the demons.

### 32. He Challenges the Fishermen Again
#### (Lk. 5:1-11)

Then it came to pass that, while the crowds were pressing about him to hear the Word of God, as he was standing by the lake of Gennesaret he saw two boats moored by the shore, out of which the fishermen had come while washing their nets. And getting into one of the boats, which was Simon's, he asked him to push out a little way from the shore, and sitting down he taught the crowds from the boat. And when he had left off speaking, he said to Simon, "Launch out to where it is *deep,* and let down your nets for a catch." Simon answered and said, "Master, we have toiled all night and have taken nothing. Nevertheless, at your command I will let down the *net.*"[a]

Now when they had done so, they enclosed a huge number of fish. And their net began to break, so they beckoned to their partners in the other boat to come and help them; and they came and filled both the boats, so that they were about to sink.

And when Simon Peter saw it, he fell down at Jesus' knees, saying, *"Depart from me,* for I am a *sinful* man, Lord!" For he was astonished, and all who were with him, at the haul of fish they had taken; and so were James and John, Simon's partners, the sons of Zebedee. But Jesus said to Simon, "Fear not; you will henceforth catch *men."* And when they had brought the boats back to shore, they left *everything*[b] and followed him.

### 33. A Man Full of Leprosy Is Healed
*(Mt. 8:2-4; Mk. 1:40-45; Lk. 5:12-16)*

³ And it came to pass that while he was in one of the cities, behold, a man who was full of leprosy, when he saw Jesus, ² came to him, beseeching him; and kneeling down, ³ he fell on his face ¹ and worshiped, saying, "Lord, if you are willing, you can *make me clean.*" ² And Jesus, moved with compassion, reached out his hand and touched him, saying to him, *"I am willing; be cleansed."* And the leprosy instantly left him and he was healed. Then he sternly enjoined him and immediately dismissed him, saying, "See that you tell no one; but go and *show yourself to the priest,* and for your cleansing make the offering that Moses commanded, as a testimony to *them."*

But when he went out, he began to tell it freely and announce the news far and wide. ³ So Jesus' fame was spread abroad all the more, ² so that he could no longer go openly into a city,ᵃ but remained out in solitary places. ³ And great multitudes were gathering ² from every quarter ³ to hear, and to be healed of their infirmities; but he himself kept withdrawing into the wilderness and praying.

### 34. A Paralytic Is Forgiven and Healed
*(Mt. 9:2-8; Mk. 2:1-12; Lk. 5:17-26)*

² Now after some days he went again into Capernaum. ³ And it came to pass on a certain day that, as he was teaching, there were ¹ some of the scribes, ³ Pharisees and teachers of the law sitting by, who had come out of every town of Galilee, and from Judea and Jerusalem. ² Then the word spread around that he was at home, and [immediately] so many came together that there was no longer any room, not even about the door. And he was telling them the Word, ³ and the Lord's power was present for him to heal.

And behold, ² there came men bringing him ³ a man who was paralyzed, ¹ lying on a pallet ² which was borne by four; ³ and they sought how to bring him in and lay him before him. ² And when they could not get near him for the crowd, ³ they went up on the housetop and [2] tore open the roof above where he was; and on making an opening, [3] they lowered him with the pallet down through the tiles, right into the midst before Jesus. Seeing their faith, he said [1] to the paralytic, "Take courage, young [3] man. [2] *Your sins are forgiven you.*"

But [1] behold, [3] the scribes and Pharisees began to ponder [2] in their hearts, [3] saying, "Who is this who is speaking *blasphemies?* [2] Why does *this man* speak thus? [3] Who can forgive sins but *God alone?*" [2] Then Jesus, knowing at once in his spirit that they reasoned thus within themselves, [3] answered and said to them, [2] "Why do you ask yourselves these things? [1] Why do you think evil in your hearts? For which is easier, [2] to say to the paralytic, *'Your sins are forgiven you,'* or to say, *'Arise, and take up your pallet and walk'?* But that you may know that the Son of man *has authority*[a] on the earth to forgive sins," (he said to the paralytic) *"I say to you, arise, and take up your pallet and go home."*

And immediately he rose up before them all, [3] and taking up that on which he had lain, he went off to his home, praising God; [2] so that [1] the crowds who had seen it [2] were all seized with amazement, and glorified God [1] who had given such power to men. [3] And they were filled with awe, saying, [2] "We never saw such as this! [3] We have seen strange things today."

### 35. Tax Official Matthew Is Enlisted
*(Mt. 9:9; Mk. 2:13-14; Lk. 5:27-28)*

[3] Then after these things [1] Jesus [3] went forth [1] from there [2] again, along by the shore of the sea. And all the people kept coming to him, and he continued teaching them. Now as he was passing by, [3] he saw a publican named Levi [1] (Matthew),[a] [2] the son of Alpheus, seated at the tax office; [3] and he said to *him*, "Follow Me." And he rose up, and left everything and followed him.

\*     \*     \*

*Comment.* Note that the call of Matthew brings us already to the end of Jesus' first year of public ministry. It was at a Passover, observed by the Jews annually in spring, that His Messianic labors were begun (see Sec. 22); another Passover is now approaching. The incident in the grain fields took place on the Galilean annual First S abbath (which was the first Sabbath after Passover), specifically on the second such of His ministry (See Appendix IV).

During the first year Jesus spent much time in Judea and by the Jordan. After John's imprisonment, Jesus removed to the Galilean area, Herod's territory, and intensified His message, "Repent, for the kingdom of heaven is at hand." At Nazareth, His home town, He experienced His first general rejection, and then removed to the Capernaum area. I t was from this area that He chose nearly all His disciples during that second spring, at the conclusion of which the Pharisaic opposition began to crystallize. His final choice of Matthew, a former tax collector for Rome, was a particular outrage to the Pharisaic leaders. Thus, the year ended with John in prison and a definite tide of official opposition developing.

The brevity of the Evangelists concerning this first year may seem somewhat strange. The Synoptists skip the whole period from the temptation to His departure into Galilee after John's imprisonment. Only John's Gospel records events of that early Judean ministry, and that rather skimpily. This was while John the Baptist was "decreasing" and Jesus was "increasing." It should be noted, however, that the apostles were not evidently with Him during most of this time except on a part-time basis. Therefore, it was not a period of inactivity, though unrecorded, for He "went throughout all Galilee" that spring, teaching, preaching, and healing, followed by tremendous crowds (as noted in Sec. 31). These crowds of Galilee were to be His parish during the next year, His second year of ministry.

# PART III.

## THE YEAR OF GREAT PUBLIC FAVOR

### Chapter 6. Teaching as One with Authority

*36. In the Grain Fields on the Sabbath*
  *(Mt. 12:1-8; Mk. 2:23-28; Lk. 6:1-5)*

[2] Now [1] Jesus was then journeying by way of the grain fields on the Sabbaths. [3] And it came to pass [on the second First Sabbath] [a] that he was walking through the grain fields, [1] and his disciples were hungry and began, [2] as they went, to pluck the heads of grain [1] and to eat, [3] rubbing them in their hands. [1] But when [3] some of the Pharisees [1] saw it, they said to him, [2] "Behold, why [1] are your disciples doing [2] what is *not lawful* [b] to do on a Sabbath?"

[3] And Jesus answering said to them, [2] "Did you never read [3] even this, what David did [2] when he had need and was hungry, he and those who were with him, how he went into the house of God, when Abiathar was the high priest, [3] and took and ate *the showbread loaves*" [2] (which is not lawful but for [3] the priests alone) [2] "and gave also to those who were with him? [1] Or have you not read in the law, how on the Sabbaths the priests in the temple break the Sabbath and yet are guiltless? Now I say to you, that One greater than the temple is *here*. And if you had known what this means, *'Mercy is what I desire, and not sacrifice,'* you would not have condemned the guiltless."

[2] And he said to them, "The Sabbath was made for man, not man for the Sabbath! So then the Son of man is *Lord* also of *the Sabbath.*"

## 37. A Man's Withered Hand Is Healed
### (Mt. 12:9-14; Mk. 3:1-6; Lk. 6:6-11)

[3] Then it came to pass on another Sabbath also, [1] after he departed from that place, [3] that he went [2] again [1] into their synagogue [3] and taught; [1] and behold, there was a man there [3] whose right hand was withered, and the scribes and the Pharisees were watching him to see if he would heal [2] him on the Sabbath, that they might accuse him. [1] And they asked him, saying, "Is it lawful to *heal* on the Sabbath?"

[3] But he knew their thoughts, and said to the man with the withered hand, "Rise up, and stand before them." And he rose up and stood. Then said Jesus to them, "I will ask you this, is it lawful on the Sabbath *to do good*—or to do evil? *To save life*—or to destroy it?" [2] But they kept silent. [1] And he said to them, "What man shall there be among you who shall have one sheep, and if it fall into a pit on the Sabbath he will not take hold of it and lift it out? Then how much more is a man worth than a *sheep!* Therefore *it is lawful* on the Sabbath *to do good.*"

[3] And [2] then looking around at them all with anger, being grieved at the hardness of their hearts, he said to the man, "Stretch out your hand." And he stretched it out, and his hand was restored [1] as whole as the other. [3] But they were filled with madness, and began to consult with one another what they might do to Jesus. [2] And the Pharisees went out and immediately [1] held a council [2] with the Herodians against him, how they might destroy him.[a]

## 38. Multitudes Come; the Twelve Are Appointed
### (Mt. 12:15-21;4:24-25;10:2-4; Mk. 3:7-19a; Lk. 6:12-19)

[1] But Jesus, knowing this, withdrew from there [2] with his disciples to the sea; [1] and there followed him great throngs from Galilee and the Decapolis, and from Jerusalem and [3] all Judea, [2] and from Idumea and beyond the Jordan. [1] And his fame spread forth throughout all Syria; and men brought to him all who were sick, oppressed with various diseases and tor-

ments, the demon-possessed and epileptics and paralytics, and he healed them.

[3] And a multitude from the seacoast [2] around Tyre and Sidon, hearing what great things he was doing, came to him. So he asked his disciples to have a boat ready for him, lest the throng should overwhelm him; for he healed such a number that they pressed forward to touch him, as many as had diseases, [3] and those troubled with unclean spirits. [2] And the unclean spirits, on seeing him, fell down before him and cried out, "You are *the Son of God!*" [1] And he healed them all, although he charged them [2] strictly [1] not to make him openly known, in fulfillment of the utterance of Isaiah the prophet,

*"Behold my Servant whom I have chosen,*
*my beloved in whom my soul has delighted!*
*My Spirit will I put upon him,*
*and justice will he make known to the nations.*
*"He will not contend nor be clamorous,*
*nor will any in the streets hear his voice.*
*A bruised reed will he not break,*
*and a smoldering wick will he not quench,*
*till he bring forth justice unto victory;*
*and in his name will the nations have hope."*

[3] And it came to pass at this time that he went out upon the mountain[a] to pray, and spent all night in prayer to God; and when it was day, he summoned his disciples, [2] those whom he desired, and they came out to him. And he appointed twelve, [3] whom he also named apostles, [2] that they might stay with him, and that he should send them out to preach and to have power to [heal sicknesses and] cast out demons. [1] Now the names of the twelve apostles are these: first, Simon [3] whom he also [2] surnamed Peter, [1] and Andrew his brother, James the son of Zebedee, [2] and John the brother of James (these he also surnamed Boanerges, that is, sons of thunder); and Philip, and Bartholomew, [1] Thomas, and Matthew the publican, James the son of Alphaeus, and [Lebbaeus] [3] (Judas the son of James, [1] [whose surname was] Thaddaeus); Simon the Cananean [3] (who was called the Zealot), and Judas Iscariot, who also became the betrayer.

Then coming down with them he stood in a level place, with a number of his disciples and a great throng of the people who came to hear him and to be freed from their diseases. [3] And all the throng kept seeking to touch him, for power was coming from him and healing all.

### 39. Teaching the Twelve on the Mountain
*(Mt. 5:1-7:29; Mk. 1:22; Lk. 6:20-7:1a;16:17;12:57-59;12:22b-31;4:32)*

[1] And seeing the multitudes, he went up on the mountain; and when he was seated, his disciples came to him. [3] And lifting up his eyes on his disciples, [1] he opened his mouth and began to teach[a] them, saying,

[3] *"Blessed* are you who are poor! For yours is the Kingdom of God.

*"Blessed* are you who hunger now! For you shall be satisfied.

*"Blessed* are you who weep now! For you shall laugh.

"But *woe* to you who are rich! For you *are receiving* your comfort.

*"Woe* to you who are surfeited! For you *shall suffer hunger.*

*"Woe* to you who are merry now! For you *shall lament and weep.*

*"Woe* to you when all shall speak well of you! For their fathers did the same to the false prophets.

### True Discipleship Brings True Rewards
*(Mt. 5:3-12; Lk. 6:22-23)*

[1] *"Blessed* are the lowly in spirit. For theirs is the Kingdom of heaven.

*"Blessed* are they who mourn. For they shall be comforted.

*"Blessed* are the meek. For they shall inherit the earth.

*"Blessed* are they who hunger and thirst for righteousness. For they shall be satisfied.

*"Blessed* are the merciful. For they shall obtain mercy.

*"Blessed* are the pure in heart. For they shall see God.

*"Blessed* are the peacemakers. For they shall be called sons

of God.

"*Blessed* are they who are persecuted for righteousness' sake. For theirs is the Kingdom of heaven.

"*Blessed* are you when men shall hate you, and revile and persecute you, and say falsely all kinds of evil against you because of Me; [3] when they shall excommunicate you, and denounce your name as evil, because of *the Son of man.* Rejoice in that day, and leap for joy, for behold, your reward is great in heaven. For their fathers did these things to the prophets [1] who were before you.

### But Discipleship Requires High Conduct
#### (Mt. 5:13-20; Lk. 16:17)

[1] "You are the salt of the earth. But if the salt *has lost its saltness,* what shall make it salt again? It is no longer fit for anything but to be tossed out and trampled on by men.

"You are the light of the world. A city situated on a mountain cannot be hid; neither do men light a lamp and put it under a grain-measure, but *on the lampstand,* where it shines for everyone in the house. In this way let your light *shine before men,* that they may see your good works and give praise to *your Father who is in heaven.*

"Think not that I came to abolish the law or the prophets; I came not to annul but *to fulfill.* For verily, I say to you, till heaven and earth pass away, not one smallest letter or part of a letter shall by any means be removed from the law, *until all shall be fulfilled.* [3] And it is easier for heaven and earth to pass away than for one particle of the law to fail!

[1] "Wherefore, he that shall break one of the least of these commandments, and teach men so, shall be called least in the Kingdom of heaven; but he that shall practice and teach them, *he* shall be called *great* in the Kingdom of heaven. For I say to you, that unless your righteousness abounds more than that of the scribes and Pharisees, you shall by no means enter the Kingdom of heaven!

## It Reflects Your Attitude of Heart
### (Mt. 5:21-26; Lk. 12:57-59)

[1] "You have heard how it was said to them of old, *'You shall not murder;'* and he who commits murder shall be answerable to the court. But *I* say to you, that anyone who is *angry* at his brother [without cause] shall be answerable to the court; and anyone who calls his brother *'Emptyhead'* shall be answerable to the Sanhedrin; and he that shall say to him, *'You fool!'* shall be in danger of Gehenna's fire.

"Wherefore, if you are offering your gift at the altar and remember while there that your brother has something against you, *leave* your gift there before the altar and go away—*first make reconciliation* with your brother, and then come back and offer your gift.

[3] "And why also do you not *of yourselves* judge what is right? For when you are going with your accuser before a magistrate, give diligence [1] even while on the way with him [3] to bring about a settlement [1] quickly; [3] lest he drag you to the judge, and the judge commit you to the officer, and the officer throw you into prison. [1] Verily, I say to you, you will by no means get out of there till you have paid [3] the last fraction of a cent!

## It Means Purity, Fidelity, Simplicity
### (Mt. 5:27-37)

[1] "You have heard how it was said to them of old, *'You shall not commit adultery.'* But *I* say to you, that any man who *looks at* a woman with carnal desire has committed adultery with her already in his heart. So, if your *right eye* be the cause of your stumbling, pluck it out and throw it away from you![b] For it is better for you that one of your members perish, and not your whole body be cast into Gehenna. And if your *right hand* be the cause of your stumbling, cut it off and throw it away from you! For it is better for you that one of your members perish and not your whole body be cast into Gehenna.

"Furthermore, it was said, *'If any man put away his wife,*

*let him give her a writ of divorce.'* But *I* say to you, that if any man *put away* his wife, except for fornication, he causes her to commit adultery; and if any man marries her who has been put away, *he* commits adultery.

"Again, you have heard how it was said to them of old, *'You shall not swear falsely,'* and, *'You shall perform for the Lord what you have vowed.'* But *I* say to you, swear not at all. Not by heaven, for it is God's throne; not by the earth, for it is his footstool; not by Jerusalem, for it is 'the city of the great King.' Neither shall you swear by your head, for you cannot make one hair white or black. But let your word Yes be *'Yes,'* and your word No, *'No,'* for anything more than these comes from evil.

### It Answers Personal Enmity with Love
*(Mt. 5:38-48; Lk. 6:27-30,32-36)*

[1] "You have heard how it was said, *'An eye for an eye, and a tooth for a tooth.'* But *I* say to you, resist not the evildoer. Instead, if someone strikes you [3] upon the cheek, [1] turn to him *the other also.* If someone should sue you and take away your tunic, yield to him your cloak as well; [3] and from him who takes away your cloak, do not withhold the tunic also. [1] And if someone should compel you to go one mile, go with him *two.*

[3] "Give to everyone who may ask of you, [1] and from him who would borrow of you turn not away. [3] And from anyone who may take away what is yours, demand it not back again.

[1] "You have heard how it was said, *'You shall love your neighbor,'* (and *'hate* your enemy'). But to *you* [3] *who are hearing me,* I say, *love your enemies:* do good to those who hate you, bless those who curse you, [1] and pray for those who a-buse and persecute you, so that you may *be* sons of your Father who is in heaven. For He makes his sun to rise upon e-vil men and good, and sends rain upon the righteous and un-righteous.

"For if you love those who love you, what reward have you, [3] what credit is due you? For even the sinful love those who love them. [1] Do not even the publicans the same? And if you greet your brethren only, what are you doing more than others? Do not even the publicans so?

³"And if you help those who are helpful to you, what credit is due you? For even the sinful do the same. And if you lend to those from whom you hope to receive, what credit is yours? For even the sinful lend to the sinful, to receive the same favor in return.

"No, love your *enemies,* and do good and lend, looking for nothing in return. Then your reward will be great, and you will *be* sons of the Highest; for He is good to the ungrateful and the wicked.

"Be therefore compassionate *as your Father* also is compassionate; ¹you shall therefore be perfect, even *as your Father* who is in heaven is perfect.ᶜ

## *It Avoids Parading Its Good Works*
### *(Mt. 6:1-18)*

"Take heed not to do your good works before men to be seen by them, else you have no reward with your Father who is in heaven.

"So when you are giving alms, sound no trumpet before you, as the hypocrites do, in the synagogues and the streets, to have the applause of men. Verily, I say to you, they *are having* their full reward. But you, in giving alms, let not your left hand know what your right hand is doing, that your alms may be in secret; and your Father, who sees in secret, will himself reward you.

"And when you pray, do not be like the hypocrites; for they love to pray standing in the synagogues and on the street corners, that they may be conspicuous before men. Verily, I say to you, they *are having* their full reward. But you, when you pray, go into your inner room, and with closed door pray to your Father who is in secret; and your Father, who sees in secret, will reward you.

"And in praying do not babble over and over as the heathen do, for they think that many words will cause them to be heard. Do not, therefore, be like them; for your Father knows what you need before you ask him.

"*You* therefore should pray like this:
   'Our Father, who art in heaven,
hallowed be thy name!
May thy Kingdom come, thy will be done
on earth as it is in heaven.
   'Give us today our needful bread;
and forgive us our debts,
as we also are forgiving our debtors.
And lead us not into temptation,
but deliver us from the evil one.
   ['For thine is the Kingdom, and the power,
and the glory forever. Amen. ']d

"For if you forgive men their offenses, your heavenly Father will forgive you also; but if you forgive not men their offenses, neither will your Father forgive your offenses.

"Moreover, when you fast, be not downcast in face like the hypocrites; for they distort their appearance so that their fasting may be noticed by men. Verily, I say to you, they *are having* their full reward. But you, in your fasting, groom your head with oil and wash your face, that your fasting may not be noticed by men, but by your Father who is in secret; and your Father, who sees in secret, will reward you.

## Its Treasures Are Stored in Heaven

### (Mt. 6:19-24)

"Store not up for yourselves treasures on the earth, where moth and corrosion destroy, and where thieves dig through and steal; but store up for yourselves treasures in heaven, where neither moth nor corrosion destroys and where thieves do not dig through and steal. *For where your treasure is, there will your heart be also.*

"The body's source of light is the eye; if therefore your eye is sound, your whole body will be filled with light, but if your eye is diseased, your whole body will be filled with darkness. If therefore the *light* that is in you is darkness, how deep the darkness!

"No man can serve two masters; for either he will hate the

one and love the other, or he will hold to the one and despise the other. You cannot serve God *and* riches.

### It Trusts in the Father's Care

*(Mt. 6: 25-34; Lk. 12:22b-31)*

[1] "Wherefore, I say to you, be not anxious about your life, what you shall eat or drink, nor for your body, what you shall put on. Is not the life more than what you eat, and the body than what you wear?

"Behold the fowls of the air, how they sow not, neither reap nor gather into [3] a storehouse or granary, [1] yet your heavenly Father feeds them. Are not you worth much more than they?

"And who of you by being anxious can add the shortest measure to his life? [3] If then you cannot do what is least in importance, why are you anxious about the rest?

[1] "So why are you troubled about raiment? Consider the lilies of the field, how they grow. They toil not, neither do they spin; yet I say to you that even Solomon in all his glory was not arrayed like one of these. Now if God thus clothes the plant life of the field, which is here today and is tossed into a furnace tomorrow, will he not much more clothe you, you of little faith?

"Therefore say not anxiously, 'What shall we eat?' or 'What shall we drink?' or 'What clothing shall we have?' [3] Do not be of doubting mind. [1] For, all of these things [3] all the peoples of the world are seeking [1] and your heavenly Father *knows* that you need all these things. *But seek first the Kingdom of God and his righteousness, and all these things will be given you besides.*

"So be not anxious concerning tomorrow, for tomorrow will care for its own needs. *Today's trouble is sufficient for today.*

### It Is Generous, Humble, and Wise

*(Mt. 7:1-11; Lk. 6:37-42)*

[3] "Furthermore, judge not, [1] lest you be judged. For in the

same way you judge, you will be judged. [3] Condemn not, and you will not be condemned. Release, and you will be released.

*"Give, and it will be given to you:* good measure, pressed down, shaken together, and running over, will men pour out into your lap. For with the measure you use will it be measured to you in return."

Then he spoke to them in a similitude: "Can a *blind* man guide the blind? Will not both of them fall into a pit? A disciple is not above his teacher, and everyone perfectly taught *will resemble* his teacher.

"But why do you glare at the speck in your brother's eye, *but see not* the piece of lumber in your own eye? Or how can you say to your brother, 'Brother, let me take out the speck that is in your eye,' [1] when lo, [3] you yourself do not see the piece of lumber *in your own* eye? You hypocrite, first take out the piece of lumber from your own eye, and then will you see clearly to take out the speck from your brother's eye.

[1] "Give not that which is holy to the dogs, nor pour out your pearls before the swine—lest the latter trample on them with their feet, and they should turn around and wound you.

*"Ask, and it shall be given you; seek, and you shall find; knock, and it shall be opened to you.* For everyone who *asks* receives, and he who *is seeking* finds, and to him who *knocks* it shall be opened.

"For what man is there among you who, if his son asks for bread, will give *him* a stone? Or if he asks for fish, will give *him* a serpent? If then *you,* though evil, know how to give good gifts *to your children,* how much more will your Father who is in heaven give good things to those who ask *Him!*

## It Proves Its Reality by Its Fruit

(Mt. 7:12-20; Lk. 6:31,43-45)

[1] *"Therefore, all things that you would have men do to you, do also the same to them; for this sums up the law and the prophets.*

"Enter *by the narrow gate.* [e] For wide is the gate, and broad is the way, that is leading to destruction, and many are they who enter by it; but narrow is the gate, and difficult the way, that is leading into life, and few are they who find it.

"But beware of false spokesmen for God, who come to you in sheep's clothing but inwardly are plundering wolves. You will know them by their fruits. [3] For each tree is recognized by its own fruit. [1] Do men gather grapes from brambles, or figs from thistles?

"Thus every good tree brings forth good fruit, but a diseased tree brings forth evil fruit. [3] For [1] a good tree cannot produce evil fruit, nor a diseased tree produce good fruit. Every tree not producing good fruit is hewn down and thrown into the fire.

[3] "The good man out of the good treasure of his heart brings forth what is good, and the evil man out of the evil treasure of his heart brings forth what is evil; for out of the fulness of the *heart* his mouth speaks. [1] Indeed then by their fruits will you discern them.

### Through Obedience Its House Endures

*(Mt. 7:21-29; Lk. 6:46-49; Mk. 1:22)*

[3] "So why do you call me 'Lord, Lord!' but do not *the things I say?* [1] Not everyone who says to me 'Lord, Lord!' shall enter the Kingdom of heaven, *but he who does the will[f] of my Father who is in heaven.*

"Many will say to me in that day, 'Lord, Lord, did we not *prophesy* in your name?'...'And *cast out demons* in your name?'...'And do *many mighty works* in your name?' And then will I say to them forthrightly, 'I never knew you; *depart from me,* you who practice lawlessness!"

"Everyone therefore [3] who comes to me, [1] who hears these teachings of mine *and obeys them,* [3] I will show you whom he is like. He is like [1] a prudent man [3] building [1] his house, [3] who dug and went down deep, and laid a foundation on the rock; [1] and the rain descended, and the floods came, and the winds blew, and they lashed against that house, [3] but could not shake it. [1] It fell not, for it was founded on the rock.

[3] "But [1] everyone who hears these teachings of mine and obeys them *not* shall be likened to a foolish man who, [3] without a foundation, [1] built his house on the sand. And the rain

descended, and the floods came, and the winds blew, and lashed against that house; [3] and immediately it fell, [1] and great was its fall [3] and ruin."

[1] And it came to pass, when Jesus [3] had finished these words in the hearing of the people, [1] that the crowds stood amazed at his message; for he taught them as one with authority, [2] and not as the scribes.

## Chapter 7. Kingdom Parables and Kingly Power

### 40. A Centurion's Extraordinary Faith
#### (Mt. 8:1,5-13; Lk. 7:1b-10)

[1] And when he had come down from the mountain, great multitudes followed him, [3] and he went into Capernaum.

Now a certain slave boy, who belonged to a centurion and was very dear to him, was sick and at the point of dying. And the centurion, on hearing of Jesus [1] when he came into Capernaum, [3] sent to him some of the elders of the Jews, begging him to come and heal his servant, [1] and saying, "Lord, my servant is at the house, lying paralyzed, in terrible torment." [3] And when they came to Jesus, they besought him urgently, saying that he was worthy to have this done for him, "for he loves our nation, and built us our synagogue." [1] Jesus said, "I will come and heal him." [3] So Jesus went with them.

But when he was now not far from the house, the centurion [1] in answer [3] sent friends to him, telling him, "Trouble not, Lord, for I am not worthy to have you come under my roof— for which reason I thought myself unfit to come to you. Instead, speak but a word, and my servant will be healed. For *I*, too, am a man invested with authority, and have soldiers under myself and I say to one, 'Go,' and he goes, and to another, 'Come,' and he comes, and to my slave boy, 'Do this,' and he does it."

Now when Jesus heard these things, he marveled at him, and

turning to the multitude behind him, said, [1] "Verily, I say to you, not even in Israel have I found such extraordinary *faith!* And I say to you, that *many* shall come *from the east and west,*[a] and dine with Abraham and Isaac and Jacob in the Kingdom of heaven; but *the sons* of the Kingdom shall be cast out into the outer darkness, where there shall be wailing and the gnashing of teeth."

Then said Jesus to the centurion, "Go; and *as you have believed, so be it to you."* So his servant was healed at that hour, [3] and the messengers, when they returned to the house, found the slave boy completely well.

## 41. A Widow's Dead Son Is Restored

*(Lk. 7:11-17)*

And the next day it came to pass that he went into a city called Nain; and many of his disciples went with him, and a great throng. Now when he drew near to the gate of the city, behold, one who had died was being carried out, who was his mother's only son, and she a widow; and a large crowd from the city was with her. So when the Lord saw her, he was moved with pity toward her and said to her, *"Do not weep."*

And he came close and touched the bier, and those who bore him stood still; and he said, "Young man, I say to you, *arise!"* And he that was dead sat up, and began to speak. And he presented him back to his mother.

Then fear took hold of all, and they began to praise God, saying, *"A great prophet*[a] has risen up among us!" and, "God *has taken notice of* his people!" And this story of him spread through all Judea and all the region round about.

## 42. Jesus Is Anointed by an Outcast Woman

*(Lk. 7:36-50)*

Then one of the Pharisees asked him to dine with him, and he went into the home of the Pharisee and reclined[a] at dinner. And behold, an outcast woman of the city, who had learned that he was dining in the Pharisee's home, brought an alabaster flask of ointment and stood behind him, at the side of his feet, weeping; then with her tears she began to wet his feet, and with the hair of her head she kept wiping them, kissing and kissing his feet and anointing them with the ointment.

But the Pharisee who was his host, when he saw this, said to himself, "This man, if he were *a prophet,* would have known who and what this woman is who is touching him; for she is a fallen woman." So Jesus answering said to him, "Simon, I have something to say to you." And he said, "Teacher, speak."

"A certain money-lender had two debtors; one owed five hundred denaries,[b] and the other fifty. And as they had nothing to pay with, he in kindness forgave them both. Now which of them, would you say, will love him the more?" And Simon answering said, "He, I suppose, whom he forgave the more." So he said to him, "You have judged rightly."

Then turning to the woman, he said to Simon, "Do you *see* this woman? I came into your home; you gave no water for my feet, but she with her tears has wet my feet, and with the hair of her head she wiped them. You gave me no kiss of welcome, but she, from the time I came in, has not ceased kissing and kissing my feet. You did not anoint my head with oil, but she anointed my feet with ointment. Wherefore I say to you, her sins, though many, *have been forgiven,* for she *loved much.* But he to whom little is forgiven loves but little."

And he said to her, "Your sins have been *forgiven."* Then those dining with him began to say among themselves, *"Who is this, who even forgives sins?"* But he said to the woman, *"Your faith* has saved you;[c] go in peace."

## 43. Another Tour; He Is Accused of Demonry
### (Mt. 12:46-50; Mk. 3:19b-35; Lk. 8:1-4b,19-21;12:10)

[3] Then it came to pass soon afterward that he went about on a tour, city by city and village by village, preaching and announcing the Glad News, the Kingdom of God. And with him went the twelve, and certain women who had been healed from evil spirits and infirmities—Mary, called Magdalene, out of whom had gone seven demons, and Joanna, the wife of Her-

od's steward Chuza, and Suzanna, and many others—who kept providing for him from their means.

But when mighty throngs were gathering together and coming to him out of city after city, [2] he went into a house;[a] but again a crowd came together, so that they could not so much as eat. And his kinsfolk, when they heard of it, set out to lay hold of him, for men were saying, "He is *out of his head.*"

And the scribes who came down from Jerusalem were saying, "He has *Beelzebul,*" and, "He casts out the demons through *the Prince of the demons.*" So he called them to him, and spoke to them in analogies: "How can Satan *cast out* Satan? If a kingdom be divided against itself, that kingdom cannot stand. And if a house be divided against itself, that house is unable to stand. So if Satan has risen up against himself and has been divided, *he* cannot stand, but comes to an end. No one can go into a strong man's house and plunder his things, unless he first *binds* the strong man;[b] and *then* will he plunder his house.

"Verily, I say to you, all the sins of the sons of men can have forgiveness, and whatever blasphemies they may have blasphemed, [3] and everyone who shall speak a word against the Son of man, it will be forgiven him. [2] But he who blasphemes against *the Holy Spirit* will not be forgiven forever, but is guilty of an eternal sin." (For they were saying, "He has *an unclean* spirit.")

### His Mother and Brothers Come

[1] Now [2] therefore, [1] while he was yet speaking to the people [2] and a multitude were seated around him, [1] behold, [2] his mother and brothers arrived.[c] And standing outside, they sent to him, [1] seeking to speak to him [3] but unable to reach him for the throng. [1] [And someone said to him, "Lo, your mother and your brothers are standing outside, seeking to speak to you."]

But he answering [2] them [1] said to the one who spoke to him, *"Who* is *my mother,* and *who* are *my brothers?"* [2] And when he had looked around on those who sat about him, [1] he stretched out his hand toward his disciples and said, "Behold my mother and my brothers! ³My mother and my brothers are *these,* who are *hearing the Word of God and doing it.* ¹For whoever does the will of my Father who is in heaven, *he* is my brother, and sister, and mother."

### 44. Teaching by the Sea in Parables
*(Mt. 13:1-52; Mk. 4:1-34; Lk. 8:4c-18;13:18-21)*

²And he began again to teach by the sea; ¹and having that same day gone out of the house, he sat down beside the sea. And great crowds were gathered together around him, so that he entered the boat and sat there ²upon the sea, ¹while all the multitude stood ²on the land close by the shore. And he taught them many things in parables, and in his teaching said to them.

### Lesson of the Four Kinds of Soil
*(Mt. 13:1-9; Mk. 4:1b-9; Lk. 8:4c-8)*

²*"Hearken!* Lo, the sower went forth to sow ³his seed. ²And it came to pass as he sowed, that some fell upon the roadside; ³and it was trampled on, and the birds of the air ²came and devoured it. ¹And some fell on the rocky places, ²where it had not much earth; and it sprouted up at once, as it had no depth of earth, but when the sun rose, it was scorched, and because it had no root ³and lacked moisture, it withered away. And some fell into the midst of the thorns; and the thorns sprang up with it and choked it, ²and it produced no returns. But some fell into the *good* soil; and growing up and increasing, it brought forth results, some thirtyfold, some sixty, and some a hundredfold." ³And when he had said these things, he exclaimed ²to them, *"He who has ears to hear, let him hear!"*

### "Why Speak to Them in Parables?"
*(Mt. 13:10-17; Mk. 4:10-12; Lk. 8:9-10)*

²Now when he was alone,ª they who were about him, with

the twelve [1] disciples, came and [3] asked him, saying, "What does this parable mean? And [1] why are you speaking in parables *to them?*"

And he answered and said to them, "Because *to you* it has been given to know the mysteries [3] of the Kingdom of God, but to the others [1] it has not been given. *For this reason* I speak [2] everything in parables to those who are outside:[b] that 'looking they may see but not perceive,' and 'listening they may hear but not comprehend,' 'lest they be turned back' and they should be forgiven. [1] For in them is fulfilled Isaiah's prophecy which says,

*'Listening you shall hear, but will not comprehend,*
*and looking you shall see, but not at all perceive.*
*For the heart of this people has grown fat,*
*and with their ears they have listened drowsily,*
*and their eyes they have utterly closed—*
*lest with their eyes they should see,*
*and with their ears they should hear,*
*and with their heart should comprehend*
*and be turned back that I might heal them.'*

"But *blessed* are *your* eyes, for they are seeing, and *your* ears, for they are hearing! For verily, I say to you, many prophets and righteous men yearned to witness the things which you are seeing, and did not see them, and to hear the things which you are hearing, and did not hear them."

### *"The Seed Sown Is the Word"*

(Mt. 13:18-23; Mk. 4:13-20; Lk. 8:11-15)

[2] Then said he to them, "Do you not understand this parable? Then how will you understand *all* the parables? [1] Hear therefore the parable of the sower; [3] the message of the parable is this:

"The seed is the Word of God; [2] *the Sower* is sowing the *Word.* [1] When anyone hears the Word of the Kingdom and does not comprehend it, then [2] at once Satan, [1] the wicked one, comes and snatches away what was sown in his heart, [3] lest he should believe and be saved. [1] This is he who received seed upon the roadside.

[2] "And likewise [1] he who received seed on the rocky places, this is he who hears the Word and at once receives it gladly; yet he has no root in himself, and [3] believes and [2] continues only a little while. Then later, when adversity arises, or persecution on account of the Word, he is caused to stumble immediately, [3] and falls away.

[1] "He also who received seed among the thorns is he who, [3] on hearing [2] the Word, [3] goes his way; [2] and the cares of this world [3] and the pleasures of life, [2] the seductiveness of riches, and passionate desires for other things, enter in and choke the Word and it is made unfruitful—[3] it brings no fruit to completion.

[1] "But he who received seed upon the *good* soil is he who, [3] hearing the Word in an honest and good heart, [2] welcomes [1] and understands it [3] and holds it fast, and with patience [1] bears fruit indeed and brings forth, [2] some thirtyfold, some sixty, and some a hundredfold."

## Lesson of the Wheat and Darnel

### (Mt. 13:24-30)

[1] Another parable put he before them, saying, "The Kingdom of heaven has become like a man who scattered good seed in his field, but while men slept his enemy came and sowed darnel in the midst of the wheat, and went away; so when the blades had sprouted up and produced heads of grain, then the darnel was manifest also.

"So the bondservants of the owner of the house came and said to him, 'Sir, did you not scatter good seed in your field? Why then has it the *darnel?*' And he said to them, 'An *enemy* did this!' And the bondservants said to him, 'Do you want us then to go out and gather it up?' But he said, 'No, lest in gathering the darnel you should root up the wheat with it also. Let them both grow together till the harvest; and at harvest time I will say to the reapers, *First collect the darnel, and bind it in bundles to be burned; but gather up the wheat into my granary.*'"

## Of Things Hidden, and How to Listen

*(Mt. 13:12; Mk. 4:21-25; Lk. 8:16-18)*

[2] He also said to them, [3] "Now [2] is the lamp brought to be put under the grain-measure or under the couch? [3] No one on lighting a lamp covers it with a vessel or puts it under a couch, but he sets it *on a lampstand*, so that those who come in may see the light. For nothing is covered up that shall not be disclosed, nor hidden that shall not come to light. [2] *If anyone has ears to hear,* let him *hear!"*

[2] And he said to them, [3] "Take heed therefore how you listen; [2] give attention to what you hear. With the measure that you use will it be measured back to you, and more will be given you who *hear.* For anyone who has, to him shall be given, [1] and he shall possess abundance. But anyone who has not, from him shall be taken away even what he has—[3] that which he *seems* to have."

## Of a Harvest; of Mustard; of Leaven

*(Mt. 13:31-35; Mk. 4:26-34; Lk. 13:18-21)*

[2] And he said, "So is the Kingdom of God, as if a man should scatter the seed on the soil, then should sleep and rise night and day; and the seed should sprout and grow up (*he* knows not how, for the soil of itself brings forth a crop, first the blade, then the ear, then the full grain in the ear), and when the crop is ripe, he at once puts forth the sickle, because the harvest time has come."

And [1] another parable put he before them by saying, [2] "Unto what shall we liken the Kingdom of God; by what comparison shall we portray it? [1] The Kingdom of heaven[c] is like a mustard seed, [3] which a man took and cast into his garden; [1] which indeed, [2] when sown in the ground, is one of the tiniest seeds, but it grows up [1] and is the greatest of the garden plants—[3] it becomes a tree [2] and puts forth large branches, [1] so that the birds of the air [2] can [1] come and roost [2] in its shade."

[3] Again, [1] he gave them another comparison: [3] "Unto what shall I liken the Kingdom of God? [1] The Kingdom of heaven is like leaven which a woman took and hid in three measures of

flour, till the whole of it was leavened."

All these things Jesus spoke in parables to the multitude,
[2] and with many such comparisons he kept telling them the
message, according as they were able to hear it. [1] And he was
telling them nothing without a parable, that there might be
fulfilled what was spoken by the prophet,

*"I will open my mouth in parables;*
*I will utter things kept hidden*
*from the foundation of the world."*

[2] But in private he explained all things to his disciples.

### Kingdom Lessons to the Twelve

(Mt. 13:36-52)

[1] Jesus then dismissed the crowds and went into the house;
and his disciples came to him, saying,[d] "Explain to us the parable of the darnel of the field."

And he answering said to them, "He that sows the *good*
seed is the Son of man, the field is the world, and the good
seed are the sons of the Kingdom. But the darnel weeds are the
sons of the wicked one, and the enemy who sowed them is the
Devil; the harvest is the consummation of the age, and the
reapers are angels. As the darnel therefore is collected and consumed with fire, so will it be in the consummation of this age;
the Son of man will send forth his angels and they will gather
out of his Kingdom all the things that cause stumbling, and
those who practice iniquity, and they will cast them into the
furnace of fire, where there shall be wailing and the gnashing
of teeth. Then shall the righteous *shine forth as the sun* in the
Kingdom of their Father. *He who has ears [to hear],* let him
*hear!*

"Again, the Kingdom of heaven is like a treasure hid in a
field, which a man on finding conceals it, and in his joy goes
and sells all that he has, and buys that field.

"Again, the Kingdom of heaven is like a merchant seeking
beautiful pearls, and on finding one pearl of extremely great
value he went and sold all his possessions and bought it.

"Again, the Kingdom of heaven is like a dragnet, which was

cast into the sea and gathered up of every kind; and when it was filled and hauled up on shore, men sat down and sorted out the good into baskets, but the bad they threw away. So will it be in the consummation of this age; the angels will go forth and sort out the wicked from the righteous, and will cast them into the furnace of fire, where there shall be wailing and the gnashing of teeth."

Jesus said to them, "Have you understood all these things?" They said to him, "Yes, Lord." Then said he to them, "Therefore every instructor trained for the Kingdom of heaven is like a man who is the master of a house, who brings forth out of his treasure *things new and old.*"

## 45. Ruler of the Winds and Sea
### (Mt. 8:18,23-27; Mk. 4:35-41; Lk. 8:22-25)

[2] Then the same day when it was evening, [1] Jesus, seeing great crowds about him, gave commandment [3] and said, "Let us cross over to the other side of the lake." So [1] his disciples, [2] dismissing the throng, [1] followed him into the boat. And [2] they took him with them as he was, [3] and sailed forth; [2] and there were other small ships with him also.

[3] But as they sailed, [1] behold, [2] a great windstorm [3] came down upon the lake; [2] and the waves began breaking into the boat, so that it [1] was being swamped [2] already [3] and they were in peril. [2] But he himself was in the stern, on the cushion, sleeping. [1] So his disciples came [3] and aroused him, saying, *"Master, Master! We are perishing!'...* [1] *"Lord, save us!"...* [2] "Teacher, *don't you care* that we are *perishing?"* [1] And he said to them, "Why are you *fearful,* you of little faith?"

Then he arose and rebuked the winds [3] and the raging of the water, [2] and said to the sea, "Peace; *be still."* And they ceased, and there came a great calm. And he said to them, [3] "Where is your *faith?* [2] How is it you have *no faith?"* [1] And the men were filled with wonder [2] and were awed beyond measure, [3] saying to one another, [1] "What kind of man is *He?* [3] WHO then is He, that *He commands even the winds and the water, and they obey him!"*[a]

## 46. Conqueror of the Gerasene Demons

*(Mt. 8:28-34; Mk. 5:1-20; Lk. 8:26-39)*

[3] So they sailed on down to the country of the Gerasenes, which is across from Galilee. And when he stepped out on shore, [2] immediately [1] there met him [3] from the city [1] two with demon possession, coming out from the tombs, extremely fierce, so that no one could pass along that way; [3] a man in particular[a] who had long had demons and wore no clothes, and who lived not in a house but in the tombs. [1] And behold, [2] when he saw Jesus from a distance, [3] he cried out [2] and ran, and [3] fell down before him and [2] worshiped him. [3] And he said in a loud voice, [1] *"What are you doing to us,* [2] *Jesus, Son of the most high God?* [1] Did you come here to torment us *before the time?* [2] Before God I implore you, *torment me not!"*

[3] For he had begun to order the unclean spirit to come out of the man. For many times had it laid hold of him, [2] and no one was able to bind him, not even with chains. For he had often been restrained with shackles and chains, but the chains had been wrenched apart by him and the shackles broken in pieces, and no one was able to subdue him; [3] and he was driven by the demon into the wilderness, [2] and continually, night and day, he was in the mountains and among the tombs, uttering cries and cutting himself with stones.

[3] Then Jesus asked him, "What is your name?" [2] And he answered saying, "My name is *Legion;* for we are many" [3] (for many demons had entered into him). [2] And he began to beg him much not to order them away from that region [3] into the abyss.

[1] Now at a distance from them, [2] on the mountain side, a great herd of swine were feeding; and all the demons besought him, saying, [1] "If you cast us out, let us go away into the herd of swine."[b] [2] And Jesus at once granted them leave, [1] and said to them, "Go." [2] So the unclean spirits [3] came out of the man [1] and went off into the herd of swine. And behold, the whole herd [2] of about two thousand stampeded down the steep slope [3] into the lake and were choked [1] in the waters.

[3] Now when those who fed them saw what happened, they

fled; [1] and they went away into the city [2] and countryside [1] and told everything, and concerning the demoniacs also. And behold, the whole city came out to meet Jesus [3] and to see what had come to pass.

So they came [1] and saw [3] Jesus; and they found the man [2] who had been demon-possessed [3] sitting at Jesus' feet clothed and in his right mind—[2] even he who had had the legion!—and they were frightened. [3] They also who had seen it related to them how the demoniac had been restored, [2] and about the swine. [3] Then the whole throng from the Gerasene country [2] began to ask him to depart from their district, [3] for they were seized with a violent fear; so he went back again.

[2] Now as he boarded the boat, [3] the man from whom the demons had gone out began to beg to stay with him. [2] But Jesus would not let him, [3] and sent him away, saying, [2] *"Go home to your own kinsfolk,* and tell *them* the things the Lord [3] God has done for you, [2] and how he pitied you." [3] So he departed, and began to proclaim [3] throughout the whole city, and [2] in the Decapolis, all the things Jesus had done for him; and everybody marveled.

### 47. Eating with Capernaum's Outcasts
*(Mt. 9:1,10-17; Mk. 5:21a;2:15-22; Lk. 8:40;5:29-39)*

[3] And it came to pass that when Jesus [1] crossed over and [3] returned [1] to his own city, [3] the people welcomed him gladly, for they were all looking hopefully[a] for him.

[3] And Levi held a great banquet for him in his home. [1] And it came about that as he was reclining at table, behold, [3] quite a multitude of publicans and other [1] persons of ill repute, who had come, were reclining at the table with Jesus and his disciples; [2] for there were many such and they were following him. [3] So the Pharisees and their scribes, [2] when they saw him eating with these publicans and other outcasts, [3] began to criticize his disciples, saying, "Why do you eat and drink *with publicans and sinners?* And [1] why does *your teacher?"*

But Jesus on hearing it [3] answered them and said, "They who are well do not need a physician, but they who are *sick.*

[1] And go you and learn what *this* means: *'Mercy is what I desire, and not sacrifice.'* For I have not come to call the 'righteous,' but *sinners,* to repentance."

## Feasting While Others Fasted

[2] Now [1] at that time [2] the disciples of John, and those of the Pharisees, were keeping a fast. So [1] the disciples of John came up to him [2] and asked him, [1] "Why do we, [3] and likewise the disciples of the Pharisees, fast often and make petitions, [2] but *your* disciples *do not fast—*[3] yours eat and drink?"

[2] And Jesus said to them, [3] "Can you make the young men of *the wedding party* fast? [1] Can they mourn while the bridegroom is with them? [2] But days are coming when the Bridegroom will have been taken away from them, and *those* are the days when they will fast."

[3] And he also spoke a parable to them: "No one [2] sews a piece of [3] new, [2] unshrunk cloth on *an outworn garment.* [1] For the patch pulls away from [2] the old [1] garment and a worse rent is made; [3] it tears the new cloth, and the new piece does not match the old. And no one puts new wine into *old wineskins,* else the new wine will rupture the skins and be spilled, and the skins will be made useless. But new wine must be put into *new* wineskins, [1] so that both are preserved together. [3] And no one, after drinking old wine, cares [at that time] for new; for he says, *'The old is better.'"*

## 48. A Woman Is Healed, a Dead Girl Raised
### (Mt. 9:18-26; Mk. 5:21b-43; Lk. 8:41-56)

[1] While he was speaking these things to them,[a] [2] a great multitude gathered about him; and he was near the shore of the sea. [3] And behold, there came a man whose name was Jairus, [2] one of the officials of the synagogue; and when he saw him, [3] he fell down at Jesus' feet and [1] worshiped him, [3] and besought him to come to his home. For he had an only daughter, about twelve years of age, and she was dying. [2] So he pleaded with him earnestly, saying, "My young daughter is [1] right now [2] at the point of death. Come, I pray you, and lay your hands

upon her, that she may be healed and live."

[1] Then Jesus arose [2] and departed with him, [1] and so did his disciples. [3] And as he went, [2] a great crowd kept following and thronging about him.

[1] Then behold, [2] a certain woman [1] who had been diseased with a flow of blood for twelve years—who had suffered much under many physicians [3] but could not be cured by any, [2] and had spent all she had and was in no way improved but instead had grown worse—having heard about Jesus, came up in the throng behind him. And she touched [1] the border of his garment, for she was saying to herself, "If I may but *touch* [2] *his clothes,* I shall be cured." And instantly her flow of blood was dried up, and she knew in her body that she was healed of the affliction.

Then immediately Jesus, knowing in himself that the power had gone forth from him, turned about in the throng and said, [3] "Who was touching me? [2] Who touched my clothing?" [3] With all denying it, Peter and [2] the disciples [3] who were with him said [2] to him, [3] "Master, [2] you see the crowd that is pressing all around you, and yet you are saying, 'Who touched me?'" [3] But Jesus said, *"Somebody touched me;* for *I* knew that *power* went forth from me." [2] And he started to look around to see the one who had done this.

So the woman, frightened and trembling, knowing what had been done to her, [3] when she saw that she was not hid, [2] came and fell down before him and told him all the truth, [3] declaring before all the people why she had touched him and how she was instantly healed. And he said to her, [1] "Be of good courage, daughter; *your faith* has healed you. [2] Go in peace, and be well of your scourge."

*"Why Make a Tumult?"*

While he was yet speaking, there came some from the home of the synagogue official. [3] One of them said to him, "Your daughter *has died;* trouble not the Teacher [2] further." [3] But Jesus, having heard [2] the word that was spoken, said to the official of the synagogue, "Fear not; *only believe,* [3] and she shall be restored." [2] And he allowed no one to go along with him but Peter and James and James' brother John.

So he came to the home of the synagogue official, and beheld [1] the flute players and the crowd making a tumult, [2] weeping and wailing greatly [3] and beating their breasts for her. [2] And when he had gone in, he said to them, [1] *"Off with you!* [2] Why make a tumult, and weep? [3] Weep not, [1] for the maiden did not die but is sleeping." [3] And with scorn they laughed at him, knowing that she was dead.

[2] But when he had put them all out, he took the father of the maiden, and the mother, and those who were with him, and went in where the child was lying. [3] And taking her by the hand, he called [2] to her, [3] saying, [2] "Talitha *cumi"* (that is, "I say to you, maiden, *arise"*). [3] And her spirit returned, [2] and the young girl rose up at once and started walking; [3] and he directed that something be given her to eat. [2] And they were seized with overwhelming amazement; but he charged them strictly [3] to tell no one what had occurred. [1] But the news of it went out into all that region.

### 49. Two Blind Men and a Dumb Demoniac
#### (Mt. 9:27-34)

Now as Jesus went on from there, two blind men were following him, calling out and saying, "Have pity on us, *Son of David!"*

And when he had gone into the house, the blind men came to him and Jesus said to them, "Do you *believe* that I can do this?" They said to him, *"Yes, Lord!"* Then touched he their eyes, saying, "According to your faith[a] *be it done to you."* And their eyes were opened. And Jesus enjoined them strictly, saying, "See that you let no one know." But going forth they made him known in all that district.

And as they were leaving, behold, there was brought to him a dumb man who was possessed by a demon; and when the demon had been cast out, the dumb man spoke. And the crowds were filled with wonder, saying, *"Never* was it so seen in Israel!" But the Pharisees kept saying, "He *is casting* out the demons *through the Prince of the demons."*

## 50. *Jesus Answers John the Baptist*
### *(Mt. 11:2-19; Lk. 7:18-35;16:16)*

[3] Now the disciples of John brought him word [1] in the prison [3] of all these [1] works of the Messiah. [3] Then John, summoning a certain two of his disciples, sent them to Jesus, saying to him, *"Are you* that One who is coming? Or are we to look for another?"* So the men, when they had come[a] to him, said, "John the Baptist has sent us to you, saying, *'Are you* that One who is coming? Or are we to look for another?'"

But in that same hour he healed many from their diseases and afflictions and evil spirits, and to many who were blind he granted sight. So Jesus answering said to them, "Go and report to John *the things you have seen and heard.* [1] The blind are receiving sight, the crippled are walking, the lepers are being cleansed, and the deaf are hearing, the dead are being raised, and the lowly are being told the Glad News. And blessed is he who does not *stumble* because of Me!"

[3] Then, when John's messengers had left, he began to address the multitude concerning John: [1] "What went you out into the wilderness to see—a reed tossed about by the wind? No! So what went you out to behold—a man arrayed in soft apparel? Lo, they who wear the soft, [3] fine raiment and are living in luxury are in [1] *kings'* [3] *palaces!*

"So what went you out to behold? A prophet? Yes, I say to you, and *much more* than a prophet! [1] For this is he of whom it was written,

> *'Behold, I send my messenger before thy face,*
> *who shall prepare thy way before thee.'*

[3] For [1] verily I say to you, among those born of women there has not risen a greater [3] prophet than John the Baptist (although the lowliest in *the Kingdom of God* is greater than he).

"And on hearing him all the common folk, and the publicans, justified God by being baptized with *the baptism of John,* while the Pharisees and the doctors of the law *disregarded* the counsel of God toward themselves by refusing to be baptized by him. [1] And from the days of John the Baptist *until now* [3] the Kingdom of God *is being preached—*[1] the Kingdom of heaven is being won by storming walls of opposition, [3] and all entering it are forcing their way.

[1] "For all the prophets and the law prophesied till the time of *John*. And, if you are willing to receive it, *he is Elijah*[b] who was to come. *He who has ears to hear,* let him *hear!"*

[3] And the Lord said, "To what then shall I liken the men of this generation? Now to what can they be compared? They are like small children, sitting in the marketplace and calling to one another, saying,

> 'We fluted to you, and you did not dance;
> we wailed to you, and you did not weep.'

For John the Baptist came neither eating bread nor drinking wine, and you say, 'He has *a demon.'* The Son of man has come both eating and drinking, and you say, 'Behold *a glutton and a wine drinker, a friend of publicans and sinners!'* So wisdom was being *justified* by all *her* children."

### Chapter 8. Answering Jerusalem's Leaders

### 51. An Invalid at the Pool of Bethesda Healed
#### (Jn. 5:1-47)

After these things there was a feast of the Jews, and Jesus went up to Jerusalem. Now there is in Jerusalem by the Sheep Gate a pool called in the Hebrew tongue Bethesda, which has five entrance-ways. In these lay a crowd of afflicted folk, the blind, the crippled, the paralyzed, [waiting for the moving of the water. For "an angel came down from time to time into the pool and disturbed the water, and whoever first stepped in after the troubling of the water became well of whatever affliction he had."][a]

And a certain man was there who had been an invalid for *thirty-eight years.* Jesus saw him lying there and, knowing that he had been a long time in that plight, said to him, "Do you wish *to get well?"* The afflicted man answered him, "Sir, I have no man, when the water is troubled, to put me into the pool; and while I am coming someone else steps down before me." Jesus said to him, *"Rise; take up your pallet and walk."* And immediately the man was made well, and he picked up his pallet and started walking.

But that day was the Sabbath; so the Jews said to the healed man, "It is *the Sabbath;* it is *unlawful* for you to carry the pallet." He answered them, "The man who made me well, *he* said to me, 'Take up your pallet and walk!'" They asked him therefore, "Who is this man who said to you, 'Take up your pallet and walk'?" But the healed man did not know who it was; for Jesus had betaken himself away, because of the throng in the place.

Later Jesus found him in the temple, and he said to him, "Behold, you have been healed; sin no more, lest some worse thing befall you." The man departed, and told the Jews that it was Jesus who had made him well. For this reason the Jews continued persecuting Jesus and seeking to kill him, because he was doing such things on the Sabbath.

But Jesus answered them, *"My Father* is continuing to work until now; *I, too, am working."* The Jews because of this kept seeking all the more to kill him, for not only was he "breaking the Sabbath"[b] but was also calling God his own Father, "making himself equal with God."

*"All Should Honor the Son"*

Jesus therefore answered and said to them, "Verily, verily, I say to you, the Son can do nothing from himself, but only what he may see *the Father* doing; for whatever things *He* is doing, the Son does likewise. For the Father loves the Son, and shows him all the things he himself is doing.

"And greater works than *these* will he show him, *so that you may marvel.*[c] For as the Father raises up the dead and makes them alive, so the Son also makes alive whom he will. For not even is the Father judging anyone, but he has given all judgment to *the Son,* so that *all men should honor the Son even as they honor the Father.* He who is not honoring the Son *is not honoring the Father who sent him.*

"*Verily, verily, I say to you, he who hears my Word and believes Him who sent Me, has everlasting life and does not come into judgment but has passed out of death into life.*

"Verily, verily, I say to you, that an hour is coming, and now is, when *the dead will hear the voice of the Son of God, and those who have heard will live.* For as the Father has life in himself, so he granted the Son also to have life in himself; and he gave him authority to administer judgment, because he is the Son of man. Marvel not at this, for an hour is coming when all who are in the graves will hear his voice and come forth, they who have done good unto resurrection of life, and they who have done evil unto resurrection of judgment.

"From myself I can do nothing; according as I *hear,* I judge. And my judgment is righteous, because I seek not my own will but *the will of the Father who sent me.*

### Attested by Four Truthful Witnesses

"*If I testify in my own behalf,* my testimony *'is not true'?* There is *another* who testifies of me, and I know that the witness which he bears of me is true; you yourselves have sent to *John,* and *he* has borne witness to the truth. Not that My credentials are from a man, but I say these things that you might be saved. He was *the lamp,* a burning and shining one, and *you* were willing to rejoice a short while in his light.

"But *I* have a greater attestation than John's; for *the works* which the Father gave me to accomplish, *the very works which I am doing,* bear witness of me that the Father has sent me.

"And *the Father who sent me* has himself borne witness of me. His voice you have never heard and his form you have not seen—and his Word you do not have abiding in you, because the One whom He sent you believe not!

"You search *the Scriptures,* because in them you think to have eternal life—*and it is they that bear witness of Me!* And you are unwilling to come to Me that you might have *life.*

"Glory from men I am not receiving; but I have known you, that you have not the love of *God* within you. *I* have come in *my Father's* name and you welcome me not; if another comes in his own name, him you will welcome! How can you believe, who welcome glory from one another, but the glory from the only God you do not seek?

"Think not that *I* will accuse you to the Father; one there is who is accusing you, namely *Moses,* in whom *you* have trusted. For had you believed Moses, you would have believed Me; because he wrote concerning Me. But if you believe not *his writings,* how will you believe my words?"

## 52. His Second Visit at Nazareth

*(Mt. 13:53-58; Mk. 6:1-6a)*

[1] And Jesus withdrew from there[a] [2] and came to his boyhood town; and his disciples were following him. And with the coming of the Sabbath [1] he began to teach them in their synagogue. [2] And many on hearing him were astonished, saying, "Where did *he* get [1] all these things?" [2] and, "What is the wisdom that is given *him,* that such mighty works are wrought by his hands? Is not this the carpenter, [1] the son of the carpenter? Is not his mother called Mary, and his brothers James and Joseph and Simon and Jude? And his sisters, are they not all [2] here with us?" And to them he was a cause of stumbling.

Then said Jesus to them, "A prophet is not without honor but in his home town, and among his kinsfolk, and in his own home!" And he could not perform there any [1] mighty works, because of their *unbelief,* [2] except that he laid his hands on a few sick folk and healed them. And he marveled over and over at their unbelief.

# Chapter 9. The Climax of Israel's Acclaim

## 53. *The Twelve Are Sent Out to Preach*

*(Mt. 9:35-10:1,5-16,24-33,37-11:1; Mk. 6:6b-13; Lk. 9:1-6)*

[1] Then Jesus journeyed about to all the cities and the villages,[a] teaching in their synagogues and continuing to proclaim the Glad News of the Kingdom, and healing every sickness and infirmity among the people.

But when he saw the multitudes, he was moved with compassion toward them, for they were harried and desolated like sheep that had no shepherd. Then said he to his disciples, "The harvest is plentiful indeed, *but the laborers are few.* Pray therefore the Lord of the harvest that he thrust out laborers into his harvest."

[3] So he summoned [1] his twelve disciples to him, [3] and gave *them* power and authority over all the [1] unclean spirits, to cast them out, and to heal all kinds of sickness and infirmity. These twelve began Jesus to send out [2] two by two, [3] to proclaim the Kingdom of God and to heal those who were sick.

### *"Go to the Lost Sheep of Israel"*

*(Mt. 10:5b-15; Mk. 6:8-11; Lk. 9:3-5)*

[1] And he commanded them, saying, "Go not out into Gentile neighborhoods, and go not into any city of Samaritans, but go rather *to the lost sheep of the house of Israel.* And as you go, make a proclamation, saying, *'The Kingdom of heaven is at hand!'*

"Heal the sick, cleanse the lepers, raise the dead, cast out demons. Without paying, you received; without pay, give. [3] Take nothing for the journey [2] but only a staff. [1] Provide neither gold nor silver nor copper [2] in your money belt, and no bread, [1] nor a provision bag; [3] neither have two tunics, [1] nor pairs of sandals, nor staves [2] (but be shod with sandals). [1] For the workman deserves his subsistence."

[2] And he said to them, [1] "Into whatever city or village you enter, inquire in it who is worthy; [3] and into whatever home

70

you enter, there remain [2] till you depart from that place. [1] And when you enter the home, say a greeting; and if the home indeed be worthy, let your blessing come upon it, but if it be not worthy, let your blessing return to you.

"And as many as will not welcome you or hear your message, when you depart from that home or that city shake off [3] even the dust from [2] under your feet [3] as a witness against them. [1] Verily, I say to you, it shall be more tolerable for the land of Sodom and Gomorrah in the day of judgment than for that city!

### *"Fear Them Not, Therefore"*
#### *(Mt. 10:16,24-31)*

"Lo, it is *I* who send you forth—as sheep in the midst of wolves. Be wise therefore as the serpents, and guileless as the doves.[b]

"A disciple is not above his teacher, nor a bondman above his lord. It is enough for the disciple that he become like his teacher, and the bondman like his lord. If they called the Master of the house Beelzebul, how much more will they those of his household!

"For this reason *you should fear them not:* for there is nothing covered up that shall not be disclosed, nor hidden that shall not be known. What I am telling you in the darkness, speak out in the light, and what you are hearing whispered, proclaim upon the housetops.

"And fear not those who kill the body but are unable to kill the soul, but rather fear him who can destroy both soul and body in Gehenna. Are not two sparrows sold for one copperpiece? Yet not one of them will fall to the ground without your Father. And as for you, the very hairs of your head are all numbered. Fear not, therefore; *you* are worth more than *many* sparrows!

### *Witnessing and Service to Be Rewarded*
#### *(Mt. 10:32-33,37-42)*

*"Whoever therefore shall confess Me before men, him will I*

*also confess before my Father in heaven; but anyone who shall deny Me before men, him will I also deny before my Father in heaven.*

"He who loves *father or mother* above Me, he is not worthy of me; and he who loves *a son or daughter* above Me, he is not worthy of me. And he who takes not *his cross* and follows Me, he is not worthy of me.

*"He who has found his life will lose it, and he who has lost his life for My sake shall find it.*

"He who receives you *receives Me;* and he who receives Me *receives Him who sent me.* He who receives a prophet because he is a prophet will receive a prophet's reward; and he who receives a just man because he is a just man will receive a just man's reward. And he who gives but a cup of cold water to drink, to one of these lowly ones because he is a disciple, verily, I say to you, shall not at all lose his reward."

## Seven Simultaneous Preaching Tours

*(Mt. 11:1; Mk. 6:12-13; Lk. 9:6)*

[1] And it came to pass that, when Jesus had finished commissioning his twelve disciples, he departed from there to teach and preach in their cities. [3] And they went forth and made their way among the *villages,* announcing the Glad News and healing everywhere. [2] And they proclaimed that men must repent; and they cast out many demons, and anointed with oil many persons who were sick, and healed them.[c]

## 54. John the Baptist Is Martyred

*(Mt. 14:1-13a; Mk. 6:14-29; Lk. 9:7-9)*

[3] Now [1] at that time [2] king Herod [3] the tetrarch heard of all the things being done by [1] Jesus; [2] for his name was becoming famous. [3] And Herod was perplexed, [3] and said, "John I *beheaded,* so who is *this,* of whom I am hearing such things?"

[3] For by some it was being said that [2] John "the Baptizer" [3] had been raised from the dead, [2] others were saying [3] that Elijah had appeared, [2] others also [3] that a prophet [2] like one [3] of

the old prophets had arisen. [2] But Herod on hearing it said [1] to his servants, "This *is* John the Baptist, [2] whom I beheaded! He has risen from the dead, [1] and this is why these mighty powers are working in him." [3] So he began to seek to see him.

[2] For Herod had himself sent forth and arrested John, and had bound him in prison for Herodias' sake,[a] his brother Philip's wife, because he had married her. For John kept saying to Herod, *"It is not lawful* for you to have your brother's wife." So Herodias held a grievance against him and wanted to kill him, but she could not. For Herod held John in awe, knowing him to be a righteous and holy man; so he was keeping him safe, and, when he heard him, did many things told him and kept listening gladly. [1] Even when minded to put him to death, he feared the people, for they held him to be a prophet.

But when [2] an opportune day arrived, and Herod on his birthday held a banquet for his courtiers and high captains and the chief men of Galilee, Herodias' own daughter came in and danced [1] in their midst. [2] And she gave pleasure to Herod and those at table with him; [1] for which cause [2] the king said to the maiden, "Ask of me anything you wish, and I will give it you." And he swore to her [1] with an oath, [2] "No matter what you may ask of me, I will give it you, up to half of my kingdom!"

Then went she out and said to her mother, "What shall I ask for?" And she said, "The head of *John the Baptist."* So she came in at once with haste to the king, [1] and said, [2] "I desire that you give me [1] here [2] at once on a platter the head of John the Baptist."

And the king was very unhappy, [1] but because of his oaths and those at table with him, [2] he would not refuse her; and immediately the king sent a guardsman and ordered that his head should be brought and [1] presented. So [2] he went and beheaded John in the prison; [1] and his head was brought on a platter and presented to the maiden, and she brought it to her mother.

[2] And when his disciples heard of it, they came and took up his body, [1] and buried it [2] in a tomb. [1] Then they went and told Jesus; and when Jesus heard of it, he withdrew[b] from where he was.

## 55. Five Thousand Are Miraculously Fed
### (Mt. 14:13b-23; Mk. 6:30-46; Lk. 9:10-17; Jn. 6:1-15)

³ Now the apostles on returning ² gathered together with Jesus, and reported to him all the things they had done and taught. Then said he to them, "Come away by yourselves to a wilderness place and *rest* for a little while." For there were many coming and going, and they had no leisure time even to eat. ³ And he took them and withdrew privately ² in the boat ⁴ to the other side of the Sea of Galilee (or Sea of Tiberias) ³ to a wilderness spot belonging to a city called Bethsaida.

But the crowds learned of it and ² saw them leaving, and many recognized him; and together on foot they hurried in that direction from all the towns. ³ They followed him ⁴ because of seeing the miraculous signs which he wrought on those who were sick. ² They even arrived there before them, and came together toward him; so when Jesus came ashore, he beheld a great throng. But he was moved with compassion toward them, as they were like sheep that had no shepherd. ³ And he welcomed them, ² and began to teach them many things; ³ and he talked to them about the Kingdom of God, and healed those who had need of healing.

² Now when the day was far spent,ᵃ ⁴ Jesus went up on the mountain and sat down there with his disciples. And the Passover, the Jewish feast, was at hand.ᵇ So when Jesus raised his eyes and saw a great multitude approaching him, he said to Philip, "Where shall we buy loaves of bread, so that these people may eat?" (But this he said to test him, for he himself knew what he would do.) Philip answered him, *"Two hundred denaries' worth of loaves* would not be enough for them each to receive just a little." One of his disciples, Andrew, Simon Peter's brother, said to him, "Here is a young lad who has five barley loaves and two small fish; but what are these among *so many?"*

### "Bring Them Here to Me"

³ Then came the twelve and they said to him, ¹ "The place ³ here ¹ is a wilderness, and the hour already late; ³ send the

multitude away, that they may go into the villages and countryside round about, and lodge, [1] and buy themselves food.
[2] For they have nothing to eat." But he answered and said to
them, [1] "They need not go away; *you* give them something to
eat."

[2] And they said to him, "Shall we go and buy *two hundred
denaries'* worth of loaves, and give them to them to eat?" But
he said to them, "How many loaves do you have? Go and see."
And on finding out they said [1] to him, "We have here just five
loaves and two fish—[3] unless indeed *we* go and *buy* food for all
this throng!" [1] But he said, *"Bring them here to Me."*

[4] Then said Jesus [3] to his disciples, [4] "Have the men recline
for eating, [3] in companies of fifty." [4] Now there was abundant
grass in the place, [3] and they did so, having them all recline
[2] on the green grass; and they reclined in rows, by hundreds
and by fifties. [3] Then took he the five loaves and two fish, and
looking up toward heaven he blessed them; [4] and having given
thanks, [2] he broke the loaves and [4] distributed [3] to the disciples to set before the throng. [4] And likewise of the [2] two
[4] small fish [2] divided he among them all, [4] as much as they
wished; [1] and all of them ate and were satisfied.

[4] And when [3] all were filled, [4] he said to his disciples, "Gather up the fragments that remain, that nothing be lost." So they
gathered them and filled *twelve baskets* with fragments from
the five barley loaves [2] and the fish, [4] which were left by those
who had eaten. [1] And those who had eaten were *about five
thousand* men, besides women and children.

### Ready to Make Him King

[4] Then those men, having seen the miraculous sign which Jesus wrought, kept saying, "This surely is the *Prophet* who is
coming into the world." Jesus therefore, perceiving that they
were ready to come and seize him *to make him king,* [2] immediately constrained his disciples to board the boat to precede
him to the other side, to Bethsaida, while he should send the
multitude away. And when he had taken leave of [1] the crowds,
he [4] withdrew again up the mountain, by himself alone, [2] to
pray.

## 56. His Pre-dawn Walk on the Sea

(Mt. 14:24-36; Mk. 6:47-56; Jn. 6:16-21)

[4] Then with evening come, his disciples went down to the sea and boarded the boat, and started to go across toward Capernaum. It was now dark, and Jesus had not come to them; and the sea was getting rough from a strong wind that blew.

[2] And he, [1] there alone [2] on the land, saw[a] them hard-pressed in their rowing; [1] the boat was now out in the middle of the sea, being pounded by the waves, for the wind was contrary to them. So in the fourth quarter of the night, [4] when they had rowed between three and four miles, [1] Jesus went toward them, walking on the sea.

[2] And he was making to come alongside of them, but [1] when the disciples saw him walking on the sea [4] and drawing close to the boat, [1] they were alarmed, saying, "It is *a spirit!*" And they cried out for fear, [2] for all saw him and were terrified. [1] Then immediately Jesus spoke to them, saying, *"Have courage!* It is 'I AM;'[b] do not fear."

Peter answered him and said, "Lord, if it is *You,* bid me come to you on the water." And he said, "Come." So Peter climbed down from the boat and walked on the water toward Jesus. But seeing the wind turbulent he was frightened, and commencing to sink he cried out, *"Lord, save me!"* Then Jesus quickly stretched out his hand and caught him, and said to him, "You Little-faith, what made you doubt?"

And when they came up into the boat, the wind ceased; [4] therefore [1] those in the boat [4] were ready to welcome him. [2] And inwardly they were filled with amazement and awe (for they understood not about the loaves, since their hearts were unreceptive) [1] but they came and made obeisance before him, saying, *"Truly You are* the Son of *God."*

### Excitement in Gennesaret

[4] Then at once the boat [2] drew to the shore [4] toward which they were headed, [2] having crossed to the land of Gennesaret. And upon their disembarking, [1] the men of that place [2] recognized him immediately; and running throughout that whole

countryside, they began to carry about on pallets the folk who were ill, to wherever they heard he was.

And in every place he entered, in villages, cities, or the country, they kept laying the sick in the marketplaces[c] and begging that they might only touch the border of his garment; [l] and as many as touched it were made completely well.

* * *

*Comment.* The episode of feeding the 5000 across the Sea and its sequel brought to a consummation the second twelve months of Jesus' public labors, a year that began with the Passover season disclosed in Sec. 36. It was a period of great activity and wide public favor.

Although this second year is reported more fully than the first, the writers still present only a few outstanding highlights of that period. Several of these events may be noted as especially significant in bringing that phase of His ministry to a climax. The year began just after the Lord called His twelve disciples to be with Him and after the second Passover season in which Jesus antagonized the religious leaders on an issue of the disciples' Sabbath breaking. From this point the leaders sought how they might destroy Him, whether by character or in body. His ministry then was focused almost entirely on the general populace of the Galilean region, meeting both physical and spiritual needs.

A most crucial event which occurred that second summer was the giving of the Sermon on the Mount. This was given, not as a way of salvation, but to clarify forever the true nature of righteousness and God's Kingdom. In it He struck a sharp distinction between mere hand ritual and heart righteousness. The Sermon constituted a virtual "declaration of war" with the Pharisaic leaders, rejecting their hypocritical system *in toto.* Then, following another Galilean tour that summer in which He displayed His Messianic credentials by numerous miracles, Jesus' powers were castigated by the leaders as being necromancy or Satan-inspired. So serious was this charge that Jesus altered His approach and commenced the disclosure of a new interadvent Kingdom program through the means of parables. This change turned His primary attention from the rejecting nation, as such, to receptive individuals who were responding to Him.

That year was climaxed by two other significant rejections. During this period, John the Baptist was sealed up in Herod's prison at Machaerus and was beheaded the following spring. This was an outrage to the whole movement which John had begun and it spoke of the intransigency of wickedness in high places. Then shortly after, Jesus, on vacation with His disciples, fed the 5000 and seemingly so gained the acclaim of the Galilean populace that they sought to make Him king. The genuineness of this acclaim Jesus tested the next day at Capernaum by offering Himself as "the Bread of life." They responded to this by a mass desertion. It should be noted that this almost universal rejection demonstrated the crass materialism of their thinking and the basic superficiality of the reformation that began with John the Baptist and was carried on by the Lord in His ministry of miracles. Their interests were primarily material and political rather than spiritual.

This rejection at Capernaum then disclosed the fact that the leaders were not alone in their rejection of Him. Though the populace rejected Him for other reasons, they demonstrated the fact that they also had little appetite for the spiritually-oriented program He presented. From this point on He will move more to the outcasts and outlying areas, ministering grace to individuals and instructing the apostles for their future work.

# PART IV.

## CRUCIAL REJECTIONS BY ISRAEL

### Chapter 10. Repudiated at Capernaum

#### 57. He Discourses on the Bread of Life
##### (Jn. 6:22-71)

The next day the people remaining on the other side of the sea, when they saw that no other boat had been there but the one his disciples had entered, and that Jesus had not boarded the boat with his disciples but that they went off alone—although some other boats from Tiberias landed near where they ate the bread after the Lord had given thanks—when the people therefore saw that neither Jesus nor his disciples were there, they themselves boarded the boats[a] and came to Capernaum, seeking Jesus.

And on finding him across the sea, they said to him, "Rabbi, when did you come *here?*" Jesus answered them and said, "Verily, verily, I say to you, you seek me, not because you saw miraculous signs, but because you *ate of the loaves, and were filled.* Labor not for the food that perishes, but for the Food which abides *unto everlasting life;* which the Son of man will give you, for on Him has God the Father placed His seal."[b]

They said therefore to him, "What must we *do,* to work the works that God requires?" Jesus answered and said to them, "The work that God requires is this, that you *believe upon the One whom He sent."*

They asked him therefore, "What miraculous sign are *you* producing, that we may see it and believe you? What work are you *performing?* Our *fathers* ate the *manna* in the wilderness, as it is written, *'Bread out of heaven gave he them to eat.'"* Jesus therefore said to them, "Verily, verily, I say to you, *Moses*

79

did not give you the bread out of heaven. It is *my Father* who is giving you the true bread out of heaven; for the Bread from God is that which *is coming down* out of heaven and *is giving life* to the world."

They said therefore to him, "Sir, evermore give us this bread!" And Jesus said to them, *"I am* the Bread of life. He who comes to *Me* shall never hunger, and he who believes upon *Me* shall never thirst. But I said to you, that you also *have seen me and do not believe!*

*"All that the Father gives me* will come to me. *And him who comes to Me I will by no means cast out.*

"For I have come down from heaven, not to do my will but the will of the One who sent me. Now *this* is the will of the Father who sent me: that of all that He gave me I should lose none, but should raise it up at the last day. And *this* is the will of Him who sent me: *that everyone who sees the Son and believes upon Him should have everlasting life;* and *I* will raise him up at the last day."

### *"How Can He Give His Flesh?"*

The Jews[c] began therefore to mutter against him, because he said, *"I am* the Bread which came down out of heaven," and they kept saying, "Is he not Jesus, the son of Joseph, whose father and mother we know? How then does he say, 'I have come down *out of heaven'?"* Jesus therefore answered and said to them, "Mutter not among yourselves. No one can come to me unless the Father who sent me draw him. *And him will I raise up at the last day.*

"It is written in the prophets, *'And all men will be taught by God.'* So everyone who has listened to the Father *and has learned* comes to Me. (Not that anyone has *seen* the Father—except that the One who is from God, *He* has seen the Father.)

*"Verily, verily, I say to you, he who believes upon Me has everlasting life.* I am the Bread of *life.* Your fathers in the wilderness ate the manna and yet died; *this* is the Bread which comes down out of heaven that anyone may eat of it *and not die.*

"I am *the Living Bread* which came down out of heaven. If anyone eat of this Bread, he shall live forever. Moreover, the Bread that *I will give* is *my flesh,* which I will give *for the life of the world."*

The Jews therefore began to dispute with one another, saying, "How can he give us his flesh *to eat?"* Jesus therefore said to them, "Verily, verily, ! say to you, *unless* you eat the flesh of the Son of man and drink his blood, *you have no life in you.* He who eats my flesh and drinks my blood *has everlasting life; and I will raise him up at the last day.*

"For my flesh is *food* indeed and my blood is *drink* indeed. He who eats my flesh and drinks my blood[d] dwells in Me, and I in him. As the living Father sent me and I live through the Father, so the one who eats me shall also live through me. *This* is the Bread which came down out of heaven. Not as your fathers ate the manna and yet died; he who eats this Bread shall *live forever."*

### *"Do You Also Wish to Go Away?"*

These things he was speaking while teaching in the synagogue in Capernaum. Many of his disciples therefore on hearing them said, "This is a difficult message; who can accept it?" But Jesus, knowing within him that his disciples were murmuring about this, said to them, "Does *this* offend you? Then what if you should see the Son of man ascending to where he was before? *It is the spirit that gives life—the flesh avails nothing. The words* which I speak to you *are spirit and life.*

"But there are some of you who believe not!" For Jesus knew from the very first who they were who did not believe, and who it was that would betray him. And he said, *"Because of this* is it that I have said to you, that no one can come to Me unless it be granted him from my Father."

From that time many of his disciples turned back and no longer went about with him. Jesus therefore said to the twelve, "Do *you* also wish to go away?"

Then Simon Peter answered him, "Lord, *to whom* shall we go? *You have words of eternal life!* And *we* have come *to be-*

*lieve,* and have known, *that You are the Holy One of God."*

Jesus answered them, "Was it not *I* who chose you twelve? And one of *you* is a devil!" He was speaking of Judas, son of Simon Iscariot, for it was he that would betray him, though one of the twelve.

## 58. Men's Traditions Versus God's Commands

### *(Jn. 7:1; Mt. 15:1-20; Mk. 7:1-23)*

[4] Even after these things Jesus kept going about in Galilee; for he was unwilling to go about in Judea, because the Jews were seeking to kill him.

[2] Then there assembled about him the Pharisees, and some of the scribes, who had come *from Jerusalem;* and when they saw some of his disciples eating with defiled (that is, unpurified) hands, they found fault. For the Pharisees and all the Jews, unless they scrub the hands with the fist, do not eat, thus continuing their forbears' tradition; and on coming from the marketplace, unless they purify themselves, they do not eat. And there are many other things which they received to observe, like the purifying of cups and pots, bronze utensils, [and dining couches].

The Pharisees and the scribes accordingly asked him, [1] *"Why* do your disciples *disregard the tradition of the elders?* For they do not purify their hands before eating." [2] But he answering said to them, [1] *"You hypocrites!* Well did Isaiah prophesy concerning *you,* when he said, [2] as it is written,

[1] *'With their mouth do this people draw near to me,*
*and with their lips are they honoring me,*
*but their heart is far off from me;*
*and in vain are they worshiping me,*
*teaching as doctrines commandments of men.'*
[2] For, *disregarding the commandment of God* you hold to the tradition of men, like the purifying of pots and cups; and many other such things are you doing."

And he said to them, "Is it right for you to set aside the commandment of *God,* that you may observe your *tradition?* For Moses said—[1] for *God* commanded—[2] *'Honor your father and your mother,'* and, *'He who speaks evil of father or mother, let him be put to death;'* but *you* say that, if a man tells his father or mother, 'That by which you might be helped from me is a gift to God,' [1] even if in no way he will honor his father or mother, [2] you no longer will let him do anything for his father or mother. [1] Thus have you set aside the commandment of God, [2] *making void God's Word* by your tradition which you have handed on. And *many* such things are you doing."

## Man's Defilement Is from Within

And when he had summoned all the people, he said to them, "Hear me, all of you, and understand: there is nothing from without a man that going *into* [1] his mouth [2] can defile him; but the things that come [1] *out of* his mouth, [2] it is they that *defile* a man. *[If anyone has ears to hear, let him hear!]"*

[1] Then came his disciples and said to him, "Do you know that the Pharisees were offended by that statement?" But he answering said, "Every plant which my heavenly Father has not planted shall be uprooted. Let them alone; they are *blind leaders* of the blind, and if blind men *lead* the blind, *both will fall into a pit."*

[2] Now when he went into a house from the crowd, his disciples asked him about the parable, [1] and Peter said to him, *"Explain* the parable to us." And Jesus [2] said to them, "Are *you also* thus [1] still without understanding? Do you not yet perceive, [2] that whatever from without [1] goes into the mouth, [2] *it* cannot defile a man? For it enters not into his heart but his *body,* and so goes on out" (he thereby making *all foods clean).* [a]

And he said, [1] "But the things which go forth *from* the mouth [2] of a man [1] come *from the heart,* and *these* defile a man. [2] For from within, out of the heart of men, come forth the *evil purposes–* [1] murders, adulteries, sex vices, thefts, false testifying, blasphemies, [2] envyings, malicious deeds, deceit, licentiousness, a sinful eye, conceit, foolishness–*all* of these corruptions come forth *from within,* and [1] *these* are the things that defile a man. But eating *with unpurified hands* does not defile a man."

# Chapter 11. A Ministry in Gentile Regions

## 59. Crumbs from the Children's Table
### (Mt. 15:21-28; Mk. 7:24-30)

[1] Then Jesus [2] arose from that place and journeyed off into the region of Tyre and Sidon.[a] And he went into a house, and he would have no one know it, but could not be hid. For [1] behold, a Canaanite woman of that region, [2] whose small daughter had an unclean spirit, having heard of him came and fell at his feet.

And the woman was a *Gentile,* a Syro-Phoenician by race, [1] but she cried to him, saying, "Have pity on me, Lord, *Son of David.* My daughter is sorely afflicted with a demon." [2] And she begged him to cast out the demon from her daughter. [1] But he answered her not a word; and his disciples came and besought him, saying, "Dismiss her, for she is crying after *us.*"

Then he answering said, "I was not sent but to the lost sheep of the house of *Israel.*" But she made obeisance to him, saying, *"Lord, help me!"*

[2] And Jesus said to her, "Let the *children* get filled up first; for it is not good to take the children's bread and throw it to the little dogs." But she answered and said to him, *"Oh yes, Lord!* For even the little dogs eat of the children's crumbs [1] that fall from their masters' table."

Then Jesus answering said to her, "O woman, great is your *faith!* [2] For this answer [1] your request is granted. [2] Go your way; the demon has gone out from your daughter." [1] So her daughter was restored from that hour, [2] and on going back home she found that the demon had gone out, and her daughter was lying on the bed.

## 60. A Deaf Man, and Many, Healed
### (Mt. 15:29-31; Mk. 7:31-37)

[2] Then again, leaving the district of Tyre and Sidon, he came toward the Sea of Galilee through the midst of the Decapolis

region. And they brought him a deaf man who had an impediment in his speech, and besought him to lay his hand on him.

So taking him aside from the multitude, he put his fingers into his ears, and spat and touched his tongue; and looking up toward heaven, he groaned and said to him, *"Ephphatha,"* which means, *"Be opened."* And immediately his ears were opened, and the stricture of his tongue was released and he began speaking clearly.

Then he charged them not to tell anyone, but the more he charged them the more they kept proclaiming it. And they were amazed beyond measure, saying, "He has done *all* things well! He makes even the deaf to hear and the dumb to speak."

[1] Then Jesus came along by the Sea of Galilee, and he went up on a mountain[a] and sat down there. And there came to him great multitudes, bringing with them the lame, the blind, the dumb, the maimed, and many others, and they hastened to place them at Jesus' feet, and he healed them; so that the crowds marveled at seeing the dumb speaking, the maimed restored, the lame walking, and the blind seeing, and they glorified the God *of Israel.*

## 61. Four Thousand Hungry Gentiles Fed

### (Mt. 15:32-38; Mk. 8:1-9a)

[1] Now [2] in *those* days,[a] there being a great multitude with nothing to eat, Jesus summoned his disciples and said to them, "I am moved with compassion on the multitude, for they have been with me now three days and have nothing to eat. [1] And I will not send them off hungry [2] to their homes, [1] lest they grow faint on the road; [2] for some of them came a long way."

So his disciples answered him, [1] "Where shall we find loaves enough [2] *here* [1] in a desolate place to satisfy so great a multitude?" And Jesus [2] asked them, "How many loaves do you have?" And they said, "Seven, [1] and a few little fish."

Then he commanded the throng to recline on the ground. [2] And taking the seven loaves [1] and the fish [2] and giving thanks, he broke them and gave to his disciples to serve, and they set them before the people. [1] So all ate and were filled, and they took up seven basketfuls of the fragments that remained; [2] and those eating were about *four* thousand men, [1] besides women and children.

## 62. The Leaven of Error Is Reproved
### (Mt. 15:39-16:12; Mk. 8:9b-21)

[1] He then sent away the multitude, [2] and immediately boarding the boat with his disciples went to the district of Dalmanutha, [1] to the neighborhood of Magdala. Then came forth to him the Pharisees and Sadducees, [2] and they began to cavil at him, demanding [1] that he show *them* a miraculous sign from heaven, [2] making a test of him.

[1] But he answering said to them, "In the evening you say, 'It will be fair weather,' for the sky is red; and in the morning, 'It will be a stormy day,' for the sky is red and menacing. *You hypocrites,* the face of the sky you indeed know how to read, but the signs *of the times*[a] you cannot recognize!" [2] And groaning deeply in his spirit he said, "Why is *this* generation demanding a sign? [1] A generation that is *wicked and adulterous* is demanding a miraculous sign, and [2] verily, I say to you, [1] no sign will be given it but the sign of the prophet *Jonah."* [2] And he left them, and boarding the boat once more went off to the farther shore.

Now they had forgotten to take bread, and except for one loaf they had none with them in the boat. [1] And when his disciples reached the farther shore, Jesus [2] warned them, saying, [1] "Take heed and beware of the leaven of the Pharisees and the Sadducees, and [2] of Herod." So they began to question with one another, saying, [1] "Is it because we brought no loaves?"

[2] But Jesus perceiving it said to them, [1] "Why question with one another, you of little faith, because you did not bring *loaves?* [2] Do you not perceive yet, nor understand? Are your hearts still unresponsive? Do you have eyes, but do not see? And ears, but do not hear? And do you not remember? When I broke the five loaves for the five thousand, how many baskets full of fragments did you take up?" They answered him, "Twelve." "And when the seven for the four thousand, how

many basketfuls of fragments took you up?" And they said, "Seven."

So he said to them, "How is it you do not understand?[b] [1] Why do you not see that it was not concerning *bread* I told you to beware of the leaven of the Pharisees and Sadducees?" Then they understood that he had not warned them of the leaven of bread, but of the *teaching* of the Pharisees and Sadducees.

### 63. At Bethsaida a Man Is Given Sight
#### (Mk. 8:22-26)

Then came he to Bethsaida, and men brought to him a blind man and besought him to touch him. And taking the blind man by the hand, he led him out of the village; then he put spittle on his eyes, and laying his hands upon him asked if he saw anything. And looking up he said, "I see *the men!* They appear like walking trees." Then he laid his hands upon his eyes again and had him look up, and he was restored and beheld them all clearly. So he sent him off to his home, saying, "Go not into the village, [nor tell anyone in the village]."[a]

### Chapter 12. Fiercely Rebuffed at Jerusalem

### 64. He Is Challenged to Display Himself
#### (Jn. 7:2-10)

Now the Jews' feast of the Tabernacles was at hand.[a] His brothers said therefore to him, "Depart from here and go off to Judea, that your disciples also may *witness* your works which you are doing. For no one does his works in secret when he seeks to be publicly known. If you are doing these things, *display yourself to the world.*" For not even did his brothers believe upon him.

Jesus said therefore to them, "My time is not yet here. But

*your* time is always ready! The world cannot hate you; but it does hate me, because I testify of it that its works are evil. As for you, go on up to this feast; *I* am not [yet] going up to this feast, for my time has not yet fully come."

With these words he remained in Galilee; but when his brothers had gone up, then he likewise went up to the feast, not publicly, but as though in secret.

## 65. *Teaching at the Feast of Tabernacles*

### *(Jn. 7:11-36)*

The Jews therefore were looking for him at the feast, and kept saying, *"Where is* that man?" There was also much muttering among the people concerning him. Some indeed were saying, "He is a *good* man," but others, "No, *he is deceiving the people."* None, however, spoke about him openly for fear of the Jews. But then, at the midpoint of the feast, Jesus went up into the temple and began to teach.

And the Jews were filled with wonder, saying, "How does this man possess learning, when he has had *no learned teaching?"* Jesus answered them and said, "The teaching I give is not mine, but comes from *Him who sent me. If anyone purposes to do His will, he shall know of the teaching, whether it is from God or whether I am speaking from myself.*

He who speaks from himself seeks his own glory; but he who is seeking the glory of *Him who sent him,* he is *true,* and no unrighteousness is in him. Has not *Moses* given you the law? Yet none of you is *keeping* the law—why are you seeking *to kill me?"*

The people answered and said, "You have a demon! Who is seeking to kill you?" Jesus answered and said to them, "I wrought one work,[a] and you all marvel. Now Moses gave you *circumcision*—not that it is from Moses, but from the fathers— and you circumcise a male on the Sabbath. If a male is circumcised on the Sabbath, that the law of Moses should not be broken, are you angry at me for healing a man's whole body on the Sabbath? Judge not according to appearance, but render *righteous* judgment."

## *"I AM from Him"*

Some therefore of Jerusalem were saying, "Is not he the one they are seeking to *kill?*[b] And behold, he is speaking openly and they say nothing to him! Have the rulers perhaps recognized that he is indeed *the Messiah?* Yet we know *this* man, where he is from, while the Messiah, when he comes, no one knows where he is from." Jesus therefore, as he taught in the temple, cried out and said, "So you 'know' me and you 'know' where I am from!' Yet it is not on my own authority I have come, but *He who sent me* is true—*Whom you do not know;* but *I* know Him, *for I AM from Him, and it is He who sent me."*

They kept seeking therefore to arrest him, although no one laid a hand on him, for his hour had not yet come. But many of the crowd believed upon him, and kept saying, "The Messiah, *when he comes,* will he do any greater miraculous signs than these which *this* man wrought?"

The Pharisees heard how the people were muttering these things about him, so the Pharisees and the chief priests sent officers to arrest him. Jesus therefore said to them, "Yet a little while am I with you; then I am going unto Him who sent me. You will seek me but will not find me, and where *I* am *you cannot come."* The Jews therefore said to one another, "Where does he intend to go, that we shall not find him? Will he go to those who are dispersed among the Greeks, and teach the Greeks? What does he mean by saying, 'You will seek me but will not find me, and where *I* am *you cannot come'?"*

## 66. *The Great Day of the Feast*

*(Jn. 7:37-8:1)*

Then on the last day of the feast, the "Great Day," Jesus stood and cried out, saying,

> *"If anyone is thirsty,*
> *let him come unto Me and drink!*
> "He who puts his trust in Me,
> *out of the depths of his being shall flow*

(even as the scripture said)
*'rivers of living water.'"*

Now this he said concerning *the Spirit,* whom those believing upon him would receive; for the Holy Spirit had not yet come, since Jesus had not yet been glorified.

Many of the people, therefore, on hearing this utterance said, "Truly this is *the Prophet."* Others said, *"He is the Messiah!"* But some said, "No, for does the Messiah come from *Galilee?*[a] Has not the scripture said that from the offspring of David, and from *Bethlehem,* the village where David was, the Messiah is coming?"

A division therefore arose among the people concerning him; and some of them wanted to seize him, yet no one laid hands on him. So the officers went back to the chief priests and Pharisees; and they asked them, "Why did you not bring him?" The officers answered, *"No man ever spoke like this one!"* The Pharisees therefore answered them, "Have *you, too,* been deceived? Have any of the *authorities* believed upon him, or have any of the *Pharisees?* But this rabble, who know not the law, are accursed!"

Nicodemus, the man who came to him by night and was one of their number, said to them, "Does our law judge a man before first giving him a hearing and learning what he is doing?" They answered and said to him, "Are *you also* from Galilee? Search and see, that *no prophet has arisen* out of Galilee." [Then they went everyone to his home. Jesus went to the Mount of Olives.]

## 67. *An Adulteress and Her Accusers*

### *(Jn. 8:2-11)*

[At dawn, however, he came again into the temple; and all the people were gathering around him, so he sat down and began to teach them.

Then the scribes and the Pharisees brought to him a woman, one who had been taken in adultery. And when they had stood her in the midst of the people, they said to him, "Teacher, this woman was taken in *adultery,* in the very act. Now in the law Moses commanded us that such should be stoned; what therefore do *you* say?" But this they said only to put him to the test, to find an accusation against him.

But Jesus, stooping down, began to write with his finger upon the ground. Then as they kept asking him, he raised himself up and said to them, "He that is *without sin* among you, let *him* cast the first stone at her." And stooping down once more, he continued writing on the ground.

Now at hearing this, and being convicted by conscience, they went out one by one, beginning with the eldest and even down to the last; and Jesus was left alone with the woman, standing in the midst of the people.

Then when Jesus straightened up and saw none but the woman, he said to her, "Woman, where are those who accused you? Did no one keep on condemning you?" And she said, "No one, Sir." And Jesus said to her, "Neither do *I* condemn you. Go your way, *and sin no more.*"] [a]

### 68. *"I Am the Light of the World"*
#### *(Jn. 8:12-59)*

Jesus therefore once more spoke to them, saying, "I am *the Light of the world.* He who follows *Me* shall not walk in the darkness, but shall have the light of Life."

The Pharisees said therefore to him, "You are witnessing *concerning yourself;* your testimony is not valid." Jesus answered and said to them, "Though I am witnessing concerning myself, my testimony *is valid.* For I know where I came from and where I am going, while you know *not* where I came from or where I am going—*you* judge according to *the flesh.*

As for myself, *I* am judging no one. And if *I* also am judging, *my judgment is valid;* for I am not alone, but it is *I and the Father who sent me.* Furthermore, it is also written in your law that the testimony of *two* men is valid. *I* am one witnessing concerning myself, and *the Father who sent me* is witnessing concerning me."

They said therefore to him, *"Where is* your father?" Jesus answered, "You know neither Me nor my Father. If you had

known Me, you would have known *my Father also."* These
words Jesus uttered in the treasury, while teaching in the temple; yet no one put him under arrest, because his hour had not
yet come.

## *"You Will Die in Your Sins"*

Jesus therefore addressed them once more: *"I* am going
away, and you will search for me; and in your sin you will die
—where *I* am going *you cannot come."* Therefore said the
Jews, "Will he perhaps kill himself, since he says, 'Where *I* am
going *you cannot come'?"* So he said to them, *"You* are from
beneath; *I* am from above. *You* are of this world; *I* am not of
this world. Therefore I told you that you will die in your sins.
For if you believe not that I AM HE,[a] *you will die in your
sins."*

They said therefore to him, "Who *are* you?" And Jesus said
to them, "Altogether that which I also told you! Many things
have I to say and to judge concerning you. But He who sent
me is true; and for my part, the things which I heard from *Him*
are what I am saying to the world."

That he was speaking to them of the Father they did not
grasp. Jesus said therefore to them, "When you shall have *lifted up* the Son of man, then will you know[b] that I AM HE, and
that I do nothing on my own, but am saying these things as
*my Father* instructed me. And He who sent me *is with me;*
the Father did not leave me alone. *For I am always doing the
things which are pleasing to Him."*

## *"Why Do You Not Believe Me?"*

By his saying these things many believed upon him. Then
said Jesus to the Jews who had believed him, *"If you continue
in my Word, my disciples are you indeed, and you shall know
the truth and the truth shall make you free."*

They made answer to him, "We are offspring of *Abraham,*
and have never been in bondage to anyone. How do *you* say,
'You will be made *free'?"* Jesus answered them, "Verily, verily, I say to you, *everyone who is practicing sin is a bondslave*

to the sin. Now the bondslave dwells not in the home evermore, but the son dwells evermore. If therefore *the Son* shall
set you free, you will be *free indeed.*

"That you are offspring of Abraham, I know; but you are
seeking *to kill* me, because my Word has no entrance in you.
*I* am declaring what I have seen in the presence of *my* Father,
and *you* therefore are doing what you have seen in the presence of *your* father."

### *"You Are from Your Father the Devil"*

They answered and said to him, *"Abraham* is our father."
Jesus said to them, "If you were children of Abraham, *the
works* of Abraham you would do. Instead now you are seeking
*to kill me*—a man who has told you the truth which I heard
from God—*this* Abraham did not do! *You* are doing the works
of *your* father."

They said therefore to him, *"We* were not born from fornication!ᶜ *One* Father have we, even *God."* Jesus said therefore
to them, "If God were your Father, you would have loved *Me*;
for from God came *I* forth and have come. For not on my own
have I come, but *He* sent me. Why do you not comprehend
what I say? Because you cannot *give heed* to my message.

*"You* are from your father *the Devil,* and the desires of
*your* father *you desire to do.* He was a murderer from the beginning, and for the *truth* he has not stood, because there is no
truth in him. When he speaks falsehood, it is from his nature
he speaks, for he is a liar and the *father* of falsehood.

"Yet because *I speak* the truth, you do not believe me! Who
among you convicts Me of sin? But if I do speak the truth,
why do *you* not believe me? He who is of God heeds God's
words. It is for this reason *you* do not heed them: *because you
are not of God."*

### *"Before Abraham Was, I AM"*

The Jews therefore answered and said to him, "Say *we* not
well *that you are a Samaritan*ᵈ *and have a demon?"* Jesus answered, *"I* have not a demon; instead, I am honoring my Fath-

er—and you are dishonoring me. But *I* am not seeking my glory; One there is who is seeking it and judging.

*"Verily, verily, I say to you, if anyone shall keep my Word,*
*he shall not at all see death forever."*

The Jews said therefore to him, "Now we *know* that you
have a demon! Abraham died, and the prophets died, yet *you*
say, 'If anyone shall keep my Word, he shall not at all taste
death forever.' Are *you* greater than *our father Abraham,* who
died? And *the prophets* died. *Whom do you make yourself to*
*be?"*

Jesus answered, "If I glorify *myself,* my glory is nothing; it
is *my Father* who glorifies me—of whom you say that he is
*your God,* yet you have not known him! But *I* know him. And
were I to say that I do not know him, I should be a liar like
you; but I do know him, and am keeping his Word. Your father Abraham exulted in that he would see My day; and he saw
it, and rejoiced."

The Jews therefore said to him, "You are not yet *fifty*[e]
years old, and have you seen *Abraham?"* Jesus said to them,
"Verily, verily, I say to you, before Abraham *was,* I AM."

Upon this they picked up stones to hurl at him; but Jesus
hid himself and, [going through their midst,] departed from
the temple [and went thus on his way.]

### 69. *Sight Is Given a Man Born Blind*
#### *(Jn. 9:1-10:21)*

Now as he was passing along,[a] he saw a man who had been
blind from birth; and his disciples asked him, saying, "Rabbi,
who sinned, this man or his parents, so that he was born
blind?" Jesus answered, "It is not because this man sinned, or
his parents, but that the works of God might be shown forth
in him. It behooves me *to be doing* the works of Him who sent
me, while it is day; night is coming, when no one can work. *As*
*long as I may be in the world, I am the Light of the world."*

Upon saying these things he spat on the ground and formed
mud with the spittle, then he applied the mud to the blind
man's eyes and said to him, "Go and wash in the Pool of Silo-

am" (which means *sent).* He went off therefore and washed, and came back seeing.

The neighbors therefore, and those who had known him as a blind man, said, "Is not this he who was sitting and begging?" Some said, "It is he," but others, "He is like him." The man himself said, *"I am he."* They said therefore to him, "How were your eyes opened?" He answered and said, "A man called Jesus formed mud, and he put it on my eyes and said to me, 'Go off to the Pool of Siloam and wash.' So I went off and washed, and received sight." They said therefore to him, "Where is he?" He replied, "I do not know.".

## *"He Does Not Keep the Sabbath!"*

They brought to the Pharisees the man who had been blind. Now it was on a Sabbath that Jesus had formed the mud and opened his eyes. So the Pharisees also began to ask him once more how he had received his sight, and he said to them, "He put mud on my eyes, and I washed, and I now see." Some of the Pharisees therefore said, "That fellow is not from God, for he does not keep the Sabbath!" Others said, "How can a *sinner* work miraculous signs?" So there was a division among them. They said again to the blind man, "What do *you* say concerning him, since he opened your eyes? And he said, "He is *a prophet."*

The Jews, however, did not believe about him that he had been blind and had received sight, till they called the parents of the one who received sight, and asked them, "Is this your son, who *you* say was *born* blind? How is it he can now see?" His parents answered them and said, "We know that this is our son, and that he was born blind; but how he now can see we do not know, or who opened his eyes we know not. He is of age, ask him; he shall speak for himself." These things his parents said because they were afraid of the Jews. For the Jews had already agreed together that, if anyone should acknowledge him as *the Messiah,* he should be banished from the synagogue; this was why his parents said, "He is of age, ask him."

*Excommunicated for Truthfulness*

So a second time they summoned the man who had been blind, and they said to him, "Give praise to *God. We* know that this man *is a sinner."* He answered therefore and said, "Whether he is a sinner, I do not know; one thing I do know: I was blind, but *I now see."*

And they spoke to him once more: "What did he do to you? *How* opened he your eyes?" He answered them, "I told you already, and you did not listen. Why do you wish to hear it again? Do *you* also wish to become his disciples?" Then they railed at him and said, *"You* are *his* disciple; but *we* are disciples of *Moses. We know* that *God* has spoken to Moses, but as for this fellow, we know not where he is from."

The man answered and said to them, "This truly is a marvel, that *you* know not where he is from, yet he opened my eyes. Now we know that God does not hear sinners, but if anyone is a worshiper of God and does his will, him he hears. Not in all time has it ever been heard that anyone opened the eyes of one born blind. If this man were not from God, he could do nothing." They answered him and said, *"You* were utterly born in *sins,* and are *you* teaching *us?"* And they thrust him out.

*"Lord, I Believe"*

Jesus heard of their thrusting him out, and when he had found him, said to him, *"Do you believe upon the Son of God?"* He answered and said, "Who is he, Sir, that I may believe upon him?" And Jesus said to him, "You have both seen Him and it is He who is speaking with you." And he said, *"Lord, I believe."* And he bowed in worship before him.

And Jesus said, "For judgment *came I*[b] into this world, that those not seeing might see, and that those 'seeing' might be made blind." And those of the Pharisees who were present heard these things, and said to him, "Are *we* blind also?" Jesus said to them, "If you were blind, you would not have sin. But now you are saying, *'We see,'* so your sin remains.

### *"I Am the Good Shepherd"*

*(Jn. 10:1-21)*

"Verily, verily, I say to you, he who enters not the sheep-fold by the door, but climbs up some other way, such a one is a thief and a robber. But he who enters in by the door is the *shepherd* of the sheep; to him the gate-keeper opens, and the sheep hear his voice, and his own sheep he calls by name and leads them out.

"Even when he pushes out his own sheep, he goes his way *before* them, and the sheep follow him because they know his voice. But a stranger they will not at all follow, but will flee from him, because they know not the voice of strangers."

This allegory Jesus directed at them, but they did not grasp what it was·that he was telling them. Jesus spoke therefore to them again: "Verily, verily, I say to you, *I am* the Door of the sheep. All who ever came before Me are thieves and robbers; but the sheep did not hear them. I am the *Door;* if anyone enters through Me, he shall be saved, and shall go in and out, and find pasture. The thief comes not but to steal and kill and destroy; I came that they might have *Life,* and might have it abundantly.

"*I am the good Shepherd;* the good Shepherd *lays down his life for the sheep.* But the hired man, who is not a shepherd, to whom the sheep are not his own, sees the wolf coming and leaves the sheep and flees, and the wolf seizes and scatters the sheep. The hired man flees because he is a hired man and cares not himself about the sheep.

### *"My Life I Am Laying Down"*

"*I am the good Shepherd and know those who are mine;* and I *am known by mine,* just as the Father knows me and I also know the Father. And *my* life I am laying down for the sheep. And other sheep have I, which are not of this fold; those also must I bring, and *they* will hear my voice, and there will be one flock, one Shepherd.

"Because of this does the Father love me, *that I am laying down my life*—so that I may claim it again. No one is taking it away from me; of my own accord am I laying it down. I have authority to lay it down, and authority to claim it again; this command received I from my Father."

Because of these words, therefore, a division arose again among the Jews. And many of them said, "He has a *demon* and is mad; why do you listen to him?" But others said, "These are not the words of a demon-possessed man. Can a demon *open the eyes of the blind?*"

## 70. The Dedication; Stoning Again Threatened
### (Jn. 10:22-42)

Now the feast of the Dedication was being observed at Jerusalem, so it was winter; and Jesus was walking about in the temple, in the Colonnade of Solomon. The Jews accordingly gathered around him, and they said to him, "How long are you holding our soul in suspense? If *you* are *the Messiah,* tell us plainly."

Jesus answered them, "I told you, and you do not believe. *The works* which I am doing in the name of my Father, *these* are bearing witness of me. But *you* do not believe because you are *not of My sheep.*

"As I said to you, *my sheep hear my voice, and I know them, and they follow me. And I give to them eternal life, and they shall in no wise ever perish, nor shall anyone snatch them out of my hand. My Father, who gave them me, is greater than all, and no one can snatch them from the hand of my Father. I* and the Father *are One.*"

Because of this the Jews again began to pick up stones to stone[a] him. Jesus answered them, "Many good works showed I you from my Father; for which of these works are you stoning me?" The Jews answered him, saying, "For a *good* work we are not stoning you, but for *blasphemy,* because you, a man, are *making yourself God.*"

Jesus answered them, "Is it not written in your law, *'I said, You are gods'?* If he called *them* 'gods,' to whom the word of God came—and the Scripture cannot be broken—do *you* say to the One whom the Father sanctified and sent into the world, *'You are blaspheming,'* because I said that I am *the Son* of

God? If I am *not* doing my Father's works, do not believe me; but if I am, even though you believe not Me, *believe the things which I am doing,* that you may perceive and believe *that the Father is in Me and I in Him."*

They again sought therefore to put him under arrest, but he went forth out of their hand.

### A Fruitful Period in Perea

*And he departed once more to the other side of the Jordan,* to the area where John was at first baptizing; and there he dwelt,[b] and many came to him. And they said, "John indeed wrought no miraculous sign, but all the things which John said of this man *were true."* And many believed upon him there.

* * *

*Comment.* This third year of Jesus' ministry, like the first, is a comparatively neglected period as far as the Synoptic records are concerned. Luke's voice is wholly silent, and Matthew and Mark are heard in less than one-third of the pages. For both human and divine reasons, they did not elaborate on the events of this particular time period. They moved more directly to the climactic issues of the final year during which Jesus turned His face decisively toward the cross. He had come as Israel's Messiah and King, but now He begins to speak of His death. What brought about this change of direction in His ministry is not fully explained by the Synoptists. For instance, in recording the feeding of the 5000, they do not describe the mass rejection that followed in the aftermath at Capernaum.

Although the Synoptists speak sparingly of the events of the third year, that year did involve crucial events that precipitated the change in Jesus' ministry. In John's Gospel are described a number of these significant third-year occurrences, and, with the records interwoven, the reason for His basic change in ministry becomes quite apparent. The key is the fact repeatedly shown, that though Jesus was sent to be Israel's righteous King. *He would not force Himself on anyone.* John declared at the beginning of His Gospel:

He came to his own creation, and his own people received him not.
But as many as received him, those who put their trust in his name,
to them gave he the high estate of being made children of God.

In pursuing this theme, John recorded how that when the religious leaders were outraged at Jesus' zeal in cleansing the temple, He *withdrew* to the country districts. When jealousy developed with respect to His relation to John the Baptist, He *withdrew* to Galilee. When His hometown rejected Him, He *withdrew* to a friendlier city. When His second visit at Jerusalem met rejection, He *withdrew* again to Galilee. And when at the beginning of the third year, His adopted city of Capernaum repudiated Him, He *withdrew* to Gentile regions of Palestine. In a later visit to Jerusalem to display His resurrection power in the raising of Lazarus, He again *withdrew* to outlying areas to foil a plot to destroy Him.

In the face of this general rejection, the question might be posed, "To whom would He now go?" The answer is implied in what next occurred: He would *withdraw from the entire world of men.* The fulfillment of the prophesied Messianic Kingdom on earth would be denied to that generation and actualized in a future generation bringing forth the fruits thereof. In the meantime, His eternal purpose of bearing the sins of the world would be accomplished, and the criminal execution of that death would be perpetrated by the very people He came to deliver. His death was certainly no "afterthought" in the plan of God. But its outworking in terms of human responsibility did follow a progressive pattern of development.

With these key points of rejection made clear, the subsequent preparations and revelations in the following sections unfold quite logically. At His first specific announcement concerning His death, Jesus will also announce His plan to build His Church. And as He progressively discloses this new program, He will also give intensive training to His corps of apostles who will constitute the foundation for that newly-- announced, interadvent Kingdom program (Eph. 2:20).

# PART V.

## HIS FACE TURNS TO THE CROSS

### Chapter 13. Disclosing that He Must Die

#### 71. *Peter Declares Jesus' Messiahship*
##### *(Mt. 16:13-20; Mk. 8:27-30; Lk. 9:18-21)*

[2] Then Jesus and his disciples went forth [1] and came [2] into the villages of Caesarea Philippi.[a] And on the journey [3] it came to pass that, while he was praying alone, the disciples were with him and he questioned them, [1] asking, "Who [2] do men say that *I,* [1] *the Son of man, am?"*

[3] And they answered, [1] "Some say John the Baptist, and others Elijah, and others Jeremiah; or [3] that *some* prophet of old has arisen." But he said to them, "But you—who do *you* say that I am?" [1] And Simon Peter [2] answering said to him, [1] "You are THE MESSIAH,[b] THE SON OF THE LIVING GOD."

And Jesus answered and said to him, *"Blessed* are you, Simon Bar-Jona! For flesh and blood did not reveal it to you, but my Father who is in heaven. And this also *I* say to you, that you are *'Petros,'* a piece of *rock;* and on this kind of *bedrock*[c] I will build my *Church,* and against it the gates of Hades shall not prevail. And to you will I give the *keys* of the Kingdom of heaven; and everything you bind on earth shall have been bound in heaven, and everything you loose on earth shall have been loosed in heaven."[d]

[3] But he strictly admonished [1] his disciples, commanding them to tell no one at that time [2] concerning him [1] that he was *the Messiah.*[e]

## 72. *"The Son of Man Must Be Killed"*

### *(Mt. 16:21-28; Mk. 8:31-9:1; Lk. 9:22-27)*

[1] From that time Jesus began to disclose to his disciples that he must journey *to Jerusalem,*[a] [3] saying that, "The Son of man must suffer many things, and be rejected by the elders and chief priests and scribes; *and he must be killed, and on the third day* [2] *rise again;'* and he was saying this plainly.

So Peter seized him face to face and began to reprove him, [1] saying, "Mercy on you, Lord! *This* shall never happen to You." But he, [2] turning about and looking at his disciples, rebuked Peter, saying, ' Get behind me, Satan! [1] You are a stumbling-block in my way; [2] for you are not seeking the things of God, but those of *men."*

[1] Then [2] calling the people to come near with his disciples, [1] Jesus said [3] to them all, *"If anyone would come after me, let him put himself aside, and take up his cross every day and follow me. For whoever would save his life shall lose it; but whoever shall lose his life for My sake,* [2] *and for that of the Glad News, shall save it—*[1] *he shall find it.*

*"For what is a man profited if he gains the whole world but* [3] *destroys himself or* [2] *loses his soul? Or what exchange shall a man give for his soul?*

"For whoever is ashamed of Me and of My words in this adulterous and sinful generation, of him will also *the Son of man* be ashamed, [3] when he shall come in his glory and that of his Father and the holy angels. [1] For the Son of man *is going to come* in the glory of his Father, with his angels; and then will he render to everyone according to his deeds."

[2] And he said to them, "Verily, I say to you, there are *some standing here* who shall not at all taste of death [1] till they have seen the Son of man coming in his Kingdom, [2] the Kingdom of God *having come in power.'*[b]

## 73. *Three See a Preview of His Glory*

### *(Mt. 17:1-13; Mk. 9:2-13; Lk. 9:28-36)*

[3] Now it came to pass that [1] six days [3] after these words Je-

sus took Peter and James [1] and his brother John [2] and led them up on a high mountain, by themselves alone, [3] to pray. And it came to pass that, as he was praying, the appearance of his countenance was changed and [2] he was transfigured before them. [1] His face shone like the sun, [2] and his garments became lustrous, extremely white like snow, as no fuller on earth could whiten them, [3] a brilliant white [1] like the light.

And behold, there appeared unto them [3] two men, who were Moses and Elijah; who, appearing in radiance [2] and conversing with Jesus, [3] talked of his departure which he was going to fulfill at Jerusalem. (Now Peter and his companions had been overcome with sleep, but becoming wide awake, they saw his glory and the two men who were standing with him.)

Then it came to pass that, as these men were departing from him, [1] Peter answered and said to Jesus, "Lord, it is good for us to be here. If You are willing, let us make here three booths, one for You, one for Moses, and one for Elijah" [3] (not being aware what he was saying; [2] for he knew not what to say, for they were much afraid).

[3] But even as he was speaking thus, [1] behold, [3] there came [1] a bright cloud [3] and it overshadowed them; and they were frightened as they were enveloped in the cloud. [1] And lo, [3] there came a Voice from out of the cloud, saying, [1] *"THIS IS MY BELOVED SON, IN WHOM I HAVE DELIGHTED; HEARKEN TO HIM."*

Now on hearing it the disciples fell on their faces in terror. But [3] when the Voice had ceased, [2] suddenly [1] raising their eyes [2] and looking around, they saw no one any more but Jesus only with themselves. [1] And Jesus came to them and touched them, saying, "Rise up, and be not terrified."

## *"Elijah Has Come Already"*

Then as they made their descent from the mountain, Jesus charged them [2] to tell no one the things they had seen, till the Son of man should rise from the dead. [3] So they kept it close and told no one in those days any part of the things they had seen. [2] And they kept to themselves what he had said, asking each other, , "What is *the rising from the dead?*"

They also asked him, saying, [1] "Why then do the scribes say that *Elijah must first come?*"[a] And Jesus answering said to them, "Elijah indeed is coming first and will put all things in order. But I say to you, [2] that Elijah *has also come* [1]*already;* and they recognized him not, but did to him whatever they desired, [2]just as it is written of him.[b] [1]In the same way also will the Son of man suffer at their hands. [2]And how is it written of the Son of man? That *He* should suffer many things and be despised!"

[1]Then the disciples comprehended that it was of John the Baptist he had spoken to them.

## 74. "I Believe—Help My Unbelief!"
### (Mt. 17:14-21; Mk. 9:14-29; Lk. 9:37-43a)

[3]Now it came to pass the next day, after their descent from the mountain, that [2]when he came to the disciples he saw a great crowd around them and some scribes disputing[a] with them. And immediately all the people, greatly amazed at seeing him, ran up to him and welcomed him. And he asked the scribes, "What are you questioning with them?"

[3]And behold, a man [2]in answer [1]came up to him [3]from the crowd, [1]and falling on his knees to him, [3]cried out, saying, "Teacher, I beseech you, look upon *my son!* [1]Have mercy on my son, [3]for he is my only child. [2]I brought my son to You, [1]Lord, because he is an epileptic and suffers grievously [2]from a dumb spirit. And wherever it seizes him, [3]lo, he suddenly cries out, [2]and it throws him down [3]in convulsions [2]and he foams and grinds his teeth, [3]and only after a bruising struggle does it leave him. [2]And he is wasting away; so [1]I brought him to your disciples and [3]begged *them* to cast it out, but [1]they could not cure him."

Then Jesus answered and said, "O unbelieving and perverse generation, how long shall I be with you? How long shall I bear with you? [3]Bring your son [1]here to me." [2]So they brought him to him; [3]but while he was yet approaching, [2]when the spirit saw Jesus it immediately convulsed the boy, and he fell on the ground and wallowed, foaming.

¹ Then Jesus ² asked his father, "How long has this been with him?" And he said, "From childhood. And many times has it cast him both into fire and into waters to destroy him. But if You *can* do anything, have pity on us and help us." And Jesus said to him, "If you *can believe! All things are possible to him who believes.*" And immediately the father of the child cried out and [with tears] said, "Lord, I *do believe*—help my unbelief!"

So Jesus, seeing that a multitude was gathering on the run, rebuked the foul spirit, saying to it, "You dumb and deaf spirit, *I* command you, come out of him; and enter not into him again." ¹ Then the demon, ² shrieking out and convulsing him sorely, ¹ came out of him. ² And he became as if dead, so that many said that he *was* dead. But Jesus took him by the hand and began to lift him up, and he arose; ³ and he gave him back again to his father. ¹ So the lad was restored from that moment, ³ and they all marveled at the majesty of God.

*"Why Could Not We?"*

² Now upon his going into a house, his disciples ¹ came to Jesus privately and ² asked him, "Why could not *we* cast it out?" ¹ And Jesus said to them, "Because you *are lacking in faith.* For verily, I say to you, if you have faith as large as a grain of mustard seed, you will say to *this mountain,*[b] 'Move from here to yonder place,' and it will move; and nothing will be impossible to you. ² But this kind can come out by nothing but by prayer [and fasting]."[c]

## 75. *Foretelling His Death Again*
### *(Mt. 17:22-23; Mk. 9:30-32; Lk. 9:43b-45)*

³ But while all were amazed at all that Jesus was doing, he said to his disciples, "As for you, let *these words* sink into your ears: for *the Son of man is going to be delivered into the hands of men!*"

² And they departed from there and made their way through Galilee, but he would not that anyone should know it.[a] For

[1] during their sojourn in Galilee [2] he continued teaching his disciples and saying to them, "The Son of man [1] is going to be delivered into men's hands, [2] and they will kill him; and after he is killed, [1] he will be raised up on the third day."

And they were deeply distressed, [3] yet they did not comprehend this statement. It was also veiled from them to keep them from seeing its meaning, and they feared to ask him concerning the statement.

## 76. Paying the Overdue Temple Tax

### (Mt. 17:24-27; Mk. 9:33a)

[2] So he came to Capernaum; [1] and on their arrival in Capernaum the collectors of the half-shekel tax confronted Peter and said, "Is not your teacher paying *the half-shekel?*"[a] He replied, "Yes."

And when he came into the house, Jesus spoke of the matter first, and said to him, "What do you think, Simon? *From whom* do the kings of the earth collect customs or tribute, from their sons or from the outsiders?" Peter said to him, "From the outsiders." Jesus said to him, "Then the *sons* indeed go *free.* But lest we be a cause of stumbling to them, go to the sea and cast in a hook, and take the first fish that comes up. On opening its mouth you will find a silver coin; take that and give it to them for me and for you."

## 77. He Discourses on Humility and Forgiveness

### (Mt. 18:1-19:2; Mk. 9:33b-10:1; Lk. 9:46-50)

[1] At that time the disciples came to Jesus [2] in the house, [1] saying, "Who then is *the greatest* in the Kingdom of heaven?" [3] But Jesus, perceiving the thought of their heart, [2] asked them, "What were you *disputing* about among yourselves on the way?" And they were silent, for they had disputed with one another on the way who should be the greatest.

So sitting down, he called all twelve and said to them, "If anyone *wishes* to be first, he shall be *last of all, and servant of all.*" [1] Then Jesus called to him a young child [3] and placed him by his side [1] in their midst, and said, "Verily, I say to you, unless you turn about and become like the little children, you *shall not at all enter the Kingdom of heaven.* Whoever therefore *humbles* himself as this little child, *he* is the greatest in the Kingdom of heaven. [3] For *he that is least* among you all, *he* shall be great."

[2] And when he had taken him in his arms, he said to them, [1] "And whoever receives one such little child *in My name* receives Me; [2] *and whoever receives Me receives not Me but Him who sent me.*"

## Avoid Giving Cause to Stumble

*(Mt. 18:6-9; Mk. 9:38-50; Lk. 9:49-50)*

[3] And John answering [2] him [3] said, "Master, we saw a man casting out demons in Your name, and we forbade him because he is *not following with us.*" [2] But Jesus said [3] to him, [2] "Forbid him not; for there is no one who shall do a mighty work in my name who can readily speak evil of me. [3] For he that is not against us is for us. [2] For verily, I say to you, whoever may give you in my name *a cup of water to drink* because you are Christ's, shall by no means lose his reward.

[1] "But whoever causes stumbling to one of these little ones who believe upon Me, it would be better for him were a great millstone hung about his neck and he were sunk in the depth of the sea! *Woe* to the world for the causing of stumbling! For it is necessary for causes of stumbling to come, but woe to that man by whom the stumbling comes!

"Now if your hand or your foot makes you stumble, cut it off and throw it away from you! It is better for you to enter life maimed or lame than, having two hands or two feet, to be cast [2] into Gehenna, [1] the eternal fire, [2] [where their worm does not die and the fire is not quenched]. [1] And if your eye makes you stumble, pluck it out and throw it away from you![a] [2] It is better for you with one eye to enter the Kingdom of God than with two eyes to be cast into the Gehenna of fire, where their worm does not die and the fire is not quenched.

[1] "For everyone shall be salted with fire, [and every sacrifice shall be salted with salt]. Salt is good, but if the salt has

become saltless, with what will you season it? Have salt in yourselves and *be at peace with one another.*

## Do Not Despise the Lowly
*(Mt. 18:10-20)*

"See that you *despise not* one of these little ones;[b] for I tell you that their angels in heaven continually behold the face of my Father who is in heaven.

*"[For the Son of man came to save that which was lost.]* What do you think; if a man has a hundred sheep, and one of them has gone astray, does he not leave the ninety-nine and go out on the mountains and seek the one that went astray? And if it be that he finds it, verily, I say to you, he rejoices more over it than over the ninety-nine that went not astray. So it is not the will of your Father who is in heaven that *one* of these little ones *should perish.*

*"Now, if your brother sins against you,* go and tell *him* his fault between you and him alone; if he will hear you, you have gained your brother. But if he will not listen, take with you one or two others, that *'at the mouth of two or three witnesses'*[c] every word may stand confirmed. And if he will not listen to them, tell it to the assembly. But if he will not listen even to the assembly, let him be to you as a pagan and a publican.

"Verily, I say to you, everything you bind on earth shall have been bound in heaven, and everything you loose on earth shall have been loosed in heaven. Again, I say to you, that if *two* of you agree on earth concerning anything they shall ask, *it will be done for them* by my Father who is in heaven. *For where two or three are gathered together in My name, there am I in the midst of them."*

## "How Many Times Forgive?"
*(Mt. 18:21-35)*

Then Peter came up to him and said, "Lord, *how often* shall my brother sin against me and I forgive him? Till seven times?" Jesus said to him, "I say to you, not till seven times, but till *seventy times* seven!

### Forgive as You Have Been Forgiven

"The Kingdom of heaven therefore may be likened to a man who was a king, who wished to call his bondmen to account. And when he had begun the reckoning, one was brought to him whose debt was ten thousand talents;[d] and as he was unable to pay, his lord ordered that he be sold, and his wife and children, and all that he had, and payment to be made.

"The bondman therefore fell down and made obeisance, saying, 'Sir, have patience with me, and I will pay you all.' And the lord of that bondman, moved with compassion, released him and forgave him the debt.

"But that bondman went out and found one of his fellow bondmen who owed him a hundred denaries, and seizing him he took him by the throat and said, *'Pay me what you owe!'* So his fellow bondman fell down at his feet and besought him, saying, 'Have patience with me, and I will pay you all.' And he would *not,* but went and flung him into prison until he should pay the debt.

"Now when his fellow bondmen saw what had occurred, they were greatly aggrieved and went and told their lord all that had happened. Then calling him before him, his lord said to him, 'You wicked bondman, I forgave you all that debt, since you entreated me; should not you therefore have shown *your* fellow bondman mercy, even as *I* showed mercy *to you?'*

"And with anger his lord turned him over to the jailers till he should pay all that was owed him. Thus also will my heavenly Father do to you, unless you each from your heart *forgive* your brother for his offenses."

### He Ministers Again in Perea
(Mt. 19:1-2; Mk. 10:1)

[1] And it came to pass that, when Jesus had finished these words, [2] he arose from there and [1] withdrew from Galilee, and came into the region of Judea [2] on the farther side of the Jordan. [1] And great crowds [2] came together about him again [2] and [1] followed him; [2] and again, as was his custom, he taught them [1] and healed them there.

## Chapter 14. A Great Final Teaching Tour

### 78. His Face Is Set Toward Jerusalem

*(Mt. 8:19-22; Lk. 9:51-62)*

[3] But it came to pass, with the days approaching when he should be received up, that he steadfastly set his face to journey to Jerusalem.[a]

And he sent messengers to go before him, and they went and entered a village of Samaritans to make ready for him. But these would not receive him, because his face was as though he were going to Jerusalem.

Now at seeing this his disciples James and John said, "Lord, will You have us call fire to come down from heaven and consume them, [as Elijah also did]?" But he turned and rebuked them, [and said, "You know not what spirit you are of! For the Son of man came not to destroy men's lives, but to save them."] And they went to another village.

And it came to pass, as they were going on their way, that [1] a certain scribe came up to him and said, ' Teacher, [3] Sir, I will follow You wherever you may go." And Jesus said to him, "The foxes have holes, and the birds of the air nests, but *the Son of man has no place to lay his head.*"

And he said to another [1] of his disciples, [3] *"Follow Me."* But he said, "Lord, let me first go to bury my father."[b] And Jesus said to him, "Leave the *dead* to bury their own dead; and as for *you,* go forth and proclaim the Kingdom of God!"

And another also said, "I will follow You, Lord, but first let me bid farewell to those in my home." But Jesus said to him, "No one who has put his hand to the plow *and looks back* is fitted for *the Kingdom of God.*"

### 79. Heralds Are Sent to Thirty-five Places

*(Mt. 11:20-30; Lk. 10:1-24)*

[3] Now also after these things the Lord appointed *seventy* others, and sent them two by two to go before him into every

110

city and place where he himself was going to come.[a]

He said therefore to *them:* "The harvest is plentiful indeed, but the laborers are few. Pray therefore the Lord of the harvest that he thrust forth laborers into his harvest.

"Go on your way; behold, *I* send you forth, as lambs in the midst of wolves. Carry no purse or provision bag or sandals; and greet no one on the way. And into whatever home you enter, first say, *'Peace* to this home.' And if indeed a son of peace is there, upon him your peace shall rest; but if not so, to you shall it return. And in the same home remain, eating and drinking the things they provide (for the laborer is worthy of his wages); do not move from home to home.

"And into whatever city[b] you may enter and they receive you, eat the things set before you; and heal the sick who are there, and say to them, 'The Kingdom of God has drawn near you.' But into whatever city you may enter and they receive you not, go out into its streets and say, 'Even the dust of your city that clings to us, we are wiping it off against you. Nevertheless know this, that *the Kingdom of God has drawn near you.'* And I say to you, it shall be more tolerable [1] in the day of judgment for the land of Sodom [3] than for that city."

## Woes Pronounced on Three Cities

[1] Then began he to upbraid the cities in which most of his *mighty works* had been done, because they did not repent. *"Woe* to you, Chorazin! *Woe* to you, Bethsaida! For if the mighty works which were done in you had been done in Tyre and Sidon, they would have repented long ago, [3] sitting in sackcloth and ashes. [1] I say to you, it shall be more tolerable for Tyre and Sidon in the day of judgment than for *you!* And you, *Capernaum,* who have been exalted up to heaven, down to Hades shall you be thrust! For if the mighty works done in you had been done in *Sodom,* it would have remained till this day. So I say to you likewise, it shall be more tolerable for the land of Sodom in the day of judgment than for *you.*

[3] *"He who hears you hears Me, and he who rejects you rejects Me; and he who rejects Me rejects Him who sent me."*

### The Return of the Seventy Heralds

And the seventy returned with joy, saying, "Lord, even the demons are subject to us through *Your name!*" And he said to them, "I saw Satan falling like lightning out of heaven. Behold, I give you authority to tread on serpents and scorpions,[c] and over all the power of the enemy, and nothing shall in any way hurt you. Nevertheless, rejoice not in this, that the spirits are made subject to you, but rather rejoice because *your names are written in heaven.*"

In that same hour Jesus rejoiced in the Holy Spirit, and answered and said, "I praise thee, O Father, Lord of heaven and earth, that thou hast hid these things from the learned and worldly-wise, and hast revealed them unto babes; yes, Father, for thus it was well pleasing in Thy sight."

[And turning to the disciples, he said,] *"All things were delivered unto Me by my Father.* And no one knows who the Son is but the Father, or who the Father is, except the Son, and he to whom the Son may choose to reveal him.

### His Invitation to All Mankind

[1] *"Come unto Me, all you who labor and are heavy-laden, and I will give you rest. Take My yoke upon you, and learn of Me; for I am meek and lowly in heart, and you shall find rest for your souls. For My yoke is easy, and My burden is light."*

[3] Then turning to the disciples in private, he said, *"Blessed* are the eyes that see the things which you are seeing! For I say to you, that many prophets and kings *desired* to see the things which *you* see, and did not see them, and to hear the things which *you* hear, and did not hear them."

### 80. The Example of the Good Samaritan
#### (Lk. 10:25-37)

Now behold, a certain lawyer stood up and made a test of him, saying, "Teacher, what shall I do *to inherit eternal life?"* And he said to him, "What has been written *in the law?* How do you read it?" And he answering said, *"You shall love the*

*Lord your God with all your heart, and with all your soul, and with all your strength, and with all your mind; and your neighbor as yourself."* And he said to him, "You have answered rightly; this *do,* and you shall live."

But he, desiring to justify himself, said to Jesus, "And who is *my neighbor?"*

And Jesus, accepting the challenge,[a] said, "A certain man journeyed from Jerusalem down to Jericho; and he fell among robbers, who stripped him and wounded him, and went away, leaving him half dead. And by chance a certain priest was proceeding down that road; but when he saw him, he passed by on the other side. Likewise also a Levite, on arriving at the place, came and saw him, and passed by on the other side.

"But a certain *Samaritan,* as he journeyed, came to where he was. And when he saw him, he was moved with compassion; and he went to him and bound up his wounds, dressing them with oil and wine. Then he set him on his own beast, and brought him to an inn and took care of him. And when he left on the morrow, he took out two denaries and gave them to the keeper of the inn, and said to him, 'Take care of him; and whatever more you spend, when I return *I* will repay you.'

"Which therefore of these three, do you think, was the *neighbor* to him who fell among the robbers?" And he said, "He that showed him kindness." Jesus therefore said to him, "Go; and *you* do likewise."

## 81. Mary's Choice Was to Hear His Word
### (Lk. 10:38-42)

And it came to pass, as they proceeded, that he[a] went into a certain village; and a certain woman named Martha received him into her home. And she had a sister called Mary, who also sat at the feet of Jesus and kept listening to his Word.

But Martha was distraught with much serving; and she came to him and said, "Lord, don't You *care* that my sister has left me to get the work done *alone?* Then speak to her, that she help me." But Jesus answered and said to her, "Martha, Martha, you are anxious and troubled about many things. Only one thing is *needful,* and Mary has chosen the good part, which shall not be taken away from her."

## 82. *"Lord, Teach Us to Pray"*
### *(Lk. 11:1-13)*

Then it came to pass that, as he was praying in a certain place, when he ceased one of his disciples[a] said to him, "Lord, teach *us* to pray, even as John also taught his disciples."

And he said to them, "When you pray, say,

'Our Father, who art in heaven,
hallowed be thy name!
May thy Kingdom come, thy will be done
on earth as it is in heaven.
'Give us each day our needful bread;
and forgive us our sins,
for we also forgive everyone indebted to us.
And lead us not into temptation,
but deliver us from the evil one."

### *Don't Be Diffident About Asking*

And he said to them, "Who among you shall have a friend, and shall go to him at midnight and say to him, 'Friend, lend me three loaves, because a friend of mine has come to me from a journey and I have nothing to set before him;' and he will answer from within and say, 'Do not trouble me—the door is now shut, and my children are with me in bed; I cannot get up to give you anything'? I say to you, even if he will not get up and give to him because he is his friend, yet because of his *shamelessness* he will rise and give him as many as he needs.

"And to *you* I say, *ask,* and it shall be given you; *seek,* and you shall find; *knock,* and it shall be opened to you. For everyone who *asks* receives, and he who *is seeking* finds, and to him who *knocks* it shall be opened.[b]

"And which of you who is a father, if his son asks for [bread, will give *him* a stone? Or if for] fish, will give *him* a serpent? Or if for an egg, will give *him* a scorpion? If then *you,* though evil, know how to give good gifts *to your children,* how much more will the heavenly Father give *the Holy Spirit* to those who ask *Him!"*

### 83. A Blind and Dumb Demoniac Restored
#### (Mt. 12:22-37,43-45; Lk. 11:14-15,17-28)

[1] Then there was brought to him one possessed by a demon, blind and dumb, and he healed him; so that [3] it came to pass, with the demon gone out, [1] the one blind and dumb spoke and saw. And all the people were amazed [3] and filled with wonder, [1] and said, *"Is not this the Son of David?"*

[3] Yet some of them, [1] the Pharisees, on hearing it said, *"This fellow does not cast out the demons; it is only by Beelzebul, the Prince of the demons."* But Jesus, knowing their thoughts, said to *them,*[a] "Every kingdom divided against itself is brought to desolation, and a city or house divided against itself will in no case stand. So if Satan is *casting out Satan,* he is divided *against himself;* how then shall his kingdom stand?

[3] "For you say that I cast out the demons *by Beelzebul.* Now if *I* am casting out the demons by Beelzebul, by whom do *your sons* 'cast out'? [1] Because of this shall they be your judges. But if I *by the Spirit of God* cast out the demons [3] by the finger of God, then *the Kingdom of God has come upon you!*

[1] "Or how can anyone enter into the *strong* man's house and plunder his goods, unless he first *binds* the strong man? It is *then* that he will plunder his house. [3] When the strong man, who is armed, is protecting his own dwelling, his possessions are in peace; but when the *stronger* man than he comes upon him and overpowers him,[b] he takes away his armor in which he had trusted, and divides his spoils.

### The Sin without Forgiveness

[1] *"He who is not with me is against me,*[c] *and he who gathers not with me scatters.* Because of this I say to you, every sin and blasphemy will be forgiven men, but the blasphemy against the *Spirit* will not be forgiven men. And whoever

speaks a word against the Son of man, to him it will be forgiven; but whoever speaks against *the Holy Spirit,* to him it will not be forgiven, either in this age or the age to come.

"Either make the tree good and make its fruit good, or make the tree corrupt and its fruit corrupt; for the tree is known from *its fruit.* You offspring of vipers, how can you speak good things, when you are *evil?*

"For out of the abundance of the *heart* the mouth speaks. The good man out of the good treasure of the heart brings forth things that are good, and the evil man out of the evil treasure brings forth things that are evil. And I say to you, that *every idle word* that men may speak, they shall render account thereof in the day of judgment. For by your words shall you be justified, and by your words shall you be condemned.

[1] "Now when the unclean spirit has gone out of a man, it passes through waterless places seeking rest, [3] and finding none it [1] then says, 'I will *return* to my house out of which I came.' And when it comes, it finds it empty, swept, and decorated. Then it goes and takes along with it seven other spirits, more wicked than itself, and they enter and dwell there; and the last state of that man becomes worse than the first. Thus also shall it be with *this wicked generation.* "

## *His Mother Is Again Spoken Of*

[3] And it came to pass, as he spoke these things, that a woman from the crowd raised her voice and said to him, "Blessed is the womb that bore *you,* and the breasts at which *you* were nursed!" But he said, "No; instead, blessed are those who are *hearing the Word of God and keeping it.* "

## 84. *"None Except the Sign of Jonah"*
### *(Mt. 12:38-42; Lk. 11:16,29-36)*

[1] Then certain of the scribes and Pharisees answered, saying, "Teacher, we want to *see* a miraculous *sign* from you." [3] And others *as a test* sought from him a sign from heaven.

[3] So when the crowds were thronging together, he began to

say [1] to them in answer, [3] "This generation is a *wicked* one!
[1] *An evil and adulterous generation* is seeking a *sign,* and *no*
sign shall be given it except *the sign of the prophet Jonah.*
[3] For as Jonah became a sign to the people of Nineveh, so also
shall the Son of man be to this generation. [1] Just as Jonah was
in the belly of the sea monster for three days and three nights,
so shall the Son of man be *in the heart of the earth for three
days and three nights.* [a]

"The men of Nineveh will stand up at the judgment with
this generation and *condemn* it; for they repented at the
preaching of Jonah, and behold, a greater than Jonah is *here.*
The queen of the south will rise up at the judgment with this
generation and *condemn* it; for she came from the farthest
reaches of the earth to hear the wisdom of Solomon, and behold, a greater than Solomon is *here.*

[3] "Now no one, on lighting a lamp, puts it in a hidden place
or under a grain-measure, but on the lampstand, so that they
who enter may *see* the light. The lamp of the body is the eye;
when therefore your eye is sound, your whole body also is
full of light, but when it is diseased, your body also is dark.
Take heed therefore lest the *light* that is in you be darkness! [b]
If on the other hand your whole body is light, having no part
of it dark, it will be wholly light as when a *lamp's* radiance is
giving you light."

## 85. Warnings to Pharisees and Lawyers

### (Lk. 11:37-54)

Now as he was speaking, a certain Pharisee invited him to
dine with him, and he went in and reclined at table. When the
Pharisee saw this, however, he was amazed that he did not cer-
emonially wash before dinner.

But the Lord said to him, "Now you *Pharisees* make clean
the outside of the cup and of the platter, but inwardly you are
filled with extortion and wickedness! You fools, did not he
who made the outside make the inside also? Now rather, *give
away as alms* those things which are within you, and behold,
all things are clean for you.

"But *woe* to you, Pharisees! For you pay tithes of mint and rue and of every kind of herb, and you disregard justice and love for God! *These* things should you have done, while not leaving those undone. *Woe* to you, Pharisees! For you love the most prominent seats in the synagogues and the salutations in the marketplaces. *Woe* to you, scribes and Pharisees—*hypocrites!* For you are like unmarked graves, which men are walking over unknowingly."

Then answered one of the lawyers[a] and said to him, "Teacher, *we too* are reproached by your saying these things." But he said, *"Woe* also to you lawyers! For you weigh men down with intolerable burdens, and you yourselves do not touch the burdens with one of your fingers. *Woe* to you, for you are building the sepulchres of the prophets, and *your fathers killed them!* Thus you bear witness to, and consent to, the deeds of your fathers; for they indeed killed them, and you are building their tombs.

"Because of this also the wisdom of God said, 'I will send them prophets and apostles, and some of *these* will they put to death and persecute;' that the blood of all the prophets that was shed from the foundation of the world may be required of *this generation,* from the blood of Abel to the blood of Zechariah, who perished between the altar and the sanctuary—verily, I say to you, it shall be required of *this* generation.

*"Woe* to you, lawyers! For you took away the key of knowledge; you did not yourselves enter in, and those entering in you hindered."

And upon his saying these things to them, the scribes and Pharisees began to assail him violently and to provoke him to speak of many things, lying in wait for something from his mouth that might ensnare him.

### 86. *"Everyone Who Shall Confess Me..."*
#### *(Lk. 12:1-9)*

In the meantime, when such myriads of people were gathered together[a] that they trampled on one another, he began to

say, first to his disciples, *"Beware of* the leaven of the Pharisees, which is *hypocrisy.* But there is nothing covered up that
shall not be disclosed, or hidden that shall not be known. Everything therefore that you have said in the darkness shall be
listened to in the light, and what you have whispered in the
inner rooms shall be proclaimed upon the housetops.

"And I say to *you,* my friends, fear not those who kill the
body, and after that have no more that they can do. Instead, I
will show you whom to fear: fear him who, after he has killed,
has power to cast into Gehenna; yes, I say to you, fear him!
Are not five sparrows sold for two copper-pieces? Yet not one
of them is overlooked by God. No, even the hairs of your head
have all been numbered! Fear not, therefore; *you* are worth
more than *many* sparrows.

"And to *you* I say, *"Everyone who shall confess Me before
men will the Son of man also confess before the angels of God,
but he who has denied Me in the presence of men will be denied in the presence of the angels of God."*[b]

### 87. God's Question to a Rich Fool
#### (Lk. 12:13-21)

Then one from the multitude said to him, "Teacher, bid my
brother to divide *the inheritance* with me." But he said to him,
"Man, who made Me a judge or a divider over you?" And he
said to them, ' Take heed, and beware of *covetousness;* for a
man's life *consists not in the abundance of his possessions."*

And he addressed to them a parable, saying, "The land of a
certain rich man brought forth abundantly; and he reasoned
within himself, saying, 'What shall I do? For I have nowhere to
store my crops.' So he said, 'This will I do; I will pull down my
barns and build greater ones, and there will I store all my produce and my goods. And I will say to my soul, Soul, you have
much goods laid up for many years; take your ease—*eat, drink,
and be merry.'* But God said to him, *'Fool!* This night is your
soul required of you. And the things which you prepared,
*whose will they be?'*

"So is he who lays up treasure for himself and is not rich toward God."

## 88. *"Be Like Men Who Await Their Lord"*
*(Lk. 12:22a,32-40; Mt. 24:43-44)*

[3] And he said to his disciples, "Fear not, little flock; for it is your Father's good pleasure *to give you the Kingdom.* Sell what you have, and give alms; make for yourselves purses that do not grow old, a treasure unfailing in the heavens, where no thief draws near and no moth destroys. *For where your treasure is, there will your heart be also.*

"Have your clothing adjusted and your lamps burning, and be like men who await their lord's return from the wedding feast, so that when he comes and knocks they may open to him at once.

*"Blessed* are those bondservants whom the Lord when he comes finds watching; verily, I say to you, he will adjust *his* clothing and have *them* recline for feasting, and he will come and serve *them.* And if he comes before midnight, or if after midnight, and finds them so, blessed are *those* bondmen!

[1] "But know this, that if the householder had known *in what watch* the thief would come, he would have watched, and would not have let his house be broken into. [3] *You* therefore must also be ready, for in an hour when you think *not* the Son of man is coming."

## 89. *"To Whom Much Was Given..."*
*(Mt. 10:34-36;24:45-51; Lk. 12:41-53)*

[3] Then said Peter to him, "Lord, are You speaking this parable to us, or also to all?" And the Lord said, "Who then is *the faithful and wise steward* whom [1] his lord [3] will set in charge of his household, to give them the measure of food when it is due? *Blessed* is that bondservant whom his lord, when he comes, finds so doing. Of a truth, I say to you, he will set him over all that he possesses.

"But if that [1] wicked [3] bondservant says in his heart, 'My lord is *delaying* his coming,' and begins to beat [1] his fellow [3] menservants and maidservants, and to eat and drink and be drunken, the lord of that bondman will come in a day when [1] he is not expecting [3] and an hour which he does not know, [1] and will cut him in pieces [3] and appoint his portion [1] with the hypocrites, where there shall be weeping and the gnashing of teeth.

[3] "Now that bondman who knew his lord's will but did not prepare or do according to his will, shall be beaten with many stripes; but he that did not know, and did things deserving of stripes, shall be beaten with few. *So from him to whom much was given much will be required, and from him to whom much was committed will they ask the more.*

### "Not Peace but Division"

"I came to cast *fire* upon the earth; and I would that it were kindled already! And I have a *baptism* to be baptized with; and how am I distressed till it be accomplished!

"Think you that I came to give peace on the earth? No, I say to you, but rather *division;* [1] I came not to bring peace, but a sword. [3] For henceforth in one home will five be divided, three against two, and two against three. [1] I came to set at variance a man against his father, a daughter against her mother, and a daughter-in-law against her mother-in-law; [3] the father will be set against the son, the mother against the daughter, and the mother-in-law against her daughter-in-law; [1] and a man's enemies will be *his own household.*"

### 90. Parable of the Fruitless Fig Tree

*(Lk. 12:54-56;13:1-9)*

And he said also to the multitudes, "When you see the cloud rising up from the west, you immediately say, 'A shower is coming,' and thus it comes to pass; and when a south wind is blowing, you say, 'It will be hot,' and it is so. You *hypocrites,* you know how to read the appearance of earth and sky, *so how is it that you do not discern this time?*"[a]

Now at that same time there were some present who told him of the Galileans whose blood Pilate had mingled with their sacrifices. And Jesus answering said to them, ' Do you think that these Galileans were worse sinners than all the other Galileans, because they suffered such things? I tell you, *no!—but unless you repent, you shall all likewise perish!* Or those eighteen upon whom the tower in Siloam fell and killed them, do you think that these were worse transgressors than all the others dwelling in Jerusalem? I tell you, *no!—but unless you repent, you shall all likewise perish!*

And he uttered this parable: "A certain man had a fig tree that had been planted in his vineyard; and he came and sought fruit on it, and found none. Then said he to the dresser of the vineyard, 'Behold, *for three years* I keep coming, seeking fruit on this fig tree and finding none. Cut it down; why have it even use up the ground?' But he answering said to him, 'Sir, *let it alone this year also,*[b] till I dig about it and fertilize it. Then if indeed it bears fruit, all is well; but if not, *you shall afterward cut it down.*'"

### 91. A Woman Is Healed on the Sabbath
   *(Lk. 13:10-17)*

And he was teaching in one of the synagogues on the Sabbaths, and behold, there was a woman with a spirit of infirmity which she had had for eighteen years, and she was bent over and could not lift herself up completely. And when Jesus saw her, he called to her and said to her, "Woman, *you are freed* from your infirmity." Then he laid his hands on her, and at once she was made straight and began to praise God.

But the ruler of the synagogue, being angry at Jesus for healing on the Sabbath, answered and said to the people, "There are *six days* in which men ought to work; in *these* therefore come and be healed, and not on *the Sabbath day.*"

So the Lord answered him and said, *"You hypocrite!* Does not each of you on the Sabbath loose his ox or ass from the manger and lead it away to let it drink? And this woman, a daughter of Abraham whom Satan has bound, lo, for eighteen years, should not she be loosed from *this* bond on the Sabbath day?" And his saying these things made all his adversaries a-shamed, and all the crowd kept rejoicing at all the glorious things done by him.

### Chapter 15. Pressing on Toward Jerusalem

*92. "Herod Intends to Kill You"*
   *(Lk. 13:22-33)*

So he went along through cities and villages, teaching and continuing the journey toward Jerusalem.

Then said someone to him, ' Lord, are they *few* who are saved?" And he said to them, ' Strive earnestly to enter in *through the narrow gate;* for many, I say to you, will *seek* to enter in and will not be able. When once the Master of the house has risen up and shut the door, and you begin to stand outside and knock at the door, saying, 'Lord, Lord, open to us!'—and he will answer and say to you, 'I know you not; where are you from?'—then will you begin to say, 'We ate and drank in your presence, and you taught in our streets,' and he will say, 'I tell you *I know you not, where you are from; depart from me, all you workers of unrighteousness!'*

"There shall be weeping there, and gnashing of teeth, when you see Abraham and Isaac and Jacob and all the prophets in the Kingdom of God, but yourselves thrust out. And they shall come *from east and west, and from north and south,* and shall feast in the Kingdom of God. And behold, *there are last who shall be first, and there are first who shall be last.*"

That same day there came certain Pharisees, saying to him, "Get you out, and depart *from here;* for Herod intends to *kill* you." And he said to them, "Go and say to that fox, 'Lo, to-day and tomorrow I am casting out demons and accomplishing cures, and the third day[a] I am reaching the consummation.' Nevertheless, *I must press on* today and tomorrow and the day following. For it cannot be that a prophet perish anywhere but *in Jerusalem!"*

### 93. Dining with a Chief Pharisee
#### (Lk. 14:1-24)

Now it came to pass that, on his going into the home of one of the chief Pharisees to have dinner on a Sabbath, they were watching him closely, and behold, before him was a certain man who had the dropsy. And Jesus in response spoke to the lawyers and Pharisees, saying, *"Is it lawful to heal on the Sabbath?"*

But they kept silent; and he took him and healed him, and let him go. And answering he said to them, "Which of you shall have an ass or an ox fall into a pit, and will not immediately pull him out on a Sabbath?" And to these things they could not reply to him.

And he put forth a parable to those who were invited, when he noted how they were choosing the chief places, saying to them, ' When invited by someone to a wedding feast, do not recline in the place of chief honor at the table; lest some person more important than you may have been invited by him, and he who invited both should come and say to you, 'Give this man your place,' and you begin then with shame to assume the lowest place. Instead, when invited, go and recline in the *lowest* place, that he who invited you, when he comes, may say to you, 'Friend, come up higher.' Then will you have honor in the sight of those reclining with you. For everyone who *exalts* himself *will be humbled,* and he who *humbles* himself *will be exalted."*

### "Invite Those Who Cannot Repay"

Then said he also to the one who had invited him, "When you give a dinner or a banquet, do not call your friends or your brothers or your kinsfolk or rich neighbors, lest they also invite you in return and you be repaid. But when you give a feast, call the poor, the crippled, the lame, the blind; and you shall be blessed, because they cannot pay you back. *For you shall be recompensed at the resurrection of the just."*

### The Banquet Refused by the Invited Guests

And when one of those at the feast heard these things, he said to him, *"Blessed* is he that shall eat bread *in the Kingdom of God!"*

And he said to him, "A certain man was preparing a great banquet, and invited many. And he sent his bondservant at the banquet time to say to the guests, *'Come,* for everything is now *ready.'* But they all with one accord began to make excuse. The first said to him, 'i have bought a field, and I must go and see it; I pray you, *have me excused.'* And another said, 'I have bought five yoke of oxen, and am leaving to try them out; I pray you, *have me excused.'* And another said, 'I have married a wife, and therefore *cannot come.'*

"So that bondservant came and reported these things to his lord. Then the master of the house said in anger to his bondman, 'Go quickly out into the streets and lanes of the city, and bring in here *the poor, the crippled, the lame, and the blind.'* And the bondservant said, 'Sir, it has been done as you commanded, *and yet there is room.'* And the master said to the bondman, 'Go out *into the highways and hedges* and compel them to come in, that my house may be filled. For I say to you, *not one of those who were invited* shall taste of my banquet!'"

### 94. Followers Must Reckon the Cost

*(Lk. 14:25-35)*

Now there were walking with him great throngs, and he turned and said to them, "If anyone comes to me and hates[a] not his father and mother, and wife and children, and brothers and sisters, and even his own life also, he cannot be my disciple! And whoever does not *bear his cross* and come after Me cannot be my disciple.

"For which of you, desiring to build a tower, does not first sit down and reckon the cost, whether he has enough to complete it?—lest it happen that after his laying its foundation and being unable to finish it, all who see it begin to laugh at him and say, *'This man began to build, and could not finish.'*

"Or what king, going to engage some other king in war, does not first sit down and take counsel whether with ten thousand he can meet the one coming against him with twenty thousand? And if he cannot, while the other is still far off he sends an embassy and asks for terms of peace.

"Thus therefore, whoever of you does not *leave all that he has* cannot be my disciple. Salt is good, but if the salt becomes saltless, with what shall it be seasoned? It is fit neither for the land nor for the dunghill; men toss it away. *He who has ears to hear,* let him *hear!"*

## 95. *Of the Lost Sheep and Lost Coin*
### *(Lk. 15:1-10)*

Then there kept drawing near to him all the publicans and sinful outcasts to listen to him, and the Pharisees and the scribes kept muttering and saying, ' This fellow welcomes *sinners,* and eats with them!'

But he addressed to *them* this parable, saying, "What man of you who has a hundred sheep, if he loses one of them, does not leave the ninety-nine in the wilderness and go after the one that is lost, *until he finds it?*[a] And on finding it he lays it on his shoulders, rejoicing; and when he comes home, he calls together friends and neighbors, telling them, *'Rejoice with me, for I have found my sheep that was lost!'* I say to you, there will be joy likewise in heaven over one sinner who repents, more than over ninety-nine 'righteous' persons who have 'no need of repentance.'

"Or what woman who has ten silver-pieces, if she loses one, does not light a lamp and sweep the house and search carefully till she finds it? And on finding it she calls friends and neighbors together, saying, *'Rejoice with me,* for I have *found* the piece which I lost!' Likewise, I say to you, there is joy in the presence of the angels of God over *one sinner* who *repents."*

## 96. The Wayward Son Was Welcomed Home
### (Lk. 15:11-32)

And he said, "A certain man had two sons, and the younger of them said to his father, 'Father, give me the portion of the property that is coming to me;' and he divided to them his substance.

"Now not many days later the younger son gathered together everything, and went away to a distant country, and there wasted his substance in dissolute living. And when he had spent all, there arose an intense famine through all that land, and he began to be in want. So he went and hired himself to a citizen of that country, who sent him into his fields to feed swine. And he kept yearning to satisfy his hunger with the pods which the swine were eating, but no one gave him any.

"And when he came to himself, he said, 'How many of my father's hired servants have bread in abundance, while I am perishing with hunger! I will arise and go to my father, and will say to him, Father, I have sinned against heaven and in your sight, and am no longer worthy to be called your son; make me like one of your hired servants.' And he arose, and went to his father.

"But while he was yet a great way off, his father saw him and was moved with compassion, and ran and fell on his neck and kissed him over and over. And the son said to him, *'Father, I have sinned against heaven and in your sight, and am no longer worthy to be called your son!'*

"But the father said to his bondmen, 'Bring out the best robe and put it on him, and put a ring on his hand, and sandals on his feet. And bring the fatted calf and kill it, and let us eat, and be merry. For this my son was dead, but he is *alive again;* he was lost, *but has been found!''* So they began to be merry.

### But the Elder Brother Was Angry

"Now his elder son was out in the field, and as he came and drew near to the house, he heard music and dancing; and calling one of his servants, he asked what these things meant. And he said to him, 'Your brother has come! And your father has killed the fatted calf, because he has received him safe and well.'

"But he was angry, and would not go in. His father therefore came out and entreated him, but he answered and said to his father, 'Lo, these many years do I keep on serving you, and I never disregarded your command; but to me you never gave a *kid* that I might be merry with my friends. Instead, when this son of yours came who has devoured your substance with harlots, you killed for him *the fatted calf!*'

"But he said to him, 'Son, you are always with me, and all that I have is yours. But it was *fitting* that we should *be merry and rejoice.* For this your brother was dead, but he is alive again; and he was lost, but has been found.'"

## 97. The Wise Use of Wealth —— For Eternity
### (Lk. 16:1-13)

And he said also to his disciples, "There was a certain rich man who had a steward, who was reported to him as wasting his possessions. And he summoned him and said to him, 'What is this I hear about you? Render an *accounting* of your stewardship; for you may be steward no longer.'

"Then the steward said to himself, 'What shall I do, since my lord is taking the stewardship from me? I cannot dig; to beg I am ashamed. I know what I will do, so that on my removal from the stewardship men may receive me into their homes.'

"So he called to him each of his lord's debtors, and said to the first, 'How much do you owe my lord?' And he said, 'Eight hundred gallons of oil.' And he said to him, 'Take your bill, and sit down quickly and write, *Four hundred.'* Then said he to another, 'And how much do *you* owe?' And he said, 'A thousand bushels of wheat.' And he said to him, 'Take your bill and write, *Eight hundred.'*

"Now the lord commended the unrighteous steward because he had acted shrewdly. For the sons of this age are wiser with respect to their own generation than the sons of light. And I

say to you, make friends for yourselves by means of the unrighteous mammon, so that when it fails they may receive you
into the eternal dwellings."

"He who is faithful in that which is least is faithful also in
*much;* and he who is unrighteous in that which is least is unrighteous also in *much.* If therefore you have not been faithful
with the unrighteous riches, who will entrust you with the
true? And if you have not been faithful with that which is another's, who will give you what is your own?

"No servant can serve two masters; for either he will hate
the one and love the other, or he will hold to the one and despise the other. You cannot serve God *and riches."*

### 98. A Man Who Repented in Hades
*(Lk. 16:14-15,19-31)*

Now the Pharisees, who were lovers of money, were also listening to all these things, and they derided him. And he said to
them, *"You are they who justify themselves* in the sight of
*men.* But *God* knows your hearts; for that which is highly es-
teemed among men is abominable in the sight of God.[a]

"Now there was a certain rich man, who was clothed in purple and fine linen, living daily in merriment and splendor. And
a certain poor man named Lazarus was laid at his gate, full of
sores and longing to be fed with the crumbs falling from the
rich man's table; moreover, the dogs even came and licked his
sores. And it came to pass that the poor man died, and was
carried away by the angels unto Abraham's bosom.

"Then the rich man also died and was buried; and in Hades
he lifted up his eyes, being in torment, and saw Abraham far
off, and Lazarus at his bosom. And he cried out and said,
'Father Abraham, *have compassion on me,* and send Lazarus
to dip his fingertip in water and cool my tongue; for I am anguished in this flame.'

"But Abraham said, 'Child, remember that in your lifetime
you fully received your good things, and Lazarus likewise evil
things; so now he is comforted, and you are anguished. And
beside all these things, between us and you there is a great

chasm fixed, so that they who wish to cross from here to you cannot, and neither can men cross from there to us.'

"Then he said, 'I beseech you therefore, father, to send him to my father's house, since I have five brothers, *to testify urgently to them, lest they too come to this place of torment.'* Abraham said to him, 'They have Moses and the prophets; let them hear *them.'*

"But he said, 'No, father Abraham; but if someone goes to them from *the dead,* they *will repent.'* And he said to him, 'If they heed not Moses and the prophets, neither will they be persuaded though someone rise from the dead.'"[b]

## 99. Is a Servant Thanked for Obeying?
*( Lk. 17:1-10)*

Then said he to the disciples, "It is impossible that causes of stumbling should not come; but *woe* to him through whom they come! It would be better for him were a great millstone hung about his neck and he were cast into the sea, than that he should cause one of these little ones to stumble. Take heed to *yourselves.*

"And if your brother sins against you, rebuke him; and if he repents, forgive him. And if he sins against you seven times in the day, and seven times in the day returns to you saying, 'I repent,' *you shall forgive him."*

And the apostles said to the Lord, *"Increase our faith."* And the Lord said, "If you *had* faith as large as a grain of mustard seed, you might say to this mulberry tree, 'Be rooted up, and be planted in the sea,' and it would obey you.

"But will any of you, with a bondservant plowing or tending sheep, say to him on his coming in from the field, 'Never mind; recline at once at the table'? Will he not say to him rather, 'Prepare my food, and hitch up your clothing and serve me, while I eat and drink; and afterward *you* will eat and drink'? Does he *thank* that bondman because he did the things commanded him? I judge not. Thus also *you,* when you have done everything commanded you, say, 'We are unprofitable bondmen; we have done what was our *duty* to do.'"

## 100. Still Journeying; Ten Lepers Healed

*(Lk. 17:11-19)*

It came to pass also in his journeying to Jerusalem that he was traversing the border area between Samaria and Galilee, and on his entering a certain village there met him ten leprous men, who stood far off. And they lifted up their voices, saying, "Jesus, Master, have compassion on *us!*" And seeing them, he said to them, "Go on your way; and show yourselves to the priests."

And it came to pass that, as they went on their way, they were cleansed. So one of them, seeing that he was healed, turned back and with a loud voice gave glory to God; and he fell down on his face at Jesus' feet, giving him thanks. And he was a Samaritan.

And Jesus answering said, "Were not the *ten* cleansed? Where are the nine? Were none found to return and give glory to God except this 'foreigner'?" And he said to him, "Rise, go on your way; your *faith* has healed you."

## 101. When the Son of Man Will Come

*(Lk. 17:20-37)*

Now being asked by the Pharisees when the Kingdom of God would come, he answered them and said, "The Kingdom of God does not come with watching for signs; neither will they say, 'Lo, here!' or 'Lo, there!' For behold, the Kingdom of God *is in your midst.* "[a]

And to the disciples he said, "The days will come when you will desire to see one of the days of the Son of man, but will not see it. And they will say to you, 'Lo, here!' or 'Lo, there!' Do not go forth, nor follow. For as the *lightning* flashes, lighting up the sky from the one side to the other, so also will the Son of man be in his day. But first he must suffer many things, *and be rejected by this generation.*

"And as it was in the days of Noah, thus will it be also in the days of the Son of man; they were eating and drinking, marrying and being given in marriage, till the day when Noah went into the ark, and the flood came and destroyed them all.

"Likewise also, as it was in the days of Lot—they were eating and drinking, buying and selling, planting and building, but in the day when Lot went out from Sodom, it rained fire and brimstone from heaven and destroyed them all—so will it be in the day when the Son of man *is revealed.* In that day let him who is on the housetop not come down to take away his goods that are in the house; and likewise let him who is in the field not return to the things left behind. Remember Lot's wife. Whoever seeks to save his life shall lose it, and whoever loses his life shall keep it safe.

"I say to you, in that night there will be two men in one bed; one will be taken, and the other left. There will be two women grinding together; one will be taken, and the other left. [There will be two men in the field; one will be taken, and the other left.]"

And they answered and said to him, "Where, Lord?" And he said to them, *"Where the body is.* There will the *vultures* be gathered together."[b]

### *102. Persistent Prayer Will Be Rewarded*
#### *(Lk. 18:1-8)*

And he also spoke to them a parable that men ought always to pray and not become faint-hearted, saying, ' In a certain city there was a certain judge who feared not God nor had regard for man; and in that city was a widow who kept coming to him, saying, 'Give me justice against my adversary!'

"And he would not for a while, but at length he said to himself, 'Although I fear not God nor have regard for man, yet because this widow is causing me trouble, I will give her justice, lest her continual coming wear me out.'"

And the Lord said, "Hear what the unrighteous judge said. And will not *God* render justice for his elect who cry to him day and night while he delays helping them? I say to you, that he will render *swift* justice for them. Nevertheless, when the Son of man comes, *will he find the faith on the earth?"*

## 103. Two Men's Prayers in Contrast
### (Lk. 18:9-14)

Now to some who trusted in themselves as being righteous, and looked down on other men, he uttered this parable also.

"Two men went up into the temple to pray, one a Pharisee and the other a publican. The Pharisee stood and kept praying thus with himself: 'God, I thank thee that I am not, as other men are, avaricious, unrighteous, adulterous—or even like this publican. I *fast* twice in the week; I pay *tithes* of everything I get.'

"But the publican, standing far off, would not so much as lift up his eyes to heaven, but kept beating his breast and saying, 'God, be merciful to me, *the sinner!*' I tell you, *this* man went down to his house justified, rather than the other. *For everyone who exalts himself shall be humbled, but he who humbles himself shall be exalted.*"

## 104. Jesus' Teachings on Divorce
### (Mt. 19:3-12; Mk. 10:2-12; Lk. 16:18)

[2]And certain Pharisees [1]also came to him, putting him to the test and saying to him, "Is it *lawful* [2]for a husband to put away [1]his wife, no matter what the cause?" [2]But Jesus answered and said to them, "What did Moses command you? [1]Have you not read, that he who made them from the beginning made them male and female, and said, *'For this cause shall a man leave* [2]*his father and mother and be joined unto his wife, and the two shall be one flesh'?* Thus they are no longer two, but one flesh. *What therefore God has joined together, let not man put asunder.*"

[1]They said to him, "Why then did Moses command to give *a writ of divorce* and to put her away?" He said to them, "Moses on account of your hardness of heart [2]wrote for you this commandment and [1]allowed you to put away your wives; *but from the beginning it was not so.* And I say to you, that whoever shall put away his wife, except for fornication, and marry another, commits adultery; [3]and he who marries her that is

put away from her husband commits adultery."[a]

[2] And again in the house his disciples asked him about the same matter, and he said to them, "Whoever shall put away his wife and marry another is committing *adultery* against her; and if a woman puts away her husband and marries another, *she* is committing adultery."

[1] His disciples said to him, "If this is the case of the man with the wife, it is not a good thing to marry." But he said to them, "Not everyone receives what you have said, but only those to whom it has been given. For there are *eunuchs* who were born so from their mother's womb, and there are eunuchs who were made so by men; and there are eunuchs who have made themselves eunuchs for the sake of the Kingdom of heaven. He that is able to receive this, let him receive it."

### 105. *His Blessing on the Young Children*
#### *(Mt. 19:13-15a; Mk. 10:13-16; Lk. 18:15-17)*

[1] At that time there were young children being brought to him, that he might lay his hands on them and pray; [3] and they were even bringing him infants, that he might touch them. But the disciples, on seeing it, [2] began to rebuke those who brought them.

Now when Jesus saw this, he was moved with indignation, and [3] calling them to him he said [2] to them, *"Let the little children come to me; and forbid them not, [1] for of such is the Kingdom of heaven. [2] Verily, I say to you, he that will not receive the Kingdom of God as a little child* shall by no means enter therein."

And he took them up in his arms, and laying his hands on them he blessed them.

# Chapter 16. Climactic Proof of His Power

## 106. He Raises Lazarus from the Tomb
### (Jn. 11:1-44)

Now there was a certain man who was sick, named Lazarus of Bethany, the village of Mary and her sister Martha. It was the Mary who anointed the Lord with ointment and wiped his feet with her hair whose brother Lazarus was sick. The sisters therefore sent word to him, saying, ' Lord, behold, the one whom You love is sick."

But on hearing it Jesus said, "This sickness is not unto death, but for the glory of God, that through it the Son of God may be glorified." And Jesus loved Martha and her sister, and Lazarus; so when he heard that he was sick, he remained then indeed two days where he was, but after this said to the disciples, "Let us go into Judea again."

The disciples said to him, ' Rabbi, the Jews not long since were seeking to stone You, so are You going there again?" Jesus answered, ' Are there not twelve hours of daytime? Anyone walking by *day* does not stumble, since he sees the light of this world; but if anyone walks in the night, he stumbles, since the light is not in him." These things said he, and after this he said to them, "Our friend Lazarus has fallen asleep; but I am going that I may awaken him."

His disciples said therefore, "Lord, if he has fallen asleep, he will get well." Jesus, however, had spoken of his death, while they thought that he had spoken of resting in sleep.

Then said Jesus to them plainly, "Lazarus is dead. And for *your* sake I am glad that I was not there, so that you may believe; but let us go to him." Thomas, called Didymus, said therefore to his fellow disciples, "Let *us* go also, that we may die *with him.*"

### "I AM the Resurrection"

When therefore Jesus came, he found that he had been in the tomb four days already. Now Bethany was close to Jerusa-

135

lem, less than two miles distant, hence many of the Jews had
come to Martha and Mary to comfort them concerning their
brother.

Martha therefore, when she heard that Jesus was coming,
went and met him, although Mary continued sitting in the
house. So Martha said to Jesus, "Lord, if You had been here,
my brother would not have died! But even now I know that
anything You ask from God, God will give it to You."

Jesus said to her, *"Your brother will rise again."* Martha
said to him, "I know that he will rise again in the resurrection
at the last day." Jesus said to her, *"I AM the Resurrection, and
the Life. He who believes upon Me, even though he die, yet
shall he live. And everyone living*[a] *when I come, who believes
upon Me, shall not at all ever die.* Do you believe *this?"*

She said to him, "Yes, Lord! *I, too,* have believed that You
are *the Messiah, the Son of God* who is coming into the
world." And on saying these things she departed and called her
sister Mary, saying privately, *"The Teacher* has come, and is
asking for you."

At hearing this she rose up quickly and came to him. Now
Jesus had not yet arrived in the village, but was at the place
where Martha had met him. So when the Jews who were with
her in the house, comforting her, saw that Mary rose up quickly and went out, they followed her, saying that she was going
to the tomb to weep there. Mary therefore, when she came to
where Jesus was and saw him, fell at his feet and said to him,
"Lord, if *You* had been here, my brother *would not have
died."*

## *"Lazarus, Come Forth!"*

Jesus therefore, when he saw her weeping, and the Jews
who came with her, weeping also, groaned in spirit and was
troubled, and said, "Where have you laid him?" They answered him, "Lord, come and see."

*Jesus* wept.[b]

The Jews therefore said, "Behold how he loved him!" But
some of them said, "Could not he who opened the blind man's

eyes have also kept this man from dying?"

Jesus therefore, groaning in himself again, came to the tomb; and it was a cave, with a stone laid against it. Jesus said, "Take the stone away." Martha, the dead man's sister, said to him, ' Lord, by this time he is offensive—for it has been four days." Jesus said to her, "Did I not tell you that, if you would *believe,* you would see the glory of God?"

So they took the stone away from where the dead man had been laid. And Jesus lifted up his eyes and said, ' Father, I thank thee that Thou didst hear me. And *I knew* that Thou hearest me always, but because of the crowd standing around I said it, that they may *believe that Thou didst send me."*

And when he had spoken thus, he cried out with a loud voice, *"Lazarus, come forth!"* And he who had been dead came forth, bound hand and foot with burial cloths and his face wrapt around with a napkin. Jesus said to them, "Loose him, and let him depart."

## 107. The Jewish Leaders Conspire; He Withdraws
### (Jn. 11:45-54)

Many therefore of the Jews who had come to Mary, and who saw what Jesus did, believed upon him; but some of the Jews went off to the Pharisees and told them what Jesus had done. So the chief priests and the Pharisees gathered a council, and they said, "What are we accomplishing? For this man *is performing* many miraculous *signs.* If we let him go on thus, all will believe upon him, and *the Romans* will come and take away both our place and our nation."

And one of them in particular, named Caiaphas, who was the high priest that year, said to them, *"You* know *nothing,* nor recognize that *it is expedient for us that one man die for the people, and the whole nation perish not."* Now it was not from himself that he said this, but as high priest that year he was *prophesying*[a] that Jesus would die for the nation; and not for the nation alone, but also that he might gather into one God's children who had been scattered abroad.

So from that day they took counsel together how they

might put him to death. Jesus therefore no longer walked a-
bout in the open among the Jews, but went away from there
into the country near the wilderness, to a town called Ephraim, and there remained with his disciples.


### Chapter 17. The Journey through Jericho


*108. His Answer to a Rich, Young Ruler*
    *(Mt. 19:15b-26; Mk. 10:17-27; Lk. 18:18-27)*

[1] And he departed from that place; [2] and when he had gone
forth on the road, [1] behold, [3] a certain ruler[a] [2] came running
and knelt down to him and asked him, "Good teacher, what
good thing shall I do *to inherit eternal life?"* [2] But Jesus said
to him, "Why do you call me 'good'? There is no one good but
One, namely God.[b] [1] But if you would enter into life, observe
*the commandments."*

He said to him, "Which?" And Jesus said, [2] "You know the
commandments, *'Do not commit adultery, do not murder, do
not steal, do not bear false witness, do not defraud, honor
your father and mother;* [1] *and love your neighbor as yourself.'"*

[2] And [1] the young man [2] answering [1] said to him, [2] "Teacher,
*all* these have I kept from my youth up. [1] What lack I yet?"
[2] Then Jesus, [3] on hearing these things, [2] loved him, and fixing
his eyes on him said to him, *"One* thing you are lacking. [1] If
you would lack nothing, go sell [3] all that you have, and distrib-
ute to the poor, and you will have treasure in heaven. And
come, *follow Me."*

[1] But the young man on hearing these things [2] went away
very sorrowful, [1] for he had great possessions. [3] And seeing him
become very sorrowful, Jesus [2] looked about him and said to
his disciples, [1] "Verily, I say to you, [2] how hard it will be for
those who have *riches* to enter the Kingdom of God!"

And the disciples were astonished at his words, but Jesus again answering said to them, "Children, how hard it *is* [for those who trust in riches] to enter the Kingdom of God! ³For ¹again I say to you, ²it is easier for a *camel* to pass through the eye of a sewing needleᶜ than for a rich man to enter the Kingdom of God."

¹Now at hearing this they were astonished beyond measure, ²saying to one another, "Who then can be saved?" ¹But Jesus, fixing his eyes on them, said to them, ²"With men it is impossible, but not with God; for with God *all* things are possible."

### 109. Rewards Are Promised His Followers
*(Mt. 19:27-20:16; Mk. 10:28-31; Lk. 18:28-30)*

¹Then Peter in answer ²began to say to him, ¹"Behold, *we left everything* and kept on following You; what then will there be for *us?*" And Jesus ²answered and said ¹to them, "Verily I say to you, that in the regeneration, when the Son of man is to sit on the throne of his glory, *you* also, who have followed me, shall sit on twelve thrones, judging the twelve tribes of Israel."

³And he said to them, "Verily, I say to you, there is no one who has left house or parents or brothers ¹or sisters or wife or children or lands for my name's sake ²and the sake of the Glad News ³and the Kingdom of God, who shall not receive in this present age ¹*a hundredfold* ³*more,* ²houses and brothers and sisters and mothers and children and lands—with persecutions —and in the age to come ¹*inherit eternal life.*

### The Parable of the Vineyard Workers

*"But many who are first will be last, and the last first.* For the Kingdom of heaven is like a man who, as master of his house, went out in early morning to hire workers for his vineyard; and he agreed with the workers for a denary for the day, and sent them into his vineyard.

"But going out about nine o'clock, he saw others standing idle in the marketplace and said to them, 'You, too, go into the vineyard, and whatever may be right I will give you.' So they went forth. Again he went out about noon, and about three o'clock, and did the same.

"And about five o'clock he went out and found some others standing, and said to them, 'Why stand here *idle* all day?' They answered him, 'Because no one hired us.' He said to them, 'You, too, go into the vineyard, and whatever may be right you will receive.'

"And when evening came, the vineyard owner said to his overseer, 'Call the workers and give them their pay, beginning with the last and on up to the first.' Now when those hired a-bout five o'clock came, they received each of them a denary. So when the first came, they thought that they ought to get more, but they likewise received each of them a denary. And on receiving it they complained against the master of the house, saying, 'These last have worked only one hour, and you gave them equal payment with us who bore the burden, and the burning heat, of the day.'

"But in answer he said to one of them, 'Friend, I am doing you no wrong. Did you not agree with me for a denary? Take what is yours, and go; and I will give to this last one the same as to you. May I not do what I choose with what is mine? Or are you envious *because I am generous?'*

*"So it is that the last shall be first, and the first last."*

### 110. His Sufferings Are Again Foretold
*(Mt. 20:17-19; Mk. 10:32-34; Lk. 18:31-34)*

[2] Now they were on the road on their way to Jerusalem, Jesus walking in the lead, and were filled with awe and fear as they followed. And *again,* taking [1] the twelve aside in the way, [2] he began to tell them the things that would happen to him, [3] saying to them, "Behold, we are going up to Jerusalem, and everything written by the prophets concerning the Son of man will be fulfilled. For he will be betrayed [2] to the chief priests and the scribes, and they will condemn him to death and deliver him up to the Gentiles [1] to crucify him. [3] And he will be mocked and treated shamefully and spit upon, and they will scourge him and put him to death; *but the third day he will*

*rise again."*

Yet they understood none of these things; this utterance was veiled from them and they did not comprehend what was said.[a]

### 111. Another Rebuke to James and John
*(Mt. 20:20-28; Mk. 10:35-45)*

[1] Then came to him the mother of the sons of Zebedee, [2] James and John, [1] making obeisance with her sons and [2] saying, "Teacher, we desire that you do for us what we may ask." And he said to them, "What do you wish me to do for you?" [1] She said to him, "Grant that these my two sons may sit, one at your right hand and one at your left, [2] in your glory [1] in your Kingdom."

But Jesus answered and said [2] to them, "You know not what you are asking. Are you able to drink the cup [1] that *I* am going to drink, and to be baptized with the baptism with which *I* am baptized?" [2] And they answered him, "We are able." But Jesus said to them, "You will indeed drink the cup that *I* drink, and be baptized with the baptism with which *I* am baptized; but to sit at my right hand and my left is *not mine to grant*, but is for those for whom it has been prepared [1] *by my Father."*[a]

### "Came to Give His Life as a Ransom"

And when the ten heard of it, they were indignant [2] at James and John, but Jesus called them to him and said to them, "You know that the recognized rulers in the nations exercise lordship over them, and the 'great' ones among them domineer over them. [1] But it shall not be so *among you;* but whoever would become great among you, let him be your *servant*, and whoever would be chief among you, let him be the *bondslave* [2] of all—[1] *just as* [2] *even the Son of man came, not to be ministered to but to minister, and to give his life as a ransom for many!"*

## 112. A Jericho Beggar Receives Sight
### (Mt. 20:30-34; Lk. 18:35-43)

[3] Now it came to pass that, as he was drawing near to Jericho, a certain blind man was sitting at the roadside begging; and hearing a multitude passing along, he asked what this might mean. And they told him, *"Jesus of Nazareth* is passing by."* And he cried out, saying, *"Jesus, Son of David, have pity on me!"*

And those walking in front began to rebuke him, telling him to be quiet, but he cried out more and more, *"Son of David, have pity on me!"* So Jesus stopped and commanded that he be brought to him; and when he came near, he asked him, saying, "What do you wish me to do for you?' And he said, "Lord, that I may receive *sight."*

Jesus, [1] moved with compassion, [3] said to him, *"Receive sight; your faith* has healed you."* [1] And Jesus touched his eyes and he immediately received sight, and followed him, [3] glorifying God. And all the people who had seen it gave praise to God.

## 113. Jesus' Visit with Repentant Zacchaeus
### (Mk. 10:46a; Lk. 19:1-10)

[2] So they came to Jericho; [3] and he entered and was passing through Jericho, when behold, there appeared a man named Zacchaeus, who was a chief publican and was rich. And he kept seeking to see who Jesus was, but could not because of the throng, for he was small of stature; so he ran ahead and climbed a sycomore fig tree to see him, as he was to pass that way.

And when Jesus came to the place, he looked up and saw him, and said to him, "Zacchaeus, hasten and come down, for today I must sojourn *at your home."* And he hastened and came down, and welcomed him with rejoicing.

Now at seeing this they all disapproved greatly, saying, ' He has gone in *to lodge* with a man who is *a sinner.'* But Zacchaeus, standing there, said to the Lord, "Behold, Lord, *half of my possessions* will I give to the poor. And whatever I have taken from anyone wrongfully, I will restore it to him *four times over."*

And Jesus said to him, ' Today has *salvation* come to this home! For he, too, is a son of *Abraham.*[a] For the Son of man *came to seek and to save that which was lost."*

## 114. Parable of the Pounds of Silver
### (Lk. 19:11-27)

Now while they were listening to these things, he continued by uttering a parable; for he was nearing Jerusalem, and they thought that the Kingdom of God was *shortly to appear.*

He said therefore, "A certain man of noble birth went to a far country to receive for himself a kingdom, and to return. And summoning ten of his bondmen, he gave them a pound of silver each, and said to them, *'Do business till I come.'* But his citizens hated him and sent an embassy to follow him, saying, 'We will *not* have this man rule over us!'[a]

"And it came to pass that, after receiving the kingdom and returning, he commanded that those bondmen to whom he had given the money be summoned, that he might know how much business each had done. So the first came forward, saying, 'Lord, your pound of silver has produced *ten* pounds.' And he said to him, 'Well done, good bondservant! Since you were faithful in a thing of small importance, you shall have charge of ten cities.' And the second came, saying, 'Lord, your pound has produced *five* pounds.' And he said to him likewise, 'And you shall be over five cities.'

### *"I Was Afraid"*

"Then came another, saying, 'Lord, *behold* your pound, which I kept laid away in a napkin. For I was afraid of you, since you are a harsh man; you take up what you did not lay down, and reap what you did not sow.'

"And to him he said, 'Out of your own mouth will I judge you, wicked bondservant! You knew that *I* am a harsh man, taking up what I did not lay down, and reaping what I did not sow? Then why did you not put my money *in the bank,* that I might come and take it out with interest?'

"And to those who were standing by he said, 'Take from him the pound of silver and give it to him who has the ten pounds.' (And they said to him, 'Lord, he *has* ten pounds!') 'For I say to you, that to everyone who has shall be given, but from him who has not, even what he has shall be taken away. And as for those enemies of mine who would not have me rule over them, bring them here and slay them before me.'"

### 115. *Sight Is Given Bartimaeus Also*
#### *(Mt. 20:29-34; Mk. 10:46b-52; Lk. 19:28)*

³ And after saying these things he walked on before them, proceeding up to Jerusalem. ² But as he left Jericho with his disciples, ¹ and a great crowd was following him, behold, ² blind Bartimaeus, son of Timaeus, was sitting by the roadside begging. And when he heard that it was Jesus of Nazareth, *he* began to cry out and say, *"Jesus, Son of David, have pity on me!"*ᵃ

And many admonished *him* to be quiet, but he cried out the more, ¹ *"[Lord,] Son of David,* ² have *pity* on me!" And Jesus stopped and commanded that he be called; so they called the blind man, saying to him, "Have courage; *rise up,* he is calling you." And he, flinging aside his garment, rose up and came to Jesus.

And Jesus in response said to him, "What do you wish me to do for *you?"* And the blind man said to him, *"Dear Rabbi, let me receive my sight."* ¹ And Jesus was moved with compassion, and touched his eyes; ² and he said to him, "Go; *your faith* has healed you." And immediately ¹ his eyes received sight, ² and he followed Jesus on the road.

\* \* \*

*Comment.* We have now come to the end of Jesus' public ministry proper. This also marks the close of His great final journey, which included at least the thirty-five localities to which the seventy heralds were sent (Sec. 79). He began this journey perhaps nine months earlier and travelled in a zig-zag fashion throughout Galilee, Samaria, Perea, and Judea. As He journeyed, He gave instruction to His disciples and followers, and He offered a final solicitation to the outcasts (both the down-and-out and the up-and-out) to follow Him. Jericho's blind beggar and rich tax collector were equally welcomed. The "great supper" that was refused by those initially invited was to be offered to "the poor, the maimed, the halt, and the blind," that is, the spiritual outcasts.

But this offer was not to be misconstrued as a sentimental inclusion of all the outcasts and down-trodden. He still struck for decisions of the heart. Thus, as the great crowds still followed Him, Jesus sought to cull out the counterfeits from among the faithful. Stringency and sacrifice were His watchwords, and He emphasized that following Him involved also forsaking the things of the world. "Thus, therefore, whoever of you does not leave all that he has cannot be my disciple." He stressed the impossibility of serving God and "Mammon" or worldly gain. Speaking of His own cross, He also spoke of the disciples' cross. As He was to die *for* sin, they also were to die *to* sin and self. The cross was to precede the glory.

The Lord's destination in all these travels was Jerusalem, and the date of arrival was the Passover season. It has previously been noted that Jesus attended the first Passover of His ministry, but failed to attend the next three Passovers. In spite of the Jewish requirement that all males attend the Feast of Passover (Exodus 23:17), Jesus absented Himself three times following His first cleansing of the temple and their initial animosity. These Passover seasons were spent in Galilee.

At the fifth Passover, however, Jesus intended to be present, for it was a time of prophetic significance. Part VI of the harmonized narrative describes this visit to the capital city. In this account, it will be noted that Jesus' mood in this "Triumphal entry" was one of sorrow rather than of joy. He wept over the city as He approached it. Since His disciples "thought that the kingdom of God should immediately appear," (Luke 19:11) Jesus had to clarify the new program. He had to explain His extended absence from the scene of the "kingdom" before He would return to destroy His enemies and establish His Kingdom (that is, the earthly manifestation of it). But the time of this Passover was a time of anticipation for the Lord as well as for the disciples. His entrance into the city Jesus called, "this thy day," or "the time of thy visitation" (Luke 19:42, 44). It was a prophetic day.

But the recalcitrance of the leaders and people to His call for spiritual repentance changed the character of that day. It evoked the Lord's pronouncement of judgment on the city rather than blessing. He came not as a welcomed King but as a rejected King, about to go into exile. He was about to fulfill His role as the "Passover Lamb," rather than that of the "Lion of the tribe of Judah." During the era of grace, He would not lash out at His enemies as a "lion," but would deal in mercy as a "sacrificial lamb." For this purpose, then, He moved toward Jerusalem for the final Passover in a setting of unprecedented national tension.

# PART VI.

## THE HOUR IS AT HAND

### Chapter 18. He Rejects the Rejecting Nation

#### 116. *His Anointing by Mary of Bethany*
*(Mt. 26:6-13; Mk. 14:3-9; Lk. 22:1; Jn. 11:55-12:11)*

[4] Now the Jews' [3] feast of unleavened bread, called the Passover, was at hand, [4] and many went up out of the country to Jerusalem before the Passover to purify themselves. They were looking therefore for Jesus, and kept saying among themselves, while standing in the temple, "What do you think?—that he will *not come* at all to the feast?" For the chief priests and the Pharisees had issued a command that if anyone knew where he was he should make it known, that they might arrest him.

So Jesus six days[a] before the Passover came to Bethany, where Lazarus was, who had died and whom he had raised from the dead. There [1] at Bethany [4] they made him a supper therefore, [1] in the home of Simon the leper; [4] and Martha was serving, but Lazarus was one of those reclining at the table with him.

Mary therefore, taking [2] an alabaster flask of costly ointment, [4] a pound of pure nard, [1] came up to him as he reclined at the table and, [2] breaking the flask, poured it over his head; [4] and she anointed the feet of Jesus, and wiped his feet with her hair. And the house was filled with the aroma of the ointment.

[1] But when his disciples saw this, [2] some [1] became indignant [2] and said within themselves, "For *what* is this waste of the ointment? [1] For this could have been sold for much money, and given to the poor." [2] So they began to rebuke her. And [4] Judas Iscariot, who was going to betray him, said, "Why was

147

not this ointment sold for *three hundred denaries* and given to the poor?" But he said this, not that he was concerned for the poor, but because he was a thief and had the money bag, and kept taking what was put therein.

### "To Anoint My Body for Burial"

[1] Then Jesus, aware of all this, said to them, [2] "Let her a- lone. Why are you troubling [1] the woman? For she performed a good work toward me; [4] she has kept it for the day of *my burial*.[b] [2] For the poor you have with you always and can do them good whenever you will; but Me you *do not have* always. She was doing what she could; [1] for in pouring this ointment on my body [2] she came *beforehand* to anoint my body [1] for my burial. Verily, I say to you, wherever in all the world this Glad News is proclaimed, what this woman has done will also be told of as a memorial of her."

[4] A great number of the Jews therefore knew that he was there, and they came not only because of Jesus but also to see Lazarus, whom he had raised from the dead. So the chief priests took counsel how they might kill Lazarus also, since because of him a great many Jews were going away and believing upon Jesus.

### 117. His Entry of Jerusalem as Messiah
#### (Mt. 21:1-11; Mk. 11:1-11; Lk. 19:29-44; Jn. 12:12-19)

[3] And it came to pass [4] the next day, [1] when they drew near to Jerusalem and came to Bethphage [3] at the mountain called Olivet, [1] then Jesus sent two [2] of his disciples, [1] saying to them, "Go into the village that is opposite you, and immediately [2] on entering it [1] you will find an ass tied, and a colt [2] tied [1] with her [3] on which no one ever yet sat; [1] untie them and bring them to me. And if anyone says anything to you, [3] if anyone asks you, [2] 'Why are you doing this?' [3] you shall say to him, [1] 'Because *the Lord* has need of them,' and he will send them [2] here at once."

[3] So those who were sent went on their way [1] and did as Je-

sus had commanded them, [2] and found [4] a young ass [3] just as he had told them, [2] tied outside the door in the street, and they untied it. [3] And the owners of it, [2] who were standing there, said to them, "What are you doing, untying the colt?" And they told them what Jesus had commanded, [3] *"The Lord has need of it,"* [2] and they let them go. [1] So they brought the ass and the colt [2] to Jesus, [3] and throwing their garments [1] on them, [3] they set Jesus upon the colt.[a]

*"Hosanna!"*

[3] Now as he proceeded, they began to spread their garments on the road; and as he was already drawing near, at the descent of the Mount of Olives, the whole multitude of the disciples began to rejoice and praise God with a loud voice for all the mighty works which they had seen, saying, *'Blessed is the King who is coming in the name of the Lord!"..."Peace in heaven, and glory in the highest!"*

[2] And [4] a great throng who had come to the feast, when they heard that Jesus was coming into Jerusalem, [1] cut branches from the [4] palm trees and went out to meet him, [1] and strewed them on the road. And the crowds who went before him, and those who followed, [4] kept crying out, *"Hosanna!"...* [1] *"Hosanna to the Son of David!"...* [4] *"Blessed is He who is coming in the name of the Lord—the King of Israel!"...* [2] *"Blessed is the Kingdom of our father David!"... "Hosanna in the highest!"*

[1] Now all this was done that there might be fulfilled what was spoken by the prophet, saying,

> *"Tell the daughter of Zion,* [4] *'Fear not;*
> [1] *behold, your King is coming to you,*
> *meek, and mounted upon an ass,*
> *even a colt, the foal of an ass.'"*

[4] These things his disciples understood not at first, but when Jesus was glorified they remembered that these things were written of him and that they had done these things to him. Therefore the people who were with him when he called Lazarus from the tomb and raised him from the dead bore witness. For this reason also the people went and met him, be-

cause of hearing that he had wrought this miraculous sign.

## Jerusalem's Leaders Reject Him

[3] And some of the Pharisees from the multitude said to him, "Teacher, *rebuke* your disciples." But he answered and said to them. "I tell you, if these should be silent *the stones* would cry out!"

And when he drew near and beheld the city, he wept over it, saying, "If only you, yes *you,* had known at least in this your day, the things that *would bring you Peace!* But now are they hid from your eyes. For days shall come upon you when your enemies will cast up a rampart about you and encircle you and hem you in on every side, and will level you to the ground with your children within you, leaving in you not one stone upon another—*because you knew not the time of your visitation."*

[1] And upon his entering Jerusalem the entire city was a-roused, saying, "Who is *this?"* And the crowds said, "This is *Jesus the Prophet,* from Nazareth of Galilee." [4] The Pharisees said therefore to one another, "You see that you are gaining *nothing;* lo, the world has gone after him!"[b]

[2] And Jesus entered into the temple; and when he had looked around on everything, as the hour was already late he went out to Bethany with the twelve.

## 118. His Symbolic Curse on the Fig Tree
### (Mt. 21:12-19; Mk. 11:12-19; Lk. 19:45-46)

[2] Now the next morning, [1] as he was returning to the city [2] from Bethany, he was hungry, and seeing at a distance [1] by the roadside a certain fig tree [2] that had leaves, [1] he went to it [2] to see if he might find anything thereon. But when he came to it, he found nothing but leaves—for it was not the season[a] for figs. And Jesus answered and said to it, [1] "Let there be no fruit from you hereafter—[2] no one ever eat fruit from you a-gain!" And his disciples heard it; [1] and the fig tree dried up at once.

### His Messiahship Is Again Demonstrated

[2] Then came they into Jerusalem, and Jesus went into the temple [1] of God [2] and began to drive out [1] all those who were selling and buying in the temple. [2] He overturned the tables of the money changers and the seats of those selling doves, and would not allow anyone to carry a vessel through the temple;[b] and he began to teach, saying to them, "Is it not written, *'My house shall be called for all the nations a house of prayer'? But you have made it a den of robbers!'*"

And the scribes and the chief priests heard it and kept on seeking how they might destroy him; for they feared him, because all the people were struck with wonder at his teaching.

[1] And the blind and the lame came to him in the temple; and he healed them. But when the chief priests and the scribes saw the wonderful things he was doing, with the children crying out in the temple and saying, *"Hosanna to the Son of David!"* they became incensed and said to him, *"Do you hear what these are saying?"* And Jesus said to them, *"Yes!* Have you never read,

> *'Out of the mouth of babes and sucklings*
> *thou hast perfected praise'?"*

And he left them, [2] and when evening came [1] he went out of the city to Bethany and lodged there.

### 119. "Whatever You Shall Ask in Faith..."
##### (Mt. 21:20-22; Mk. 11:20-26)

[2] Now as they passed by in the morning, they saw the fig tree, dried up from the roots. And Peter remembered and said to him, "Master, behold! The fig tree that You cursed is withered." [1] And the disciples on seeing it marveled and said, "How did the fig tree dry up immediately?"[a]

[2] Jesus answered and said to them, *"Have faith in God.* For verily, I say to you, [1] if you have faith and do not doubt, you shall not only do what was done to the fig tree, but whoever shall say to *this mountain,*[b] 'Be removed, and be cast into the sea,' [2] and does not doubt in his heart but *believes that what*

*he says will come to pass,* he shall have whatever he says. Therefore I say to you, [1] *all* things whatever you shall ask in prayer, *believing* [2] that you are receiving, *they shall be yours.*

"And when you stand praying, *forgive,* if you have anything against anyone, that your Father who is in heaven may also forgive you *your* offenses. [But if you do not forgive, neither will your Father who is in heaven forgive your offenses.] "

### 120. Another Challenge to His Authority
#### (Mt. 21:23-27; Mk. 11:27-33; Lk. 20:1-8)

[2] So they came again into Jerusalem. [3] And it came to pass that, [2] as he was walking in the temple, [3] teaching the people and proclaiming the Glad News, [2] there came up to him the chief priests and the scribes and the elders [1] of the people, [2] and they said to him, [3] "Tell us, *by what authority* are you doing these things? Or, *Who is it* who gave you this authority?"[a]

[2] And Jesus answered and said to them, *I* also will ask *you* one question; now answer me, [1] and I also will tell you by what authority I am doing these things. The baptism of John—whence was it, from heaven or from men? [2] *Answer* me." And they reasoned with one another, saying, "If we say, 'From heaven,' he will say [1] to us, 'Why then did you not believe him?' But if we say, 'From men,' we fear the multitude—[3] all the people will stone us, for they are persuaded that John [2] was indeed a prophet."

So they answered and said to Jesus, "We do not know." And Jesus answering [3] said to them, "Neither do *I* tell *you* by what *authority* I am doing these things."

### 121. "Which of the Two Sons Obeyed?"
#### (Mt. 21:28-32; Mk. 12:1a; Lk. 19:47-48)

[2] And he began to speak to them in parables: [1] "Now what do you think? A certain man had two sons; and he came to the first and said, 'Son, go work in my vineyard today.' And he answering said, 'I will not;' but afterward he repented and

went. And he came to the second and said the same. And he answering said, 'I will go, sir;' but he did not go. Which of the two did the will of the father?" They said to him, "The first."

Jesus said to them, "Verily I say to you, that *the publicans and the harlots are going before you* into the Kingdom of God. For John came to you in the way of righteousness, and you did not believe him; but the publicans and the harlots believed him. And *you,* even when you saw this, did not later have a change of heart that you might believe him."

[3] And he was teaching day by day in the temple.[a] And the chief priests and the scribes and the leaders of the people kept seeking to destroy him; but they could not find what to do, for all the people were hanging upon his words.

## 122. The Vineyardists Who Killed the Son
*(Mt. 21:33-46; Mk. 12:1b-12; Lk. 21:9-19)*

[3] And he began to say this to the people: [1] "Hear another parable. There was a certain man who was the master of a house, who planted a vineyard and fenced it around, and dug in it a winepress and erected a tower; and he leased it out to vineyardists and left the country [3] for a long while. [1] Now when the time for the vintage drew near, [3] he sent a bondman to the vineyardists, that they should give him of the fruit of the vineyard. But the vineyardists [2] took him and beat him, and sent him away with no fruit.

"And again he sent to them another bondman; [3] but him also they beat and [2] stoned and wounded in the head, and [3] after shameful insults they sent him also away with no fruit. And again he sent a third; and him also they wounded and cast out. [2] Then again he sent another, and him they killed. [1] Again he sent other bondmen, [2] many [1] more than the first, and they did the same things to them, [2] beating some and killing others.

[3] "Then said the lord of the vineyard, 'What shall I do?' [2] Having therefore yet one son, his own beloved, he sent him also to them last of all, saying, [3] 'I will send *my beloved son;* it may be that, seeing [1] my son, [3] they will respect him.' [2] But those vineyardists, [1] when they saw the son, [3] reasoned among

themselves, saying, 'This is the *heir!* [2] Come, let us kill him, and the inheritance will be *ours.'* And they took him [3] and, hurling him out of the vineyard, killed him.

[1] "When therefore the lord of the vineyard comes, *what will he do to those vineyardists?"* They said to him, "He will *destroy* those wicked men with a miserable death. And he will let out the vineyard to *other* vineyardists, who will deliver him the fruits in their seasons."

## The Rejecting Nation Is Warned

Jesus said to them, [3] "He *will* come and *destroy* those vineyardists and *will give* the vineyard to others! [1] Therefore I say to you, that *the Kingdom of God* shall be taken *from you* and given to *a nation bringing forth the fruits*[a] *thereof."*

[3] And when they heard this, they said, "May *this* not be!" But fixing his eyes on them, he said, "What therefore is *this that has been written?* [1] Did you never read in the Scriptures:
> 'The stone which the builders rejected
> has become the chief cornerstone;
> this is the Lord's own doing,
> and it is marvelous in our eyes.'?
[1] [And whoever falls on this Stone shall be broken; *but on whomever it may fall, it will grind him to powder!]* "

And the chief priests [3] and the scribes [1] and the Pharisees, when they heard his parables, knew that he was speaking about *them;* [2] and they sought [3] in that same hour [2] to arrest him. But they feared the people, [1] because they looked on him as a prophet; [2] so they left him unmolested, and went away.

## 123. A King's Son's Wedding Feast
### (Mt. 22:1-14)

And again Jesus answered and spoke to them in parables, saying, "The Kingdom of heaven has become like a man who was a king, who prepared a wedding feast for his son. And he sent forth his bondmen to call those invited to the feast, but they would not come.

"Again he sent forth other bondmen, saying, 'Tell those invited, Behold, my dinner is prepared, with my bullocks and the fatlings killed, and everything ready; *come to the wedding feast.'* But they made light of it and went their ways, one to his farm, and another to his business, while the rest, on seizing his bondmen, insulted and killed them.

"Now the king on hearing of this was furious, and he dispatched his troops and destroyed those murderers and burned their city.[a] Then said he to his bondmen, 'The wedding feast is ready indeed, but those invited were not worthy. Go out therefore into the main highways and invite to the wedding feast as many as you may find.' So those bondmen went out into the highways and gathered together all whom they found, both evil and good; so the wedding hall was filled with guests.

"But when the king came in to look at the guests, he saw there a man not clothed with a wedding garment. And he said to him, 'Friend, how came you in here without having a wedding garment?' And he was speechless. Then said the king to the servants, 'Bind him hand and foot, and take him into the outer darkness, where there shall be weeping and the gnashing of teeth.' *For many are called, but few chosen.*"

## 124. *"Give Tribute to Caesar?"*

*(Mt. 22:15-22; Mk. 12:13-17; Lk. 20:20-26)*

[1] Then went the Pharisees and took counsel how they might entangle him in his talk. [3] And they watched him and sent forth spies, who should make a pretense of good faith, that they might seize upon his words and thus deliver him up to the power and authority of the governor.

[2] So they sent forth to him certain of [1] their disciples [2] and of the Herodians, and they came and [3] put to him a question, saying, [2] "Teacher, we know that you are truthful, and [3] that you speak and teach rightly and show no partiality; [2] for you pay no regard to the prominence of men but teach the way of God in truth. [1] Tell us therefore, what do *you* think: *is it lawful* [3] for us to give tribute to Caesar, or not? [2] Should we give

it, or should we not?"[a]

[1] But Jesus, knowing [2] their hypocrisy, [3] craftiness and [1] wickedness, [2] said to them, "Why do you try me out, [1] you *hypocrites?* Show me the tribute money—[2] bring a denary, that I may see it." [1] And they brought him a denary, and he said to them, "Whose is this image and inscription?" [3] And they answered and said [2] to him, "Caesar's."

[1] Then [2] answered Jesus and said to them, [1] *"Render therefore to Caesar the things which are Caesar's; and to God the things which are God's."* [3] So they could not seize upon what he said before the people, but, marveling at his answer, fell silent; [1] and they left him and went away.

### 125. Seven Who Married the Same Wife
*(Mt. 22:23-33; Mk. 12:18-27; Lk. 20:27-40)*

[3] And there came to him [1] that same day [3] certain of the Sadducees, [2] who say that there is no resurrection; and they questioned him, saying, "Teacher, Moses wrote for us [1] that, if any man dies without having children, his brother is to marry the widow and raise up children for his brother.

"Now there were with us seven brothers, [3] and the first took a wife, and died without children; and the second married her, and he died childless; and the third one took her, and likewise the seven also, and they died without leaving children. Last of all the woman died also. Therefore, [2] when they rise in the resurrection, [3] whose wife does she become? For the *seven* [1] all had her [3] as a wife."[a]

[1] And Jesus answered and said to them, "You are wrong. [2] Is it not because of *this* you are wrong, *that you know not the Scriptures nor the power of God?* [3] The sons of this world marry and are given in marriage, but they who are accounted worthy to have a part in that world and the resurrection from the dead neither marry nor are given in marriage, but are as angels [of God] in heaven. [3] Neither can they die any more; for they are equal to the angels and are sons of God, being sons of the resurrection.

[1] "Now as to the resurrection of the dead, [3] that the dead

*are raised* even Moses showed. [1] Have you not read what was spoken to you by God [2] in the book of Moses, in the part a-bout the bush, [3] when he called the Lord *'the God of Abra-ham, and the God of Isaac, and the God of Jacob'?* [2] He is not the God of the dead, but *the God of the living;* [3] for all are *liv-ing* to Him. [2] *You* therefore are greatly *in error.*

[1] And hearing this the crowds were astonished at his teach-ing; [3] and some of the scribes made answer and said, "Teacher, you have spoken well." And no longer dared they to ask him anything.

### 126. The First and Great Commandment

*(Mt. 22:34-40; Mk. 12:28-34a)*

[1] But the Pharisees, when they heard that he had silenced the Sadducees, gathered themselves together; and one of them who was a lawyer [2] of the scribes, having heard these disputa-tions and perceiving that he had answered them well, came up and [1] asked him a test question, saying, "Teacher, which com-mandment in the law is the great one? [2] What is the *first* com-mandment of all?"

And Jesus answered him, "The first of all the command-ments is, *'Hear, O Israel: the Lord our God is one Lord;*[a] *and you shall love the Lord your God with all your heart, and with all your soul, and with all your mind, and with all your strength.'* [1] *This* is the first and great commandment. And the second is like it, [2] namely this, *'You shall love your neighbor as yourself.'* [1] On these two commandments hang all the law and the prophets; [2] there is no greater commandment than these."

And the scribe said to him, "Teacher, you have well said the truth, that there is *one God* and none other but He, and that *to love him* with all the heart and with all the understanding and with all the strength, and *to love one's neighbor as him-self,* is more than all the whole burnt offerings and the sacri-fices."

And Jesus, seeing that he answered him with wisdom, said to him, *"You are not far from the Kingdom of God."*

### 127. "How Is David's Son His Lord?"
(Mt. 22:41-46; Mk. 12:34b-37; Lk. 20:41-44;21:37)

[1] But while the Pharisees were assembled together [2] and Jesus was teaching in the temple, [1] he put to *them* a question, saying, "What do you think concerning *the Messiah?* Whose *son* is he?" They said to him, "The son of *David.*"
[3] But he said to them, [2] "How can the scribes say that the Messiah is David's *son?* [1] How then does David in the Spirit call him *'Lord'?* [2] For David himself said by the Holy Spirit [3] in the book of Psalms,

'*The Lord said to my Lord,*
*Sit thou at my right hand,*
*till I make thine enemies thy footstool.*'
Therefore David [2] *himself* [3] is calling him *'Lord,'* so how is he then his *son?*"[a]
[1] And no one could answer him a word, nor from that day dared anyone to ask him another question. [2] And the great crowd of common folk listened to him gladly. [3] So by day[b] he was in the temple teaching, though going out and spending the night on the mountain that is called Olivet.

### 128. "Do Not as the Scribes"
(Mt. 23:1-39; Mk. 12:38-40; Lk. 21:38;20:45-47;13:34-35)

[3] Now all the people kept coming to him early in the morning in the temple to hear him. [1] Then said Jesus to his disciples [2] in his teaching, [3] in the hearing of all the multitude:
[2] "Take heed, [3] *beware of the scribes*—who like to walk about in long robes, [1] and who love the places of honor at the feasts and the foremost seats in the synagogues; [3] who devour the houses of widows, and for a pretense make long prayers. These shall receive a *greater* condemnation!
[1] "The scribes and the Pharisees sit in Moses' seat; all the things therefore which they tell you to observe, these observe and do. But do not copy the way they live; for they do not do what they say.
"For they bind up burdens that are heavy and hard to bear,

and lay them on the shoulders of men; but they will not move them with one finger of their own. And all of their deeds are they doing that they may be seen *by men.* They make broad their phylacteries and widen the fringes on their garments; [3] and they love salutations in the marketplaces [1] and being called *'Rabbi, Rabbi,'* by men.

"Now do not *you* be called 'Rabbi;' for One is your Teacher, *the Christ,* and you yourselves are all brethren. And call not anyone on earth your Father; for One is your Father, He who is in heaven. Neither be called masters; for One is your *Master,* the Christ. But he that is greatest among you shall be your *servant.* And whoever shall exalt *himself* will be *humbled;* and whoever shall humble *himself* will be *exalted.* [a]

*"Hypocrites!"*

"But *woe* to you, scribes and Pharisees—hypocrites! For you shut up the Kingdom of heaven against men; for you yourselves do not enter in, nor even let those who are entering go in.

*"Woe* to you, scribes and Pharisees—hypocrites! For you travel sea and land to make a single proselyte, and when he has been won, you make him twice as much a son of Gehenna as yourselves.

*"Woe* to you, you blind guides who say, 'if anyone swears by the temple, it is nothing, but if anyone swears by the gold of the temple, he must make good his oath.' You are fools and blind; for which is the greater, the gold, or the temple which hallows the gold?

"You also say, 'If anyone swears by the altar, it is nothing; but if anyone swears by the gift on the altar, he must make good his oath.' You are fools and blind; for which is the greater, the gift, or the altar which hallows the gift?

"He therefore who swears by the altar swears by it and by everything thereon; and he who swears by the temple swears by it and by Him who is dwelling therein; and he who swears by heaven swears by the throne of God and by Him who is sitting thereon.

"*Woe* to you, scribes and Pharisees—hypocrites! For you pay tithes of mint and dill and cummin, but have ignored the *weightier* things of the law—*justice, and mercy, and fidelity. These* ought you to have done, while yet not leaving those undone, you blind guides, who strain out a gnat but swallow a camel!

### "You Cleanse the Outside"

"*Woe* to you, scribes and Pharisees—hypocrites! For you cleanse the outside of the cup and the dish, but within they are filled with extortion and sensuality. Blind Pharisee, cleanse first the *inside* of the cup and the dish, that their outside also may become clean.

"*Woe* to you, scribes and Pharisees—hypocrites! For you are like whitewashed sepulchres, which appear indeed outwardly beautiful, but within are full of dead men's bones and all sorts of filth. Thus *you, too,* indeed appear outwardly to men to be righteous, but within are full of hypocrisy and iniquity.

"*Woe* to you, scribes and Pharisees—hypocrites! For you build the tombs of the prophets and beautify the sepulchres of the righteous, and say, 'Had we lived in the days of our fathers, we would not have partaken with them in the killing of the prophets.' Thus you witness concerning yourselves that you are *sons* of the murderers of the prophets; so *fill up* the measure of your fathers!

### "How Shall You Escape?"

"You serpents, you offspring of vipers, *how shall you escape* being sentenced to Gehenna? Because of this, behold, *I* am sending you prophets and wise men and scribes, and some of *these* you will kill and crucify, and some you will scourge in your synagogues and will persecute from city to city; that *upon you* may come all the righteous blood poured out on the earth from the blood of the righteous Abel till the blood of Zechariah, the son of Barachiah, whom you slew between the sanctuary and the altar. Verily, I say to you, *all these things shall come upon this generation.*[b]

*"O Jerusalem!"*

"O Jerusalem, Jerusalem!–killing the prophets and stoning those who have been sent to you! How often would I have gathered together your children as a hen gathers her brood under her wings, and you would not! Behold, your house is left to you desolate. For [3] verily, I say to you, *you shall see me no more till you shall say, 'Blessed is he who is coming in the name of the Lord!'"* [c]

### 129. A Poor Widow's Notable Gift
#### (Mk. 12:41-44; Lk. 21:1-4)

[2] And Jesus sat down across from the treasury, and he beheld how the people were dropping money into the chest and many who were rich were putting in much. [3] But looking up, he also saw a certain poor widow placing therein two tiny copper coins [2] which make less than a cent.

And he called to him his disciples and said to them, [3] "Of a truth, I say to you, this poor widow has put in *more* [2] than all those who contributed to the treasury. For they all contributed out of their abundance [3] into the offerings for God, [2] but she out of her *poverty* put in *everything she had*, even her whole livelihood." [a]

### 130. Gentiles Seek to Meet Jesus
#### (Jn. 12:20-36a)

Now there were certain Greeks among those coming up to worship at the feast; these therefore approached Philip (the one from Bethsaida of Galilee) and made request, saying, "Sir, we would see Jesus." Philip came and told Andrew, and again Andrew and Philip told Jesus.

But Jesus answered them,[a] saying, "The hour has come for the Son of man *to be glorified.* Verily, verily, I say to you, unless a grain of wheat falls into the ground and dies, it remains alone; *but if it dies, it bears much fruit. He who loves his life shall lose it, but he who hates his life in this world shall keep it unto life eternal.*

"If anyone *serves* Me, *let him follow* Me; and where *I* am, there shall also my servant be. And if anyone *serves* Me, *him will the Father honor.*

"Now has my soul been troubled; and what shall I say— 'Father, save me from this hour'? No! Because of this *came* I to this hour. *Father, glorify thy name!"*

There came therefore a Voice from heaven: *"I BOTH GLORIFIED IT AND WILL GLORIFY IT AGAIN."*

The multitude therefore who stood by and heard it, said that it had thundered; others said, "An angel has spoken to him." Jesus answered and said, "Not for My sake has this Voice come, but for your sakes. *Now* is the condemnation of this world; *now* shall the ruler of this world be cast out! *And I, when I am lifted up from the earth, will draw all men to myself."* Now this he said to signify by what death he would die.

The people answered him, "We have heard out of the law that the Messiah remains forever; how then do *you* say that the Son of man *must be lifted up?*[b] *Who is* this Son of man?"

Jesus said therefore to them, "Yet a *little* longer is the Light with you. Walk *while you have* the Light, lest darkness overtake you; for he who walks in darkness knows not where he is going. *While you have the Light, put your trust in the Light,* that you may *become* sons of *light."*

### 131. But His Own People Spurn Him
(Jn. 12:36b-50)

These things said Jesus, and he departed and hid himself from them. But although he had wrought so many signs in their presence, they did not believe upon him; that there might be fulfilled the word of the prophet Isaiah, which he uttered:
*"Lord, who has believed our report?*
*And to whom has the arm of the Lord been revealed?"*
It was on *this* account they could not believe: because Issiah said also,
*"He has blinded their eyes and hardened their heart,*
*lest with their eyes they should see,*
*and with their heart should understand,*

*and be turned back and I should heal them."*
These things Isaiah said when he saw his glory[a] and spoke concerning him.

Nevertheless indeed many even of the rulers *did* believe upon him, though because of the Pharisees they did not confess,
lest they should be put out of the synagogue; for they loved
the approval of men more than the approval of God.

But Jesus cried out and said, *"He who believes upon Me believes not upon Me but upon Him who sent me.* And he who
*beholds* Me *beholds Him who sent me.* As light have *I* come
into the world, *that whoever believes upon Me should not remain in darkness.*

"Now if anyone hears my words and does not believe, *I* am
not judging him; for I came not that I should judge the world,
but that I might *save* the world. He who rejects Me and receives not my words *has* one that judges him: *the Word* which
I spoke, *that* shall judge him at the last day.

"For *I* did not speak on my own authority; but *the Father
who sent me,* He himself gave me commandment what I
should speak, and what I should say. And I know that His
commandment is life everlasting. The things therefore which *I*
am speaking, just as *the Father* has told me, so I speak."[b]

## 132. *Jesus Tells of Things to Come*
*(Mt. 24:1-42;10:17-23;25:1-46; Mk. 13:1-37; Lk. 21:5-36;12:11-12)*

[2] Now as he was going forth out of the temple, [1] his disciples
came up to point out to him the buildings of the temple, [3] how
it was adorned with handsome stones and consecrated gifts;
[1] and [2] one of his disciples exclaimed to him, "See, Master,
*what tremendous stones, and what buildings!"*

[1] But Jesus [2] answering him [1] said to them, [2] "Are you looking at these great buildings? [1] Verily, I say to you, [3] as for these
things which you are beholding, days are coming when there
shall not be left one stone upon another, that will not be
thrown down!"[a]

[2] And as he sat on the Mount of Olives across from the temple, Peter and James and John and Andrew [1] came to him pri-

vately [3] and asked him, saying, [2] "Tell us [3] therefore, Teacher, *when* will these things be? [2] What will be the *sign* when all these things are going to [3] come to pass? [1] And what is *the sign of Your coming, and of the consummation of the age?"*

## The Remainder of the Age in Summary

*(Mt. 24:4-8; Mk. 13:5-8; Lk. 21:8-11)*

[2] And Jesus answered and began to say to them, "Take heed lest anyone mislead you. For many will come in my name, saying, 'I am He, ' [1] 'I am the Messiah,' [3] and 'The time is drawing near,' [2] and they will lead many astray. [3] Do not therefore be followers of them.

[1] "And you will hear of wars and rumors of wars; [3] but when you hear of wars and commotions [2] and rumors of wars, [3] be not terrified, [1] see that you are not disturbed. For all of these things [3] must first take place, but the end is not to be at once."

Then said he to them, [1] "For nation will rise up against nation, and kingdom against kingdom, and there will be famines and pestilences, [3] and great earthquakes in various places; [1] but all these are *the beginning* of travail. [3] *And fearful sights and great signs from heaven* shall there be.

## Persecution and Betrayals to Be Suffered

*(Mt. 10:17-23;24:9-14; Mk. 13:9-13; Lk. 12:11-12;21:12-19)*

[2] "But take heed to yourselves; [1] beware of men. For [3] before all these things [1] they will deliver you up to be afflicted, and will put you to death. [3] They will lay their hands on you and persecute you, delivering you up to the synagogues and [1] to Sanhedrins and [3] to prisons. [1] They will scourge you in their synagogues, and you will be dragged before governors and kings because of Me; [3] but it will turn out for you as a testimony [1] before them and the Gentiles.

"But when they deliver you up [2] and lead you away, [3] and bring you before the synagogues and the rulers and authorities, [2] be not anxious beforehand [3] how or what you are to answer in defense, [2] but say whatever is given you [1] in that same hour. [3] For *the Holy Spirit* will teach you what you should say; [2] it is not you who speak, but [1] the Spirit of your Father who speaks in you. [3] Settle it therefore in your hearts not to meditate beforehand what to answer; for I will give you a mouth and wisdom which none of your adversaries can reply to or resist.

[1] "And you will be hated by all the nations for My name's sake; [1] and then will many be caused to stumble, and will betray one another and hate one another. [2] Brother will deliver up brother to death, and a father his child; and children will rise up against parents and put them to death. [3] So you will be betrayed even by parents and brothers, and by kinsfolk and friends, and some of you they will put to death; you will be hated by all for My name's sake. But not a hair of your head shall perish; by your patient endurance gain your souls.

### The Gospel to All the Nations—Then the End
*(Mt. 24:12-14;10:23; Mk. 13:10)*

[1] "And many false prophets will arise, and they will mislead many; and because wickedness is multiplied, the love of many will grow cold. But he who endures to the end *shall be saved.*

[1] "But when they persecute you in this city, flee into the next; for verily, I say to you, you will not have completed the cities of Israel before the Son of man comes.[b]

[1] "And this Glad News of the Kingdom [2] must first be proclaimed [1] in all the world as a testimony to *all* the nations; *and then will the end come.*

### Jerusalem to Be Trodden Down
*(Lk. 21:20-24)*

[3] "But when you see Jerusalem encircled by armies, then know that *her desolation has drawn near.* Then those in Judea, let them flee to the mountains; and those who are in the city, let them go out; and those who are in the country, let them not go into her. For these are days of avenging, that all things that have been written may be fulfilled.

"But alas for those with child, and those with nursing babes, in those days. For there shall be great distress upon the land and wrath upon this people; and they shall fall by the edge of the sword and be led captive to all the nations. And Jerusalem shall be trodden down by the Gentiles *till the times of the Gentiles are fulfilled.*

## Then a Great Tribulation on Earth
### (Mt. 24:15-22; Mk. 13:14-20)

[1] "When therefore you see *the abomination of desolation,*[c] spoken of by Daniel the prophet, standing in the Holy Place [2] where it ought not to be" (let him who reads understand), *"then* let those who are in Judea flee to the mountains! He that is on the housetop, let him not come down into the house, or enter it to take anything out. And he that is in the field, let him not turn back [1] to take his clothes.

"And alas for those with child, and those with nursing babes, in *those* days! Pray also that your flight be not in winter or on a Sabbath. [2] For in those days [1] there shall be a great tribulation such as has not been from the beginning [2] of the creation which God created till the present time, no, nor ever shall be. And unless the Lord had shortened [1] those days, none of humankind would be saved; [2] but for the elect's sake, whom he has chosen, [1] those days will be shortened.

## As Lightning from the East
### (Mt. 24:23-31; Mk. 13:21-27; Lk. 21:25-27)

[2] "Now at that time, if anyone says to you, 'Lo, here is the *Messiah!*' or, 'Lo, he is there!' do not believe it. [1] For false Messiahs and false prophets will arise and show great signs and wonders, such as to mislead, if possible, even the elect. [2] So take heed; behold, I have told you all things beforehand.

[1] "If therefore they say to you, 'Lo, he is in the wilderness,' do not go forth; or, 'Lo, he is in the secret rooms,' do not believe it. For as the lightning comes from the east and shines as far as the west, so also will the coming of the Son of man be. For wherever the *carcass* may be, there the *vultures* will be gathered together.

"And immediately after the tribulation of those days [3] there will be signs in the sun and the moon and the stars—

¹the sun will be darkened, the moon will not give her light, ²and the stars will be falling from heaven—³and upon the earth distress of nations with perplexity, the sea and the waves roaring, men's hearts growing faint with fear and expectation of the things which are coming upon the world.

"For the powers ²which are in the heavens will be shaken, ¹and then will appear in the sky *the sign of the Son of man.* And then will all the tribes of the earth mourn, and they will see the Son of man coming upon the clouds of heaven with power and great glory. ²And then will he send forth his angels ¹with a great trumpet call, and they will gather together his elect from the four winds, ²from the farthest part of earth to the farthest part of heaven, and ¹from one end of the heavens to the other.ᵈ

### *"Watch Therefore; Be Ready"*
*(Mt. 24:32-42; Mk. 13:28-37; Lk. 21:28-36)*

³"But when these things *are beginning* to come to pass, look up and lift up your heads, for your redemption *is drawing nigh.*

And he spoke to them a parable: ²*"From the fig tree learn a lesson;* ³behold the fig tree, and all the trees. ¹When its branch has now grown tender, and ³they are coming out in leaf, you see and know for yourselves that summer already is near. So also *you,* when you see ¹all these things ³taking place, know that the Kingdom of God *is near at hand,* ¹*at the very doors.* Verily, I say to you, *this*ᵉ *generation* will by no means pass away before all these things will have been fulfilled. Heaven and earth will pass away, but my words will not pass away!

"But of that day and hour no one knows, not even the angels of heaven, ²nor the Son, ¹but my Father only. Instead, just as the days of Noah were, so also will be the coming of the Son of man. For just as in the days before the flood they were eating and drinking, marrying and giving in marriage, till the day when Noah went into the ark, and were unaware till the flood came and took them all away, so also will be the coming of the Son of man. Then will there be two men in the field;

one is taken and the other left. There will be two women grinding at the mill; one is taken and the other left.

[3] "So take heed to yourselves, lest your hearts be engrossed with dissipation and drunkenness and the cares of this life, and that day come upon you suddenly; for as a snare will it come upon all who dwell on the face of all the earth. Watch therefore unceasingly, praying that you be accounted worthy to escape all these things that are going to come to pass, and to stand before the Son of man. [2] Take heed, [1] therefore; [2] watch [and pray], [1] *for you know not in what hour your Lord is coming.*

[2] "For it is like a man who made a journey abroad, leaving his home in charge of his bondmen, giving to each of them his work and commanding the doorkeeper to be watchful. Watch therefore, for you do *not* know when the Master of the house is coming—whether in the evening, or at midnight, or at cockcrowing, or in the morning—lest coming suddenly he find you asleep. And what I say to you, I am saying to all: Watch!

## Five of the Ten Were Foolish
### (Mt. 25:1-13)

[1] "The Kingdom of heaven at that time will be like ten maidens who took their lamps and went out to meet *the bridegroom.* Now five of them were wise, and five were foolish. The foolish in taking their lamps did not provide themselves oil, but the wise took oil in flasks with their lamps.

"And while the bridegroom tarried, they all dozed off and slept. But in the middle of the night there was a cry, 'Behold, *the bridegroom is coming! Go forth to meet him.'* Then all of those maidens arose and trimmed their lamps. And the foolish said to the wise, 'Give us some from *your* oil, for our lamps are going out.' But the wise answered, saying, 'No—lest there be not enough for us and you. Go instead to those who sell, and buy *for yourselves.'*

"And while they went off to buy, the bridegroom came, and those who were ready went in with him to the wedding feast; and the door was shut. Then afterward there came the other maidens also, saying, *'Lord! Lord!* Open to *us!'* But he answering said, 'Verily, I say to you, *I do not know you.'* Watch therefore, for you know not the day nor the hour when the Son of man is coming.

## Parable of the Entrusted Talents
### (Mt. 25:14-30)

"For it is like a man making a journey abroad, who summoned his own bondmen and turned over to them his substance. And to one he gave five talents,[f] and to another two, and to another one, each according to his separate ability; then at once he took his journey.

"Then he who had received the five talents went and traded with them, and made five talents more. And likewise the one with the two also gained two more. But he who had received the one went and dug in the ground and hid his lord's silver.

"Now after a long time the lord of those bondmen came and settled with them the account. And he who had received the five talents came to him and brought five talents more, saying, 'Lord, you turned over to me five talents; behold, I have gained with them *five talents more.'* So his lord said to him, 'Well done, good and faithful bondman! You were faithful over a few things; I will set you over many. Enter into the joy of your lord.'

"And he also who had received the two talents came and said, 'Lord, you turned over to me two talents; behold, I have gained with them *two talents more.'* His lord said to *him,* 'Well done, good and faithful bondman! You were faithful over a few things; I will set you over many. Enter into the joy of your lord.'

## *"Take the Talent from Him"*

"Then came he also who had received the one talent, and he said, 'Lord, I knew you, that you are a hard man, reaping where you did not sow and gathering where you did not scatter; so I was afraid, and went and hid your talent in the ground. Behold, you have here what is yours.'

"But his lord answering him said, 'You wicked and indolent bondman, you knew that I reap where I did not sow, and gather where I did not scatter? You should therefore have placed my silver with the bankers, and when I came I should have received what is mine *with interest.* Take therefore the talent from him, and give it to him who has the *ten* talents. For to everyone who has shall be given, and he shall possess abundance; *but from him who has not, even what he has shall be taken away from him.* And as for the worthless bondman, cast him *out* into the outer darkness, where there shall be weeping and the gnashing of teeth.'

### The Son of Man to Judge the Nations
   *(Mt. 25:31-46)*

"Now when the Son of man comes in his glory, and with him all the holy angels, then will he sit upon the throne of his glory, and before him shall be gathered all the nations. And he will separate them one from another as a shepherd separates the sheep from the goats, and will put the sheep at his right hand, but the goats at the left.

"Then will the King say to those at his right hand, *'Come,* you blessed of my Father, inherit the Kingdom prepared for you from the foundation of the world. For I was hungry, and you gave me food; I was thirsty, and you gave me drink; I was a stranger, and you made me welcome; I was naked, and you clothed me; I was sick, and you visited me; I was in prison, and you came to me.'

"Then will the righteous answer him, saying, 'Lord, *when* did we see You hungering, and we fed you, or thirsting, and gave you drink? And *when* did we see You as a stranger, and we welcomed you, or naked, and we clothed you? And *when* did we see You sick or in prison, and we came to you?' And the King will answer and say to them, 'Verily, I say to you, inasmuch as you did it *to one of the least of these my brethren,*[g] you did it to Me.'

"Then will he also say to those at his left, *'Depart* from Me, you cursed, into the everlasting fire prepared for the Devil and his angels. For I was hungry, and you gave me no food; I was thirsty, and you gave me no drink. I was a stranger, and you did not make me welcome; naked, and you did not clothe me; sick, and in prison, and you did not visit me.'

"Then will they also answer him, saying, 'Lord, *when* did we see You hungering or thirsting or a stranger or naked or sick or in prison, and we did not minister to You?' Then will he answer them, saying, 'Verily, I say to you, inasmuch as you did it *not* to one of the least of *these,* you did it not to Me.' And these shall go away into eternal punishment, but the righteous into eternal life."

## Chapter 19. Preparing for His Sacrifice

### *133. The Traitor Offers His Bargain*
#### *(Mt. 26:1-5,14-16; Mk. 14:1-2,10-11; Lk. 22:2-6)*

[2] Now after two days[a] was the Passover and the feast of unleavened bread; [1] so it came about that when Jesus had finished all these utterances, he said to his disciples, "You know that after two days *the Passover* is coming—*and the Son of man is betrayed to be crucified."*

Then assembled together the chief priests and the scribes and the elders of the people in the palace of the high priest, Caiaphas, and they took counsel how they might seize Jesus by stealth and kill him. But they said, "Not during the feast, lest there be an uproar among the people;" [3] for they feared the people.[b]

Then entered Satan into Judas, surnamed Iscariot, who was counted one of the twelve. And he went away and consulted with the chief priests and the captains how he might betray him to them; [1] and he said to them, "What will you give me, if *I* deliver him to you?"

[2] And at hearing this they were jubilant, and promised to give him some money; [3] so he agreed, [1] and they allotted to

him thirty pieces of silver. And from that time he sought opportunity to betray him ²conveniently ³to them in the absence of the multitude.

### 134. Preparing to Observe the Passover
*(Mt. 26:17-19; Mk. 14:12-16; Lk. 22:7-13)*

³Then came ¹the first day of unleavened bread, ³when the Passover lamb must be killed;ᵃ ¹and the disciples came to Jesus, saying to him, ²"Where do You wish us to go and prepare ¹for you to eat the Passover?" ³So he sent off Peter and John, saying, "Go and prepare the Passover for us, that we may eat it."

And they said to him, "Where will You have us prepare it?" And he said to them, ²"Go into the city, and ³behold, ²there will meet you a *man*ᵇ carrying a pitcher of water; follow him, and wherever he may go in say to the man of the house, ³*'The Teacher says to you,* ¹My time is at hand; ²where is the guest room for me to eat the Passover ¹at your house ²with my disciples?' And he will show you a large upper room, furnished and ready; there prepare for us."

And his disciples set out and went into the city ¹as Jesus had instructed them, ³and found just as he had said to them; and they prepared the Passover.

### 135. The Passover Meal Is Begun
*(Mt. 26:20; Mk. 14:17; Lk. 22:14-18; Jn. 13:1-20)*

¹So when it was evening, ²he came with the twelve; ³and when the hour arrived, he reclined at the table, and the apostles with him. And he said to them, "With yearning have I desired to eat this Passover with you before I suffer; for I say to you, that I will not [any more] eat of it *till it be fulfilled in the Kingdom of God."* And receiving a cup, he gave thanks and said, "Take this, and divide it among yourselves; for I say to you, that I will not at all *drink of the fruit of the vine* till the coming of the Kingdom of God."

## He Portrays the Role of a Servant

[4] Now Jesus, aware before the feast[a] of the Passover that his hour had come to depart out of this world to the Father, having loved his own who were in the world, loved them to the utmost degree. So with supper begun, though the Devil already had put into the heart of Judas Iscariot, Simon's son, to betray him, Jesus, knowing that the Father had given all things into his hands and that he came forth from God and was going unto God, rose from the supper and laid aside his garments and girded a towel about himself; then he poured water into a basin and began to wash the disciples' feet, and to wipe them with the towel with which he was girded.

He came therefore to Simon Peter; and Peter said to him, "Lord, are *You* washing my feet?" Jesus answered and said to him, "What I am doing you do not know now, but you will know hereafter." Peter said to him, *"Never* may *You* wash my feet!" Jesus answered him, ' If I do not wash you, you have no part with Me." Simon Peter said to him, "Lord, not my feet only, but also my hands and my head!"

Jesus said to him, "He who has bathed needs not to wash—except his feet—but is clean all over. And you disciples are *clean,* though not you *all."* (For he knew who was going to betray him; it was for this he said, "Not *all* of you are clean.")

## "I Gave You an Example"

When therefore he had washed their feet and had taken his garments and reclined again, he said to them, "Do you know what I have done to you? *You* call me the 'Teacher' and the 'Lord,' and you speak well, for so I am. If then *I,* the Lord and the Teacher, have washed your feet, *you* also ought to wash *one another's* feet.[b] For I gave you an example, that just as *I* did to you, *you also* should do. Verily, verily, I say to you, *a bondman is not greater than his lord, nor a messenger greater than he who sent him.* If you know these things, blessed are you if you *do* them.

"I do not speak of all of you; *I* know those whom I chose.

But it is that the scripture may be fulfilled, *'He who eats bread with me lifted up his heel against me.' Now* am I telling you, *before it comes to pass,* that when it comes to pass you may believe that *I AM HE'.*[c]

"Verily, verily, I say to you, *he who receives whomever I send receives Me; and he who receives Me receives the One who sent me."*

## 136. Jesus Warns of the Betrayal
### (Mt. 26:21-25; Mk. 14:18-21; Lk. 22:21-23; Jn. 13:21-33)

[4] When Jesus had said these things [2] and while they reclined at the table and were eating, [4] he became troubled in spirit and testified, saying, "Verily, verily, I say to you, that one of you will *betray* me—[2] *one who is eating with me!"*

[4] So the disciples [1] were exceedingly grieved and [4] looked at one another, wondering of whom he spoke; [3] and they began to ask of one another who of them it might be that would do this, [2] and to say to him one by one, [1] "Lord, [2] is it *I?"*

And he answered and said to them, "It is one of *the twelve* —one who is dipping with me in the dish! [3] Behold, moreover, the hand of the one betraying me is with me on the table. And the Son of man indeed is going, as it has been determined, [1] as it is written of him. [3] But *woe* to that man by whom he is betrayed! [1] It were good for that man had he not been born."

Then Judas the betrayer answered and said, "Rabbi, is it *I?"* He said to him, "It is *as you have said."*

### *"Lord, Who Is It?"*

[4] Now there was reclining close to Jesus' bosom one of his disciples, the one whom Jesus loved; so Simon Peter beckoned to him to ask who it might be of whom he spoke. And he, leaning against Jesus' breast, said to him, "Lord, *who* is it?"[a] Jesus answered, "He it is *to whom I shall give the morsel,* when I have dipped it." And on dipping the morsel, he gave it to Judas Iscariot, son of Simon. And after the morsel, then entered Satan into him.[b]

Jesus said therefore to him, "What you are doing, *do quick-ly."* Now none of those at the table knew why he spoke to him, for some thought that, since Judas had the money bag, Jesus was telling him, "Buy the things we need for the feast,"[c] or that he should give something to the poor. Immediately therefore, after receiving the morsel, he went out; and it was night.

When he had gone out, Jesus said, *"Now has the Son of man been glorified; and God* has been glorified in him. If God has been glorified in him, God will also glorify him in himself, *and will glorify him forthwith.*

"Little children, yet a *little* while am I with you. You will seek me; and just as I said to the Jews, 'Where *I* am going *you* cannot come,'[d] I now say it also to you."

### 137. The Memorial Bread and Cup
*(Mt. 26:26-29; Mk. 14:22-25; Lk. 22:19-20)*

[1] And as they were eating, Jesus took bread, and blessed it; [3] and when he had given thanks, he broke it and gave [1] to the disciples, [3] saying, [1] *"Take, eat; this is my body,* [3] which is given *for you. This do in remembrance of Me."*

[1] And [3] in like manner after the supper [1] he took a cup, and when he had given thanks, he gave it to them, saying, *"Drink from it, all of you;"* [2] and they all drank from it.

And he said to them, "This [3] cup which is poured out for you [2] *is my blood of the New Covenant, which is poured out for many* [1] *for the remission of sins.* But [2] verily I say to you, that I will nevermore [1] drink of this fruit of the vine *till that day when I drink it new with you in the Kingdom of my Father."*

### 138. The Disciples' Strife Is Rebuked
*(Lk. 22:24-27; Jn. 13:34-35)*

[3] And there even arose a contention among them as to who of them was thought to be greatest. But he said to them, "The kings of the nations lord it over them, and those in authority

are called 'Benefactors.' But let it not be so with you; let the greatest among you become as the youngest, and he who leads *as one who serves.* For which one is the greater, he who reclines at dinner, or he who is serving? Is it not the one who reclines? But *I* am in your midst *as the one who serves.*

[4] "A new *commandment* am I giving you: that you should *love one another;* that *you* should love one another *just as I loved you.* By this will all know that you *are* My disciples: *if you have love toward each other.*

### 139. A Promise Gives Way to a Warning
#### (Lk. 22:28-34; Jn. 13:36-38)

[4] Simon Peter said to him, "Lord, *where* are You going?"[a] Jesus answered him, "Where I am going you cannot follow me now, but you shall follow me *afterward.* [3] You disciples are they who have continued with me in my trials; and even as my Father appointed me a Kingdom, so am *I* appointing *you,* that you *may eat and drink at my table*[b] *in my Kingdom and may sit on thrones judging the twelve tribes of Israel."*

[4] Peter said to him, "Lord, why cannot I follow You *now?* I will *lay down my life* for Your sake." [3] But [4] Jesus answered him, "Will you lay down your life for My sake? [3] Simon, Simon, behold, Satan demanded that he might have you disciples, that he might sift you like wheat; but *I* prayed for *you,* Peter, *that your faith may not fail.* And when you have turned back, strengthen your brethren."

And he said to him, "Lord, I am ready to go with You, both to prison and to death!" But he said, [4] "Verily, verily, I say to you, [3] Peter, *the cock will not at all crow this day till you have denied three times that you know me!*

### 140. Jesus' Great Farewell Discourse
#### (Jn. 14:1-16:33)

[4] "Let not your hearts be troubled; you believe in God, believe also in Me. In my Father's house are many abodes; if it were not so, I would have told you. I go to prepare a place for

you; and if I go and prepare a place for you, *I will come again and will receive you to myself,* that where *I* am *you* may be also. So, *where I am going*[a] you know and *the Way* you know."

Thomas said to him, "Lord, we know not where you are going, and how *can* we know the way?" Jesus said to him, "I AM *the Way—and the Truth, and the Life. No one comes to the Father but through Me.* If you had known Me, you would have known *my Father also;* and from now on you know him, and have seen him."

Philip said to him, "Lord, *show* us the Father, and we are satisfied. Jesus said to him, "Have I been so long with you all, and you, Philip, have not known Me? *He who has seen Me has seen the Father;* so how can *you* say, '*Show* us the Father'? Do you not *believe* that I am in the Father, and that the Father is in Me? *The words* which I am speaking to you all I am not speaking from myself, but *the Father,* who is dwelling in Me, *He* performs the works. *Believe me* that I *am* in the Father, and that the Father is in Me; but if not, believe me because of *the works themselves.*

"Verily, verily, I say to you, *he who believes upon Me, the works which I do shall he do also;* and *greater* works than these shall he do, because I am going to my Father. And whatever you may ask in My name *I will do,* that the Father may be glorified in the Son; *if you ask anything in My name, I will do it.*

*"If You Love Me, Keep My Word'*

(Jn. 14:15-24)

*"If you love me, keep my commandments.*

"And I will ask the Father, and he will give you another *Helper,*[b] that he may dwell with you forever, *even the Spirit of truth;* whom the world cannot receive, because it sees him not, nor knows him; but *you* know him, for he is dwelling with you, and he will be within you.

"I will not leave you orphaned; I will come to you. After a little while the world sees me no more; but *you* will see me; *because I live, you will live also.* In that day will *you* know *that I am in my Father, and you in Me, and I in you.*

"He who has my commandments *and keeps them,* he it is who *loves* me; and he who loves me will be loved by my Father, and *I* will love him and will manifest myself to him."

Judas, not Iscariot, said to him, "Lord, how is it that you will manifest yourself to us, and not to the world?"[c] Jesus answered and said to him, "If anyone loves me, *he will keep my Word.* And my Father will love him, and we will come to him and make our abode with him. He who loves me not does *not* keep my words. And the Word which you are hearing is not mine, but is that of the Father who sent me.

### *"Peace I Leave with You"*

#### *(Jn. 14:25-31)*

"These things have I told you while with you; but *the Helper, the Holy Spirit,* whom the Father will send in my name, *He* will teach you all things and bring to your remembrance everything I told you.

*"Peace* I leave with you; *my* peace am I giving you; not as the world gives do *I* give you. Let not your hearts be troubled, neither let them be afraid.

"You heard how I said to you, 'I am going away,' and 'I am coming to you.' If you loved me, you would have *rejoiced* because I said, 'I am going to the Father;' for my Father is greater than I. And now have I told you before it comes to pass, that when it comes to pass you may *believe.*

"No longer will I speak much with you, *for the ruler of this world is coming.* And he possesses nothing in Me. But, that the world may know that I love the Father and am doing just as the Father commanded me, rise up, *let us go from here.* [d]

### *The Lesson of the Vine and Branches*

#### *(Jn. 15:1-8)*

*"I am the true Vine, and my Father is the Vineyardist.* Every branch in me that does not bear fruit, he takes it away; and every branch bearing fruit, he cleanses it, that it may bear *more* fruit. Already *you* are clean through the Word which I

have spoken to you.

*"Abide in Me, and I in you.* Just as the branch cannot bear fruit by itself, unless it abides in the vine, so neither can you, unless you abide in Me. *I* am the Vine, *you* are the branches: he who abides in Me, *and I in him, he* it is who bears much fruit; *for apart from Me you can do nothing.*

"If anyone does not abide in Me, he is cast out as a branch, and withers, and they gather them and cast them into a fire, and they are burned.

*"If you abide in Me and my words abide in you, you may ask whatever you will and it shall come to pass for you.* In *this* is my Father glorified: that you should bear *much fruit;* thus will you *become* my disciples.

### *"I Have Called You Friends"*

*(Jn. 15:9-17)*

"As the Father loved me, I also loved you; continue in My love. *If you keep my commandments, you will continue in My love,* even as I also have kept my Father's commandments and continue in his love. These things have I spoken to you, so that my *joy* may continue in you and that your joy may be full.

*"This* is My commandment: that you *love* one another just as *I loved you. Greater love has no one than this, that he lay down his life for his friends.*

*"You* are *my friends,* if you do everything I command you. No longer do I call you bondservants, for the bondman knows not what his master is doing; but *you* I have called *friends,* for all things which I heard from my Father I made known to you. You did not choose me, but I chose you, *and appointed you, that you should go and bear fruit, and that your fruit should continue; that whatever you may ask from the Father in My name he may give it you.*

"These things am I commanding you so that you may *love* one another.

### "Your Persecutors Have No Excuse"

*(Jn. 15:18-25)*

"If the world hates you, you know that it has hated Me *before* you. If you were of the world, the world would love its own; but because you are not of the world, but instead *I chose you out of* the world, because of this the world hates you. Remember the word which I said to you, *'A bondman is not greater than his lord.'* If they persecuted Me, they will persecute you also; *if* they kept My word, they will keep yours also! But they will do all these things to you on account of My name—because they know not *Him who sent me.*

"If I had not come and spoken to them, they would not have had sin; but now they have no excuse for their sin—he who hates Me hates my Father also. If I had not wrought among them works which no other has wrought, they would not have had sin; but now they have both seen and hated *both Me and my Father;* that the word might be fulfilled which has been written in their law, *'They hated me without a cause.'*

### "The Helper Will Testify of Me."

*(Jn. 15:26-16:7)*

"But when the Helper has come whom *I* will send you from the Father—*the Spirit of truth* who goes forth from the Father—*He will testify concerning Me.* And *you, too,* are bearing witness, because from the first you have been with Me.

"These things have I spoken to you, that you may not be caused to stumble. They will banish you from the synagogues; indeed, an hour is coming when whoever kills you will think that he is doing *God* a service. And they will do these things to you because they know not the Father, nor Me. But I have spoken these things to you that, whenever the hour may come, you may remember that *I* told you them.

"Now I did not tell you these things at first, because I was with you; but now I am going away to Him who sent me. And none of you is asking[f] me, 'Where are you going?' Instead, because I have said these things to you, sorrow has filled your hearts. Nevertheless, I say the truth to you, it is profitable for you *that I depart;* for if I do not go, *the Helper* will not come to you, but if I go, I will send him to you.

### *"He Will Convict the World"*
#### *(Jn. 16:8-15)*

"And when he has come, *He will convict the world of sin, and concerning righteousness, and judgment:* of sin, because they believe not upon Me; concerning righteousness, because I am going away to my Father and you will behold Me no longer; and concerning judgment, because the ruler of this world has been judged.

"Many things have I yet to say to you, but you cannot bear them now. *But when He, the Spirit of truth, has come, he will guide you into all the truth;* for he will not speak on his own authority, but *whatever he hears* he will speak, and he will declare to you the things to come. *He will glorify Me,* for he will take of my things and will declare them to you. *All things* whatever the Father has *are mine;* because of *this* said I that he will take of mine and will declare them to you.

### *"Your Grief Will Turn into Joy'*
#### *( Jn. 16:16-24)*

"A little while, and you will not behold me (and again a little while, *and you shall see me)* because *I am going away to the Father."*

Some of his disciples said therefore to one another, "What is *this* that he says to us, 'A little while, and you will not behold me (and again a little while, *and you shall see me),'* and, 'because *I am going away to the Father'?"* So they kept saying, "What *is* this 'little while' of which he speaks? We know not what he means."

Jesus knew therefore that they wished to ask him, and said to them, "Are you asking one another what I meant in saying, 'A little while, and you will not behold me (and again a little while, *and you shall see me)'?* Verily, verily, I say to you, *you* will weep and lament, but the world will rejoice; *you* will sorrow, but your grief shall be turned into joy. A woman, when in travail, has sorrow because her hour of pain has come; but when she has brought forth the child, she remembers the anguish no longer for the joy that a man-child has been born into the world. *You* also therefore now indeed have sorrow, but *I will see you again*[g] *and your hearts will rejoice; and your joy shall no one take from you.* And in *that* day you will ask me *nothing.*

"Verily, verily, I say to you, *whatever you may ask from the Father in My name, he will give it you.* Hitherto you have asked nothing in My name; *ask, and you shall receive, that your joy may be made full.*

## "I Am Going to the Father"

(Jn. 16:25-28)

"These things I have spoken to you in riddles; but there is an hour coming in which I will speak to you no longer in riddles, but will inform you plainly of the Father; in *that* day you *will ask* in My name.

"And I do not say to you that *I* will beseech the Father concerning you; *for the Father himself loves you, because you have loved Me and have believed that I came forth from God.*

"*I came forth from the Father, and have come into the world; again, I am leaving the world and am going to the Father.*"

## "I Have Overcome the World"

(Jn. 16:29-33)

His disciples said to him, "Behold, You now *are speaking* plainly and not in riddles. We *now* know that You know *all things* and need not that anyone question You. *By this we believe that You did come forth from God.*"

Jesus answered them, "Do you *now believe?* Lo, an hour is coming—*and has come already!*—when you will be scattered, each to his abode, and you will leave me alone. *Yet I am not alone, for the Father is with me.* These things have I spoken to you, that in Me you may have *peace.* In the world you have tribulation; *but take courage: I have overcome the world.*"

### 141. His Prayer of Intercession

*(Jn. 17:1-26)*

When he had uttered these things, Jesus lifted up his eyes toward heaven and said, "Father, the hour has come. Glorify thy Son, that thy Son may also glorify thee; even as thou gavest him authority over all men, that to all whom thou hast given him he might give eternal life. And this is the life eternal, that they should know thee, the only true God, and Jesus the Messiah, whom Thou didst send.

"I glorified thee on the earth; I finished the work which thou gavest me to do; and now, Father, glorify thou me with thine own self, with the glory which I had with thee before the world was.

"I made known thy name to the men whom thou hast given me out of the world; thine they were, and thou hast given them me, and they have kept thy Word. Now have they known that all things are from thee, all things which thou hast given me. For the words which thou gavest me I have given them; and they received them, and knew to a certainty that I came forth from thee, and they believed that Thou didst send me.

*"Keep Them in Thy Name"*

*"I am praying for them; I pray not for the world, but for those whom thou hast given me.* For they are thine, and all mine are thine; and thine are mine, and I have been glorified in them. And now I am no longer in the world; but these are in the world, and I am coming to thee. *Holy Father, keep them in thy name, those whom thou hast given me, that they may be one, even as we.*

"While I was with them in the world, I kept them in thy name; those whom thou hast given me I guarded, and none of them perished (except the son of perdition, that the scripture might be fulfilled). But now I am coming to thee; and these things I am speaking in the world, that they may have in themselves my joy in full measure.

"I have given them thy Word; and the world has begun to hate them, because they are not of the world even as I am not of the world. I pray not that thou shouldst take them out of the world, but shouldst keep them away from the evil. They are not of the world, even as I am not of the world. Sanctify them in thy truth; *thy Word* is truth. As thou didst send me into the world, I also sent them into the world; and for their sakes I sanctify myself, that they also may be sanctified in truth.

## "That They May Be One in Us"

"And not for these only do I pray, but also for those who will believe upon Me through their word: *that they may all be one, even as thou, Father, art in me, and I in thee; that they also may be one in us, that the world may believe that Thou didst send me.*

"And the glory which thou gavest me have I given them; that they may be one, even as we are one, I in them, and thou in me; that they may be perfected into one, and that the world may know that Thou didst send me and loved them as thou lovedst me.

"Father, those whom thou hast given me, I desire that where I am they, too, may be with me; that they may behold my glory which thou gavest me in thy love for me before the founding of the world. Righteous Father, the world also knew not thee, but I knew thee, and these knew that Thou didst send me. And I made known to them thy name, and I will make it known; that the love with which Thou lovedst me may be in them, and I in them."

## 142. "Now Take Purse...and Sword"
### (Mt. 26:30-35; Mk. 14:26-31; Lk. 22:35-39; Jn. 18:1a)

[4] Now when Jesus had spoken these things, [3] he said to them, ' When I sent you forth without purse or provision bag or sandals,[a] did you lack anything?'' And they said, ' Nothing.'' He said therefore to them, "But now, let him who has a purse *take it,* and likewise a provision bag; and let him who has no sword *sell his cloak and buy one.* For I tell you, that *this* that

has been written must yet be fulfilled in me: *'And he was numbered with transgressors;'* for the things concerning me *also have a consummation."*

And they said, "Behold, Lord, here are *two swords."* And he said to them "It is *enough."*

### On Their Way to Gethsemane

[2] And when they had sung a hymn, [3] he came out and went, as his custom was, to the Mount of Olives; and his disciples also followed him.

[1] Then said Jesus to them, *"All of you* will be caused to stumble because of me this night; for it is written,

*'I will smite the shepherd,*
*and the sheep of the flock will be scattered.'*

But after my being *raised up* I will go before you into Galilee."

But Peter answered and said to him, [2] "Even if all are made to stumble [1] because of You, [2] yet not I; *I* will never be made to stumble." [2] And Jesus said to him, "Verily I say to you, that today, during this night, *before the cock crows twice,* you will deny me three times." But [1] Peter said to him [2] even more vehemently, [1] "Even if I must *die* with You, I will not at all *deny* You!" And in like manner also spoke all the disciples.

\* \* \*

*Comment:* The foregoing account of Jesus' two distinct warnings to Peter concerning his denials constitutes a most striking example of the unity and authenticity of the whole account. So far from being contradictory, these differing warnings describe precisely what took place with respect to Peter in the following chapter (See Appendix II).

Having set His face to the cross and having prepared His own for the impending ordeal, Jesus dismissed Judas the traitor to "light the fuse," so to speak, for the consummation, as He Himself had a final counsel with the Father. His supreme hour had come when He would fulfill the Father's will in redemptive sacrifice.

# PART VII.

## THE CONSUMMATION

### Chapter 20. Hour of the Power of Darkness

*143. "Not My Will, but Thine"*
*(Mt. 26:36-46; Mk. 14:32-42; Lk. 22:40-46;Jn. 18:1b)*

¹Then came Jesus with them ⁴across the brook Kidron, where there was a garden, ¹a place called Gethsemane, ⁴into which he and his disciples entered. ³And when he had arrived at the place, he said to them, ¹"Sit here, while I go yonder and pray."

And taking with him Peter and the two sons of Zebedee, ²James and John, ¹he began to be sorrowful and ²amazed, and deeply distressed. ¹Then said he to them, "My soul is exceedingly sorrowful, even unto death; remain here, and watch with me. ³*Pray, that you enter not into temptation.*"

²And going forward ³from them ²a little farther, ³about a stone's throw, he knelt down ²on the ground, ³and ¹fell on his face ²and prayed that, if it were possible, the hour might pass from him. And he said, "Abba, Father, all things are possible unto Thee; ¹*my Father, if it be possible, let this cup pass from me. Nevertheless, not as I will, but as Thou wilt.*"

And he came to the disciples and found them sleeping, and said to Peter, ²"Simon, are you *asleep?* ¹So you could not watch with me *one hour!* Watch *and pray,* that you enter not into temptation. The spirit indeed is willing, but the flesh is *weak.*"

*"Behold, the Hour Has Come"*

²And again ¹a second time he went off and prayed, saying, "My Father, ³*if Thou art willing, take away this cup from me;*

nevertheless, [1]if this cannot pass from me unless I drink it, [3]*not my will, but Thine, be done.*" And there appeared unto him an angel from heaven, strengthening him. And being in an agony he prayed the more earnestly, and his sweat became as it were great drops of blood falling down upon the ground.

And when he rose up from prayer, he came to the disciples and found them sleeping [1]again [3]for sorrow, [2]for their eyes were heavy; [3]and he said to them, 'Why do you *sleep? Rise up and pray, so that you may not enter into temptation!*" [2]And they knew not what to answer him. [1]So he left them and went off again, and prayed a third time, saying the same thing as before.

Then came he to the disciples [2]the third time, and said to them, "Are you sleeping *even now,* and taking your rest? It is enough! [1]*Behold, the hour* [2]*has come,* [1]*and the Son of man is being betrayed into the hands of sinners. Rise,* let us be going. Lo, *my betrayer* is at hand!"

## 144. The Betrayal and Desertion

*(Mt. 26:47-56; Mk. 14:43-52; Lk. 22:47-53; Jn. 18:2-11)*

[2]And immediately, while he was yet speaking, [1]behold, [2]a great crowd drew near; [3]and he who was called Judas, one of the twelve, was leading them. [4]Now Judas, who was betraying him, also knew the place, for Jesus often had resorted there with his disciples. So Judas, having received a band of soldiers, together with officers from the chief priests and Pharisees [2]and the scribes and the elders [1]of the people, [4]was coming there with torches and lanterns, and [2]with swords and clubs.

And the betrayer had given them a token, saying, "The one whom I shall kiss, he it is;[a] seize him and lead him safely away." So on arriving he at once [3]approached Jesus to kiss him. [2]And [1]Jesus said to him, "Friend, for what purpose have you come?" [1]But he came up to Jesus and said, [2]"Master, Master! [1]*Hail, Master!* And he fervidly kissed him. [3]Jesus said to him, "Judas, are you betraying the Son of man with *a kiss?*"

*"Permit Even This!"*

⁴ Jesus therefore, knowing all the things that were coming upon him, went forward and said to them, "Whom do you seek?" They answered him, "Jesus of Nazareth!" Jesus said to them, "I AM he."ᵇ (And Judas also, he who was betraying him, was standing with them.) When therefore he said to them, "I AM he," they drew backward and fell to the ground.

So again he asked them, *"Whom do you seek?"* And they said, *"Jesus of Nazareth."* Jesus answered, "I told you that I AM he. If therefore you are seeking *Me,* let *these* go *away"* (that the word which he had spoken might be fulfilled, *"Of those whom thou hast given me, I lost none").*

¹ They then came and laid ² their hands ¹ on Jesus, and seized him. ³ Now when those ² standing ³ about him saw what would follow, they said to him, "Lord, shall we strike with the *sword?"* ¹ And behold, ⁴ Simon Peter ¹ stretched out his hand and, drawing his sword, struck the high priest's bondman ⁴ and cut off his right ear. And the name of the bondservant was Malchus. ³ But Jesus answering said, *"Permit even this!"* and he touched his ear and healed him.

*"This Is the Power of Darkness"*

⁴ Jesus said therefore to Peter, ¹ *"Put back* your sword into its ⁴ sheath; ' for all who take the sword will perish by the sword. Or do you think that I cannot now call to my Father, and he will furnish me more than twelve legions of angels? But how then would the Scriptures *be fulfilled,* that it must be so? ⁴ The cup which *the Father* has given me, *shall I not drink it?"*

³ But ¹ at that same hour Jesus said to the crowds, ² and ³ to the chief priests and captains of the temple, and elders, who had come out to arrest him, "Have you come out as against a *robber,* with swords and clubs, ' to seize me? Daily I sat with you, teaching in the temple, and you did not arrest me, ³ you stretched forth no hands against me. ¹ But this has all come to pass *that the Scriptures of the prophets may be fulfilled.* ³ This is *your* hour, and *the power of darkness."*

¹ Then all the disciples forsook him, and fled. ² And a cer-

tain young man[c] was following with him, having only a linen cloth about his body, and the young men laid hold of him; but leaving behind the linen cloth, he fled from them naked.

### 145. Jesus Is Questioned by Annas
*(Mt. 26:57; Mk. 14:53; Lk. 22:54a; Jn. 18:12-14,19-24)*

[4] The band of soldiers therefore, and the chief captain and the officers of the Jews, seized Jesus and bound him; and they led him away first to Annas, for he was the father-in-law of Caiaphas, who was the high priest that year. (It was Caiaphas who had given counsel to the Jews that it was expedient that one man should die for the people.)

[4] So the high priest[a] questioned Jesus concerning his disciples and his teaching. Jesus answered him, "*I* spoke *openly* to the world; always *I* taught *in the synagogues and in the temple*, where the Jews all assemble, and I said nothing in secret. Why do you question *me?* Question those who have heard me, as to what I said to them; behold, *they* know what I said!"

Now at his saying these things one of the officers standing by struck Jesus with the palm of his hand, saying, "Do you answer *the high priest* so?" Jesus answered him, "If I spoke wrongly, bear witness of the wrong; but if rightly, why do you strike me?"

Then Annas sent him bound to Caiaphas the high priest. [1] So those who had seized Jesus led him away [3] and brought him into the high priest's house, [1] where [2] all the chief priests and the elders and the scribes [1] had gathered together.

### 146. The First Two Denials by Peter
*(Mt. 26:58; Mk. 14:54; Lk. 22:54b-55; Jn. 18:15-18,25)*

[4] Now Simon Peter kept following Jesus [1] afar off, even to the courtyard of the high priest, [4] and so did another disciple.[a] And that disciple was known to the high priest, and went into the courtyard with Jesus, but Peter stood outside the door. The other disciple therefore, who was known to the high priest, went out and spoke to the servant girl who tended the

door, and brought Peter in.

Then the servant girl who tended the door said to Peter, *"You* are not also one of this man's disciples, are you?" He said, "I am *not."*

And the bondservants and the temple guards, because it was cold, [3] had kindled [4] a fire of coals [3] in the middle of the court-yard, [4] and were standing and warming themselves. And Peter was with them [2] by the fire, [4] standing and warming himself; [3] and when they had sat down together, [2] he sat down [3] in the midst of [1] the guards to see the outcome.[b]

[4] They said therefore to him, *"You* are not also one of his disciples, are you?" He denied it, and said,*"I am not!"*

### 147. Jesus' Trial Before Caiaphas
*(Mt. 26:59-68; Mk. 14:55-65; Lk. 22:63-65)*

[1] Now the chief priests and the elders and the entire[a] Sanhe-drin kept seeking to find false witness against Jesus, so as to put him to death, but they found none; [2] for, [1] even though many false witnesses came forward and [2] testified against him, their testimony did not agree.

[1] Then at last there came forward two false witnesses, who [2] stood up and bore witness against him, saying, "We heard [1] this man [2] say, 'I will destroy this temple [1] of God [2] that is made with hands, and in three days I will build another, not made with hands.'" But not even so did their testimony agree.

### *"Are You the Son of God?"*

So the high priest stood up in their midst and questioned Je-sus, saying, "Do you answer nothing? What is it that these witness against you?" But he was silent, and answered nothing.

Again the high priest [1] [answering] said to him, [2] "Are you *the Messiah, the Son of the Blessed?* [1] I adjure you by the liv-ing God, tell us whether *you* are *the Messiah, the Son of God."* Jesus said to him, "It is *as you have said:* [2] I AM. [1] Further-more, I say to all of you, hereafter will you see the Son of man[b] *sitting at the right hand of power and coming upon the clouds of heaven."*

Then the high priest rent his garments, saying, "He has spoken *blasphemy.* Why need we any more witnesses? Behold, you have heard his blasphemy; what do you think?" And they answered and said, *"He deserves death!"* [2] And they *all*[c] condemned him as worthy of death.

*"Prophesy!"*

Then some began to spit [1] in his face, and they struck him with their fists. [3] And the men who were holding Jesus began to mock him, and when they had blindfolded him, [2] kept slaping him [3] in his face and asking him, saying, *"Prophesy!* [1] Prophesy to *us,* you *'Messiah'!* Who is it that struck you?" [3] And many other things they kept saying blasphemously against him.

### 148. *"I Do Not Know This Man"*
#### *(Mt. 26:69-75; Mk. 14:66-72; Lk. 22:56-62; Jn. 18:25a,26-27)*

[4] Now Simon Peter [1] was sitting [2] below, out in the courtyard. And one of the high priest's servant girls, seeing Peter warming himself, [3] looked at him intently as he sat in the light and said, "This man, too, was with [2] Jesus of Nazareth." [1] And she came up to him, saying, *"You, too, were with the Galilean."* [3] Yet he denied him [1] before them all, and said, [3] "Woman, *I know him not;* [2] I do not know nor even understand what you are talking about." And he went out into the fore-court; [and a cock crowed.][a]

[1] And when he had gone out into the gateway [3] a little later, [1] another woman saw him and said to those nearby, "This man, too, was with Jesus the Nazarene." [3] And another, a man who saw him, said, "You, too, *are* one of them!" But Peter [1] again made denial, with an oath, [3] "Man, I am not; [1] I do not *know* the man!"

[2] And the servant girl saw him again, and began to say to those nearby, "This man *is* one of them." But again he made denial.

*Accusers Surround the Apostle*

[3] And after the space of about an hour another man made strong affirmation, saying, "Of a truth this man also *was with him,* for he, too, is *a Galilean."* [4] One of the bondservants of the high priest, a kinsman of the one whose ear Peter had cut off, said, "Did not *I* see you *in the garden with him?"* [2] And a- gain [1] those standing nearby came up to Peter and said, "Sure- ly you also *are* one of them! [2] For you are a Galilean, [1] and even [2] [your speech confirms it] —[1] *your speech betrays you!"* [2] But [4] Peter therefore made denial [1] then [4] again, and [2] he be- gan to curse and to swear, "I know *not* this man of whom you speak; [3] *man, I know not what you are talking about!"*

And immediately, while he was yet speaking, the cock crowed [2] a second time; [3] and the Lord turned and looked at Peter. And Peter remembered the word of the Lord, how [2] Je- sus had said to him, [3] *"Before the cock crows, you will deny me three times,"* and, [2] *"Before the cock crows twice*[b] you will deny me three times." And stricken in his thoughts, [h]he went out and wept bitterly.

### 149. The Sanhedrin Confirms the Verdict
*(Mt. 27:1-2; Mk. 15:1; Lk. 22:66-23:1)*

[2] Then immediately [3] when it was day [1] all [3] the elders of the people came together, both the chief priests and the scribes, [2] and held a consultation [1] against Jesus to put him to death; [3] and they brought him up into their [2] whole Sanhedrin,[a] [3] say- ing, "If you are *the Messiah,* tell *us."*

But he said to them, "If I should tell you, you would not at all believe; and if I also should make inquiry, you would not answer me nor let me go. *Hereafter will the Son of man be seated at the right hand of the power of God!"*

Then said they all, "So *you* are *the Son of God?"* And he said to them, "It is *as you are saying,* for *I AM."* And they said, "What need have we for more testimony? For we have heard it ourselves from his own mouth!" And the entire com- pany of them arose, [2] and they bound Jesus and took him away, [1] delivering him to Pontius Pilate, the governor.

### 150. Suicide of the Betrayer
*(Mt. 27:3-10)*

Then Judas who had betrayed him, when he saw that he was condemned, was overcome with remorse; and he returned the thirty pieces of silver to the chief priests and the elders, saying, "I have sinned by *betraying innocent blood!*" But they said, "What is that to *us? You* see to that." And casting down the pieces of silver in the temple, he departed, and went off and hanged himself.[a]

Now the chief priests took the pieces of silver, and said, *"It is not lawful* to put them into the treasury, since they are the price of blood." But they counseled together and bought with them the field of the potter, as a burying ground for strangers; thus that field is called to this day "The field of Blood." Then was fulfilled what was spoken by Jeremiah the prophet, saying, *"And I took the thirty pieces of silver, the price of him on whom a price had been set by some of the sons of Israel; and I gave them for the field of the potter, as the Lord directed me."*

### 151. Jesus Is Accused Before Pilate
*(Mt. 27:11-14; Mk. 15:2-5; Lk. 23:2-3; Jn. 18:28-38a)*

[4] So they led Jesus from Caiaphas to the Roman judgment hall; [1] and Jesus stood before the governor. [4] Now it was early, so they did not go into the judgment hall, that they should not be defiled but might eat the Passover.[a]

Pilate therefore went out to them; and he said, "What accusation do you bring against this man?" They answered and said to him, "If he were not an evildoer, we would not have delivered him up to you."

So Pilate said to them, *"You* take him and judge him according to *your* law. The Jews therefore said to him, *"We* are *not permitted* to put anyone to death"—that there might *be fulfilled* what Jesus had said in signifying by what death he would die.[b]

[3] But they began to accuse him, saying, "We found this fellow perverting the nation and *forbidding to give tribute to Caesar,* saying that he himself is MESSIAH, *a king."*

[1] And the chief priests and the elders [2] continued to accuse him of many things. [1] But he answered nothing. Then said Pilate to him, [2] "Do you answer *nothing?* [1] *Do you not hear* how many things they are charging against you?" But Jesus still answered nothing even to one charge, so that the governor marveled greatly.

## *"Are You the King of the Jews?"*

[4] Pilate therefore went back into the judgment hall and called Jesus, and [1] he asked him, *"Are you the King of the Jews?"* [3] And he answered and said to him, "It is *as you are saying."* Then [4] Jesus [1] said to him, [4] "Are *you* asking this, of your own accord, or did others tell you this of me?"

Pilate answered, "Am *I* a Jew? *Your own nation and the chief priests* delivered you up to me. *What have you done?"* Jesus answered, *"My* Kingdom *is not of this world.* If my Kingdom were of this world, my attendants would fight, that I might not be delivered up to the Jews; but *now* is my Kingdom *not from here."*[c]

So Pilate said to him, *"You are* therefore *a king?"* Jesus answered, "It is *as you are saying:* that *I am* a King; *for this was I born.* And for *this* came I into the world: *that I should bear witness to the truth.* Everyone who is of the truth *heeds My voice."* Pilate said to him, "What *is* truth?"

## *152. Jesus Refuses to Answer Herod*
### *(Lk. 23:4-12; Jn. 18:38b)*

[4] And on saying this he went out again to the Jews, and [3] said to the chief priests and the crowds, "I find *no guilt* in this man." But they kept insisting, saying, *"He is stirring up the people,* teaching *throughout all Judea,* starting from Galilee and even to *this* place."

Now when Pilate heard this, he asked whether the man was a Galilean; and on learning that he was from the jurisdiction of Herod, he sent him up to Herod, who also was in Jerusalem at that time.

And when Herod saw Jesus, he was exceedingly glad; for he had wanted for a long time to see him, since he had heard many things about him and hoped to see some miraculous sign wrought by him. So he plied him with many questions; but he answered him nothing, though the chief priests and the scribes were standing there with violent accusations.

Then Herod with his soldiers, having ridiculed and mocked him, arrayed him in gaudy apparel[a] and sent him back to Pilate. And that day Pilate and Herod became friends with each other, for before this there had been enmity between them.

### 153. *"Do You Wish Barabbas, or Jesus?"*
*(Mt. 27:15-23a; Mk. 15:6-14; Lk. 23:13-22; Jn. 18:39-40)*

[3] Then Pilate called together the chief priests and the rulers and the people, and said to them, "You brought me this man as one stirring up subversion; and behold, on examining him before you *I* found in this man *no guilt* of the things of which you are accusing him; and neither did Herod, for he sent him back to us. So behold, *nothing worthy of death* has been done by him. [4] But you have a custom that I should release to you one man at the Passover; [3] I will therefore chastise him, and release him."

[1] Now at the feast the governor *was* accustomed [3] [of necessity] [1] to release for the people one prisoner, whomever they wished; and they had then, [2] bound with the fellow insurgents, [1] a notable prisoner called Barabbas, [4] a robber [3] who, for a certain insurrection in the city and for murder, had been thrown into prison.

[1] When therefore they had gathered together [2] and the multitude cried out, asking him to do as he always did for them, Pilate answered them, saying, [1] *"Whom do you wish me to release for you?*[a] Barabbas, or *Jesus,* who is called *'Messiah'?"* [2] For he knew that it was through envy the chief priests had

delivered him up; [1] and when he was sitting on the judgment seat, his wife sent word to him, saying, "Do nothing to *that righteous Man,* for I suffered many things today in a dream because of him."

*"Not This Man! Crucify Him!"*

But the chief priests and the elders [2] stirred up [1] the crowds to ask him [2] rather to release for them Barabbas, [1] and to do away with Jesus.

So the governor answered and said to them, "Which of the two do you wish me to release for you? [4] Would you therefore that I release for you *the King of the Jews?"* [1] But they said, *'Barabbas!"* [3] And [4] then again all of them cried out together, saying, *"Not this man!* [3] *Away* with this man, and release for us *Barabbas!"*

[3] Pilate therefore in a desire to release Jesus called to them again, [2] and in answer said, [1] "What then shall I do with *Jesus* who is called *'Messiah,'* [2] whom you call *'King' of the Jews?"* But they [1] all [2] cried out again, [3] saying, [1] "Let him be *crucified!"* [3] And they kept on shouting, *"Crucify! Crucify* him!"

So a third time [2] Pilate said to them, "Why, what *evil* has he done? [3] I found in him *no* guilt deserving death; so after chastising him, I *will release* him."[b]

### 154. *"He Made Himself the Son of God!"*
*(Mt. 27:23b-31;Mk. 15:15-20; Lk. 23:23-25; Jn. 19:1-16)*

[4] Pilate then took Jesus therefore and scourged him. And the soldiers wove together a crown out of thorns and placed it on his head; and they thrust a purple garment about him, and said, *"Hail, 'King' of the Jews!"* and kept giving him blows with their hands.

Pilate therefore came out again, and said to them, "Behold, I am bringing him out to you, that you may know that I find *no guilt* in him." So Jesus came out, wearing the crown of thorns and the purple garment; and Pilate said to them, *"Behold the man!"*

When therefore the chief priests and the officers saw him, they cried out, saying, *"Crucify! Crucify!"* Pilate said to them, *"You* take and crucify him; for *I* find *no guilt* in him."

The Jews answered him, *"We have a law,* and by our law he *ought to die,* because *he made himself the Son of God."*

So when Pilate heard this charge, he was the more afraid; and he went again into the judgment hall, and said to Jesus, "From where *are* you?" But Jesus gave him no answer.

Pilate therefore said to him, "You are not talking to *me?* Do you not know that I have authority to crucify you—and authority to release you?" Jesus answered, "You would have no authority at all against Me, were it not given you from above. Because of this he who delivered me up to you has the greater sin."

, At this answer Pilate kept seeking to release him, but the Jews cried out, saying, "If you release this man, you are *not a friend of Caesar.* Anyone making himself out to be the King is speaking *against Caesar!"*

*"His Blood Be on Us!"*

Pilate therefore at hearing this brought Jesus outside; and he sat down on the judgment seat in a place that is called the Pavement (but in Hebrew, Gabbatha). Now it was the Preparation day of[a] the Passover, and about six in the morning. And he said to the Jews, *"Behold your King."*

But they cried out, *"Away* with him! *Away* with him! *Crucify* him!" [3] And they were insistent, [1] and cried out all the more, [3] demanding loudly that he be crucified. [4] Pilate said to them, "Shall I crucify your *King?"* The chief priests answered, "We have no king but *Caesar!"*

[1] So Pilate, when he saw that nothing availed, but rather that a riot was building up, took water and washed his hands before the multitude, saying, "I am *innocent* of the blood of *this [righteous] man. You* will bear witness to it." Then all the people answered and said, "His blood be on *us! And on our children!"*

[3] And their voices, and those of the chief priests, prevailed; so Pilate, [2] desiring to satisfy the multitude, [3] gave sentence

that it should be as they demanded. And he released for them the man [2] Barabbas, [3] whom they asked for, who had been thrown into prison for *insurrection and murder,* but Jesus he delivered up to their will [4] that he should be crucified.

## Mockery in the Praetorium

[1] Then the soldiers of the governor took Jesus [2] and led him away into the court that is called the Praetorium; and they summoned together their whole battalion [1] to confront him. And when they had stripped him, [2] they clothed him with purple, and [1] placed around him a crimson cloak.[b]

And plaiting a crown of thorns they put it upon his head, and placed a reed in his right hand, [2] and bowing their knees in homage before him, [1] kept mocking him, saying, *"Hail, 'King' of the Jews!"* And they spat upon him, and took the reed and struck him on his head.

And after mocking him they stripped him of the cloak and [2] the purple garments, and put on him his own clothing, and led him out to crucify him.

## 155. To the Place That Is Called Golgotha
### (Mt. 27:32-38; Mk. 15:21-28; Lk. 23:26-34; Jn. 19:17-24)

[4] And he went forth, bearing his own cross. [1] But as they were proceeding on out, they found a man of Cyrene [2] who was passing by, [1] Simon by name [2] (the father of Alexander and Rufus),[a] [3] coming in from the country; [1] him [3] they seized, and laid on him the cross [2] and compelled him [3] to bear it behind Jesus.

And there were following him a great multitude of the people, and of women who also were bewailing and lamenting him. But Jesus turning to them said, "Daughters of Jerusalem, do not weep for me, *but for yourselves and for your children.* For behold, days are coming in which they will say, 'Blessed are the barren, and the wombs which never bore, and the breasts which never nursed!' Then will they begin to say to the mountains, *'Fall on us!'* and to the hills, *'Cover us!'* For if they do these things in the tree that is green, *what will happen in the dry?"*[b]

## *"Forgive Them, Father"*

And two others also, who were evildoers, were led away with him to be put to death.

And when [2] they brought him [3] to the place called the Skull, [4] which is called in the Hebrew Golgotha, [2] they offered him vinegar to drink, mixed with myrrh; but [1] when he tasted it he would not drink it. [4] There they crucified him; [2] and it was about nine o'clock.[c] [3] [But Jesus said, "Father, *forgive them,* for they know not what they do."]

[1] And with him [2] they crucified [3] the evildoers, [2] two robbers, [4] one at either side and Jesus between them; [2] [and the scripture was fulfilled which says, *"And he was numbered with transgressors."]*

## *Rome's Official Accusation*

[4] And Pilate also wrote an inscription and [1] they put it [4] on the cross [1] above his head; [2] and his accusation was written,

[1]                                THIS IS

[4]                       JESUS OF NAZARETH
                            THE KING OF THE JEWS.                          [d]

Many therefore of the Jews read this inscription, for the place where Jesus was crucified was near the city, and it was written in Hebrew, Greek, and Latin. So the chief priests of the Jews said to Pilate, "Write not, 'The King of the Jews,' but *'He said,* I am King of the Jews.'" Pilate answered, "What I have written *I have written."*

The soldiers therefore, when they had crucified Jesus, took his garments and made four parts, to each soldier a part, without the tunic, [2] casting lots as to what part each should take. [4] But the tunic was seamless, woven from the top throughout, so they said to each other, "Let us not tear it, but cast lots for *it,* to see whose it shall be;" that the scripture might be fulfilled which says,

*"They divided my garments among themselves,*

*and for my raiment they cast lots."*

## 156. The First Three Hours on the Cross
### (Mt. 27:39-44; Mk. 15:29-32; Lk. 23:35-37,39-43; Jn. 19:25-27)

[4] These things therefore the soldiers did, [1] and sitting down they kept guard of him there, [3] and the people stood beholding the sight. [2] And those passing by kept railing at him, wagging their heads[a] and saying, *"Aha!* You who would 'destroy the temple and build it in three days,' *save yourself!"...* [1] "If you *are* the Son of God, *come down from the cross!"*

And likewise also the chief priests, [2] mocking him to one another with the scribes [1] and elders, said, "He 'saved' others; *himself he cannot save!"...* [3] "Let him save *himself,* if he is *'the Christ, the Chosen One of God.'"...* [1] "If he is the 'King' of Israel, [2] let *'the Messiah, the King of Israel'* come down now *from the cross,* that we may *see* and believe [1] him."..."He trusted in *God;* let *Him* deliver him now, if He desires him, for he said, *'I AM the Son of God.'"*

[3] And the soldiers also kept mocking him, coming to him and offering him sour wine, and saying, *"If you are* the King of the Jews, *save yourself!"*

## A Repentant Robber; and Jesus' Mother

[1] Now the robbers also who were crucified with him began to reproach him in the same manner, [3] and one of the hanged evildoers kept on railing at him, saying, *"If you are* the Messiah, save yourself *and us!"* But the other answered and rebuked him, saying, "Do you not even fear *God,* since you are under the same condemnation? And *we* indeed *justly,* for we are receiving due reward for our deeds, but *this* man did *nothing* amiss." And he said to Jesus, "[Lord,] *remember* me when You come in your *Kingdom."* And Jesus said to him, "Verily, I say to you, *today* shall you be with Me *in Paradise."*[b] And it was about twelve noon.

[4] And there were standing by the cross of Jesus his mother and his mother's sister, also Mary the wife of Clopas, and Mary Magdalene. When Jesus therefore saw his mother and the disci-

ple whom he loved standing nearby, he said to his mother, "Woman, behold *your son.*" Then he said to the disciple, "Behold *your mother.*" And from that hour the disciple took her into his own home.[c]

### 157. *"It Is Finished!"*
*(Mt. 27:45-50; Mk. 15:33-37; Lk. 23:44-45a,46; Jn. 19:28-30)*

[1] Now from the noontime there was darkness over all the land till three in the afternoon, [3] and the sun was obscured.[a] [2] And at three o'clock Jesus cried out with a loud voice, saying, *"Eloi, Eloi, lama sabachthani?"* which being translated is, *"My God, my God, why hast Thou forsaken me?"* [1] And some of those standing there, when they heard it, said, [2] "Behold, [1] this man is calling *Elijah.*"

[4] Upon this, Jesus, knowing that all things were now ended, said, that the scripture might be fulfilled, *"I thirst."* Now a vessel full of sour wine[b] was standing there, [1] and one of them ran at once and, taking a sponge and filling it with the wine, put it on a [4] hyssop [1] stalk [4] and brought it to his mouth, [2] saying—[1] and the others said—[2] "Permit this;[c] let us see if Elijah *will come* to take him down, [1] to save him."

Then [4] Jesus therefore on receiving the wine [1] cried out again with a loud voice, [4] *"It is finished!"* And he bowed his head, [3] and said, "Father, into Thy hands I commit my spirit." And having said these things, [4] he yielded up his spirit.

### 158. *Awesome Wonders Follow*
*(Mt. 27:51-56; Mk. 15:38-41; Lk. 23:45b,47-49; Jn. 19:31-37)*

[3] Now the centurion [2] who stood confronting him nearby, when he saw that he [cried out] thus [and] expired, [3] glorified God by saying, "Truly this *was* a righteous man!"

[1] And behold, the veil of the temple was wrenched in two from top to bottom.[a] And the earth was shaken, and the rocks were rent and the tombs were opened, and many bodies of the saints who had fallen asleep arose; and they came forth out of the tombs after his resurrection, entering into the holy city

and appearing to many.

And the centurion and those who were with him standing guard over Jesus, when they saw the earthquake and the things that took place, were struck with fear and said, [2] "Surely this man *was* a son of a god!"[b] [3] And all the crowds who had come together to this sight, having seen the things that were taking place returned home beating their breasts.

And all those who knew him, and the women who had followed Jesus from Galilee, stood at a distance and beheld these things; [2] among whom were Mary Magdalene, and Mary the mother of James the younger and of Joses,[c] and Salome [1] the mother of the sons of Zebedee, [2] women who, when he was in Galilee, had followed him and ministered to him, and many other women who had come up with him to Jerusalem.

### The Scriptures Twice Again Are Fulfilled

Now [4] since it was the Preparation day (for that Sabbath was a special day),[d] the Jews therefore, to keep the bodies from remaining on the cross on the Sabbath, asked Pilate that their legs might be broken and they might be taken away. So the soldiers came and broke the legs of the first, and of the other who was crucified with him. But when they came to Jesus and saw that he was dead already, they did not break his legs; but one of the soldiers pierced his side with a spear, and immediately there came out blood and water.

And *he who saw it* has borne witness (and his testimony is true, and he *knows* that he is telling the truth) *so that you*[e] *may believe.* For these things came to pass that the scripture might be fulfilled, *"Not a bone of him shall be broken;"* and again another scripture says, *"They shall look on him whom they pierced."*

### 159. Entombed in Joseph's Garden
*(Mt. 27:57-61; Mk. 15:42-47; Lk. 23:50-56; Jn. 19:38-42)*

[4] And after these things, [2] when it was already evening, [1] there came [3] a man named Joseph, [1] a rich man[a] [3] from the Jewish city of Arimathea, [1] who was also himself a disciple of

Jesus, [4] but secretly for fear of the Jews; [2] who was a reputable member of the Sanhedrin, [3] a good and righteous man who had not assented to their counsel and deed and was also himself looking for the Kingdom of God. This man, [2] since it was the Preparation, that is, the day before the Sabbath, went with boldness to Pilate and asked [4] that he might take away the body of Jesus.

[2] But Pilate wondered if he were dead so soon, and calling for the centurion he questioned him whether he had been for some time dead; [1] then [2] on learning this from the centurion, he granted the body to Joseph.

He bought [4] therefore [2] cloth of fine linen, and [4] went and [3] took down the body. [4] And there came also Nicodemus (he who at the beginning came to Jesus by night), bringing a mixture of myrrh and aloes, about seventy-five pounds.[b] They took away therefore the body of Jesus [2] and wrapped him in the [1] clean [4] linen cloths with the spices, as is the Jews' burial custom.

Now in the place where he was crucified there was a garden, and in the garden a new sepulchre, [1] which Joseph had hewn [2] out of the rock and [3] where no one had ever been laid. [4] So because [3] it was the Preparation day and the Sabbath was coming on, [4] they laid Jesus there, for the sepulchre was near at hand; [1] and they rolled a great stone [2] against the door of the sepulchre [1] and departed.

[3] And the women who came with him from Galilee had followed, [1] Mary Magdalene and the other Mary, [2] the mother of Joses, [1] and sitting across from the sepulchre [3] they saw the tomb and how his body was laid; then they returned, and rested on the Sabbath day according to the commandment.

*160. The Tomb Is Made "Secure"*

   *(Mt. 27:62-66)*

[1] But on the morrow that followed the Preparation day the chief priests and the Pharisees came together before Pilate, saying, "Sir, we remember that that impostor while yet alive said, *'After three days I will arise.'* Command therefore that

the grave be made secure till the third day,[a] lest his disciples come by night and steal him away, and say to the people, *'He has risen from the dead,'* and the last deception be worse than the first."

And Pilate said to them, "You have a guard detachment; go and make it as secure as you can." So they went and made the sepulchre secure, sealing the stone[b] and stationing the guard.


## Chapter 21. Risen Victorious


### 161. *An Earth-shaking Dawn*

*(Mt. 28:1-15; Mk. 16:1-11; Lk. 23:56-24:12; Jn. 20:1-18)*

[2] Now when the Sabbath was past, [1] Mary Magdalene, and the other Mary [2] the mother of James, and Salome, bought spices that they might come and anoint him. And [3] on the first day of the week at early dawn they came, and certain others with them, [1] to see the sepulchre, [3] bringing the spices [3] and ointments [3] which they had prepared.[a]

[1] And behold, there was a great earthquake; for an angel of the Lord descended from heaven, and came and rolled away the stone from the door, and sat upon it. His appearance was like lightning, and his raiment white as snow; and for fear of him those on guard trembled, and became like dead men.[b]

[2] [Now after Jesus rose, early on the first day of the week, he appeared first to Mary Magdalene,[c] out of whom he had cast seven demons.] [4] Mary came to the sepulchre while it was yet dark, and saw that the stone had been removed from the tomb. She ran therefore and came to Simon Peter, and to the other disciple, he whom Jesus loved, and said to them, *"They took away the Lord from the sepulchre! And we know not where they laid him."*[d]

Peter therefore and the other disciple[e] [3] [arose, and] [4] went forth and ran [3] [toward the sepulchre.] [4] And they began to run together, but the other disciple outran Peter and reached the sepulchre first; and stooping down he saw the linen cloths lying there, but did not go in. Simon Peter therefore came following him, and he went into the sepulchre; [3] [and stooping down,] [4] he saw the linen cloths lying [3] [by themselves], [4] and the napkin, which had been about his head, not lying with the linen cloths but folded up in a place by itself.[f]

Then therefore the other disciple also, who had reached the tomb first, went in, and he saw and believed; for as yet they did not understand the scripture,[g] that he must rise from the dead. So the disciples departed again to their abode, [3] [wondering at what had come to pass.]

## *"Rabboni!"*

[4] But Mary kept standing outside near the sepulchre, weeping. While therefore she was weeping, she stooped and looked into the sepulchre; and she beheld two angels in white sitting, one at the head and the other at the feet, where the body of Jesus had lain.

And they asked her, "Woman, why are you weeping?" She said to them, *"Because they took away my Lord, and I know not where they laid him."* And when she had thus spoken, she turned around and saw Jesus standing, but did not know that it was Jesus.

Jesus said to her, "Woman, why are you weeping; whom are you seeking?" She, supposing him to be the gardener, said to him, "Sir, if *you* bore him away, tell me where you laid him, and *I* will take him away." Jesus said to her, *"Mary."* Turning about, she said to him, *"Rabboni!"* (which is to say, *dear Teacher!).*

Jesus said to her, "Do not hold me, for I have not yet ascended to my Father. But go to my brethren, and say to them, *'I am ascending to my Father and your Father, and to my God and your God.'"*

Mary Magdalene [2] went and told those who had been with him, as they mourned and wept, [4] that she had seen the Lord and he had spoken these things to her; [2] but they, though hearing that he was *alive* and *had been seen* by her, disbelieved it.

## At the Tomb After Sunrise

[3] Now Joanna and Mary the mother of James and the other women with them[h] [2] came to the sepulchre when the sun had risen. And they were saying among themselves, "Who will roll us away the stone from the door of the sepulchre?" (For it was very great.) But when they looked up, they saw that the stone *had been* rolled away.

Then on entering the sepulchre [3] they found not the body [of the Lord Jesus]. But it came to pass that, as they were much perplexed about this, [2] they saw a young man sitting at the right side, clothed in a long, white garment. And they were greatly amazed; [3] behold, *two* men stood by them in dazzling garments.[i]

And as they became terrified and bowed their faces to the ground, [1] the angel answered and said to the women, "Do not fear; [2] do not be amazed. [1] For I know that you seek Jesus [2] of Nazareth, who was crucified. [3] Why seek *the living* among the *dead?* [2] *He is not here,* [1] *for he has risen, as he said.* [3] Remember how he spoke to you,[j] while he was yet in Galilee, saying, 'The Son of man must be delivered into the hands of sinful men, and be crucified, *and the third day rise again.*'"

And they remembered his words; [2] and he said to them, [1] "Come, see the place where the Lord lay. [2] But go [1] quickly and tell his disciples, [2] *and Peter,*[k] [1] that *'He has risen from the dead, and behold, he is going before you into Galilee; there shall you see him,* [2] *as he said to you;*[l] lo, I have told you."

## "Rejoice!"

[2] So they went out quickly and fled from the sepulchre, for trembling and astonishment possessed them. Neither said they anything to anyone, for they were afraid; [1] and they started to run to tell his disciples.

But as they were on their way, behold, *Jesus* met them, saying, *"Rejoice!"* And they came and seized him by his feet,[m] and worshiped him. Then said Jesus to them, "Fear not; go tell my brethren to go into *Galilee,* and there shall they see me."

[3] And they returned [1] with great joy [3] and told all these

things to the eleven apostles, and to all the rest. But these words seemed to them as idle tales, and they did not believe[n] the women.

*Bribery of the Guard*

[1] Now as they were going, behold, some of the guard came into the city, and reported to the chief priests all that had come to pass. And they, when they had assembled with the elders and counseled together, gave the soldiers a large sum of money, saying, "Say that *'His disciples came by night and stole him away while we slept.'*[o] And if this comes to the governor's ears, we will 'persuade' him and free you from trouble."

So they took the money and did as they were told, and this report is spread abroad among the Jews to the present day.

*162. Jesus and Two on the Emmaus Road*

(Mk. 16:12-13; Lk. 24:13-35)

[2] [Then after these things he was revealed in another manner.] [3] And behold, that same day two of them [2] [were walking into the country,] [3] to a village called Emmaus, about seven miles from Jerusalem; and they were talking together about all these things that had taken place. And it came to pass that, as they conversed and reasoned, *Jesus himself* drew near and walked with them; but their eyes were held from recognizing him.

And he said to them, "What are these things which you are discussing with each other, as you walk with sad faces?" And one, whose name was Cleopas, answered and said to him, "Are *you* the only sojourner in Jerusalem who has not known the things that have happened there in recent days?"

And he asked of them, "What things?" And they said to him, "The things concerning *Jesus of Nazareth,* a man who was a prophet mighty in deed and word before God and all the people; and how the chief priests and our rulers delivered him up to be condemned to death, and crucified him. Now *we* were trusting that it was he who *would redeem Israel.*

"But to top it all, this is *the third day* since these things happened. And besides, certain women from among us astonished us, who were at the sepulchre early in the morning and did not find his body; and they came saying that they had even seen a vision of *angels,* who said that he was *alive!* And some of those who were with us went to the sepulchre and found it so, as the women had said, but him they did not see."

*"Believe the Prophets!"*

Then said he to them, "O foolish ones, and slow of heart to believe *all* the things which the prophets uttered! *Was it not needful* that the Messiah *should suffer these things* and enter into *his glory?"* And beginning from Moses and all the prophets he expounded to them in all the Scriptures the things concerning himself.[a]

Then they drew near to the village where they were going, and he made as though he would go farther; but they constrained him, saying, *"Lodge* with us, for it is toward evening and the day is now far spent." So he went in to lodge with them.

And it came to pass, as he reclined at table with them, that he took the bread and blessed and broke it, and began to give it to them. And their eyes were opened and they knew him; and he vanished out of their sight. Then said they to each other, "Did not our hearts burn within us, as he talked with us on the road and kept opening up to us *the Scriptures?"*

*His Appearance to Peter Convinces*

And rising up that same hour they returned to Jerusalem; and they found the eleven and those with them assembled together, saying, *"The Lord has risen indeed!* And he appeared to *Simon!"*

So they told the things that had happened on the road, and how he was known by them in the breaking of the bread; [2] [but they did not believe them.][b]

## 163. Sunday Evening with the Disciples
### (Lk. 24:36-43; Jn. 20:19-23)

[3] But as they were speaking these things, [4] it being therefore evening of that first day of the week, the doors being shut where the disciples were assembled, for fear of the Jews,[a] Jesus [3] himself [4] came and stood in their midst and said to them, *"Peace to you!"*

[3] Yet they were shocked and were filled with fear, and thought that they were beholding a spirit. But he said to them, "Why are you troubled? And why do doubtings arise in your hearts? Behold my hands and my feet, that it is *I myself*. Handle me, and see; for a spirit does not have flesh and bones, as you see *I have."* [4] And when he had said this, he showed them his hands and feet, and his side.

Then did the disciples rejoice at seeing the Lord. [3] And while they were still disbelieving for joy and were filled with wonder, he said to them, "Have you anything here to eat?" And they gave him a piece of broiled fish and of a honeycomb, and he took and ate it before them.[b]

[4] Jesus therefore said again to them, *"Peace to you! As the Father has sent Me forth, so am I sending you."* And when he had said this, he breathed on them, and said to them, *"Take the Holy Spirit.* Anyone's sins which you forgive, they have been forgiven them, and anyone's sins which you retain, they have been retained."[c]

## 164. The Convincing of Thomas
### (Jn. 20:24-29)

Now Thomas, called Didymus, one of the twelve, was not with them when Jesus came. The other disciples therefore said to him, *"We have seen the Lord!"* But he said to them, "Unless I see in his hands the imprint of the nails, and press my finger into the mark of the nails, and my hand into his side, I will *not at all believe."*

Then after eight days[a] his disciples were again indoors, and Thomas with them. Though the doors had been shut, Jesus came and stood in their midst, and said, *"Peace to you!"*

Then said he to Thomas, "Bring here your finger and look at my hands, and bring your hand and press it into my side, and be not unbelieving but *believing."* And Thomas answered and said to him, *"My Lord and my God!"* Jesus said to him, "Because you have seen me, Thomas, you have believed; blessed are they who have *not* seen and yet have believed."

### 165. With Seven Disciples in Galilee
   *(Jn. 21:1-24)*

After these things Jesus revealed himself to the disciples again, this time at the Sea of Tiberias, and he did so in this way.

There were together Simon Peter and Thomas called Didymus and Nathanael of Cana of Galilee, and the sons of Zebedee and two others of his disciples. Simon Peter said to them, "I am going *fishing.*"[a] They said to him, "We also are going with you." They went out at once and climbed into the boat. But that night they caught nothing.

But when morning had now come, Jesus was standing on the shore, though the disciples did not know that it was Jesus. So Jesus said to them, "Children, have you anything to eat?" They replied to him, "No." And he said to them, "Cast out the net on the *right* side of the boat, and you will find some." So they cast it, and now they could not draw it in for the size of the haul.

That disciple whom Jesus loved said therefore to Peter, *"It is the Lord!"* So when Simon Peter heard that it was the Lord, he thrust his coat around him, for he was naked, and flung himself into the sea. And the other disciples came in the small ship (for they were not far from shore, perhaps a hundred yards) dragging the net filled with fish.

### *"Come to Breakfast"*

When therefore they got out on shore, they saw a fire of coals that had been laid there, and fish placed upon it, and bread. Jesus said to them, "Bring some of the fish you have just caught." Simon Peter went on board and drew the net to shore, filled with one hundred fifty-three large fish. And in spite of there being so many the net was not torn.

Jesus said to them, "Come; *have breakfast."* But not one of the disciples dared ask him, "Who are *you?"* For they knew that it was the Lord. Jesus therefore came and took the bread and gave to them, and likewise of the fish. This was now the third time that Jesus was revealed to his disciples after he was raised from the dead.

### *"Do You Love Me, Simon?"*

When therefore they had eaten breakfast, Jesus said to Simon Peter, "Simon, son of John, do you *love* me, *more than these?"* He said to him, "Yes, Lord; *You* know my *affection*[b] for You." He said to him, *"Feed My lambs."*

Again a second time he said to him, "Simon, son of John, *do* you *love* me?" He said to him, *"Yes,* Lord! *You* know my *affection* for You." He said to him, *"Shepherd My sheep."*

He said to him the third time, "Simon, son of John, do you *have affection* for me?" Peter was *grieved* because of the third question, "Do you *have affection* for me?" and he said to him, "Lord, *You* know *all things; You know* that I *have affection* for You!."

Jesus said to him, *"Feed My sheep!* Verily, verily, I say to you, when you were younger, you girded yourself and walked where you desired; but when you are old, you will stretch out your hands and another will gird you and carry you where you would not go." Now this he said to signify by what death he would glorify God. And when he had spoken this, he said to him, *"Follow Me."*

### *The Story Told by John Closes*

But Peter turned about and saw following them the disciple whom Jesus loved, who also at the supper had leaned against his breast and said, "Lord, *who* is he that betrays You?" At seeing him Peter said to Jesus, "But what of *this* man, Lord?" Jesus said to him, "If I desire that he remain *till I come,* what is it to *you? Follow Me!"*

Therefore the saying spread abroad among the brethren that that disciple would not die; yet Jesus did not tell him that he would not die, but said, "If I desire that he remain *till I come, what is it to you?"* He is the disciple who testifies of these things and wrote these things, and we know that his testimony is true.

### 166. On a Mountain in Galilee

(Mt. 28:16-20)

[1] Then the eleven disciples proceeded into Galilee to the mountain[a] to which Jesus had directed them. And when they saw him, they worshiped him, though some doubted.

And Jesus came to them and addressed them, saying, *"All authority has been given unto Me in heaven and upon earth. Go therefore and disciple all the nations, baptizing them in the name of the Father and of the Son and of the Holy Spirit, teaching them to observe everything I commanded you. And lo, I am with you always, until the consummation of the age."*[b]

### 167. His Final Appearing and Ascension

(Mk. 16:14-20b; Lk. 24:44-53)

[2] [Afterward he was manifested to the eleven as they were reclining at table;[a] and he reproached their unbelief and hardness of heart, because they had not believed those who saw him after he had risen.

And he said to them, *"Go into all the world and proclaim the Glad News to the whole creation. He who believes and is baptized shall be saved, but he who disbelieves shall be condemned.*

*"And these miraculous signs will accompany those who believe: in My name will they cast out demons; they will speak in new tongues; they will pick up serpents; and if they drink any deadly thing, it will not in any way hurt them; they will lay hands on the sick and they will recover."*]

*Parting Words to the Eleven*[b]

³ And he said to them, "These are the words which I spoke to you while I was yet with you: that *all things must be fulfilled* which have been written in the law of Moses and the prophets and the psalms concerning me."

Then opened he their understanding that they might comprehend the Scriptures, and said to them, *"Thus it has been written, and so it was needful, that the Messiah should suffer and rise from the dead on the third day; and that repentance and remission of sins should be proclaimed in his name to all the nations, beginning at Jerusalem.*

*"And you are witnesses of these things. And behold, I am sending forth the promise of my Father upon you. But remain in the city of Jerusalem till you are clothed with power from on high."*

*He Ascends from the Mount of Olives*

² So then the Lord Jesus, after speaking thus to them, ³ led them out as far as to Bethany; and he lifted up his hands and blessed them. And it came to pass that, as he was blessing them, he was parted from them [and was carried up into heaven, ² and sat at the right hand of God].

³ And they [worshiped him, and] returned to Jerusalem with great joy and were continually in the temple, praising and blessing God. ² [And they went forth and preached everywhere, the Lord working with them and confirming the message by the miraculous signs that followed.]

## 168. That You May Have Life

*(Jn. 21:25; 20:30-31)*

⁴ Now Jesus also wrought in the presence of his disciples many other miraculous signs which are not written in this book; ⁴ if they were written one by one, I suppose that not even the world itself could contain the books that would be written.

[4] But these have been written *that you may believe that* Jesus is THE MESSIAH, THE SON OF GOD, and *that believing you may have life in His name.*

\* \* \*

*Comment.* This story of Christ's death and resurrection fulfills the proto-evangel promise of Genesis 3:15 that the "seed of the woman" would be crushed temporarily by the "seed of the serpent." But the cross also provided for the fulfillment of the corollary of that promise, that the serpent's head would be ultimately crushed. That final crushing of Satan will include also the destruction of his kingdom of darkness and the establishment of God's Kingdom of righteousness in the earth. In the cross, therefore, Christ provided for the fulfillment of this twofold commission from the Father—to provide redemption for men and to reclaim God's Kingdom and authority in all spheres.

During the present age, however, Christ is fulfilling the redemptive aspect of His work by calling those that will to enter His spiritual Kingdom by faith. As the human kingdom can be entered only by physical birth, so God's Kingdom can be entered only by spiritual birth. This spiritual life is offered to all men and is produced by God's Spirit as one responds positively to this, God's testimony concerning His Son. The final words summarize this redemptive purpose:

"But these [records] have been written
that you may believe that
JESUS IS THE MESSIAH, THE SON OF GOD,
and that believing,
YOU MAY HAVE LIFE IN HIS NAME."

# APPENDIX I

## THE UNIQUE PRINCIPLE OF ARRANGEMENT

### THE PRINCIPLE OF FOUR-PART HARMONY

This combination of the four Gospels is unique in several ways and is believed to be the first *true* harmony of the Gospels. Its first distinction is that it combines the four Gospels into a four-part harmony rather than presenting them in four columns as four "solos." Many such four-column "Harmonies" have been produced, but the effect has not always been harmony. Often disharmony has been the result as seeming discrepancies have been brought to light without indicating how they are resolved. Such "harmonies" have served incalculable service in bringing together the pertinent materials relative to each segment of the Gospel story; but they make no attempt at true harmony, for that is not their basic function.

### THE PRINCIPLE OF *MINUTE SUPPLEMENTATION*

The second distinction of this combination relates to its principle of interweaving the four accounts. Several attempts at interweaving the Gospels have been made during this century, but none has been produced that completely incorporates all the details. The principle that has usually guided these works is that of presenting the particular passage from the Gospel giving the fullest account and ignoring the details supplied by the shorter accounts (or placing them in the footnotes). When carefully observed, the result of such a superficial interweaving is that many pertinent details are omitted, and thus, discrepancies seem to appear. The incompleteness of such accounts may be illustrated by referring to the story of Jesus' baptism, where it is natural to use Matthew's text, the fullest account. Although he does give the fullest account of the event, there are several details supplied by Mark and Luke which are not recorded. These details may seem unimportant and minor, but they were not unimportant to the Spirit of God Who gave them.

Other interweavings have been produced which have sought to incorporate the significant details by re-phrasing or paraphrasing the accounts. This approach has been useful in smoothly portraying most of the details in popular composition, but the precise grammar itself has been sacrificed with its inspired reliability.

A significant distinction of THE LIFE OF CHRIST IN STEREO is that it accepts and incorporates everything written, omitting only actual duplications of meaning, and it makes its presentation in the Gospels' exact words and in the order indicated by the combined texts. The principle employed in this combination is the *principle of minute supplementation,* whereby the four Gospels are allowed to minutely supplement each other and the four accounts fold together without the addition of even the smallest connective word.

Several refinements of this principle may be noted as utilized herein. Where duplications between accounts are not identical, the wording selected is that with the fullest and most definite meaning, or its clearest expression. Thus, where (Sec. 73) Matthew and Mark say, "after six days," but Luke says "after about eight days," the former is used as the definite starting time. (It was one and one-half days before they reached the mountain height; hence, Luke's figure.) And where (Sec. 88) Matthew says, "in what watch," but Luke says, "In what hour," the former is employed as the fuller of the two, while retaining Luke's reference to "hour" in the next sentence. In cases where the same sayings of Jesus are recorded in different contexts, the repetitions are retained in both, recognizing that Jesus, doubtless, repeated His teachings on many occasions.

By utilizing this principle of incorporating all the details and sounding every note played on the four instruments, a harmony is exhibited that suggests a true symphony with all its movements and harmonics. And with the records thus blended, seeming discrepancies dissolve and a smooth rendering is produced. Furthermore, one's pleasure in reading the narrative is enhanced and the work of a single supernatural Hand is amazingly unfolded. Check any one of the ninety-eight sections where two or more accounts are interwoven, and the unity, consistency, and authenticity of the message will be evident.

This perfect interrelation between the Gospels strongly demonstrates the irresistible fact of their divine superintendence. The possibility of human collusion on the part of the four Evangelists is so remote as to be unthinkable, if one accepts the recorded statements of the Fathers and the obvious intent of the writers. They wrote to different racial groups of people, acquired their materials from a variety of different human sources, organized their content with different purposes in mind, utilized their own distinctive styles, and issued their publications at intervals spread over perhaps forty years. The words spoken long ago by Origen confirm themselves: "The Gospel written by four is but one Gospel."

This principle of mutual, minute supplementation is so universally applicable throughout the accounts as to suggest that it was divinely established and built into the structure of the four accounts. It signifies that a single Mind of superior intelligence superintended the writing of the more than 2100 parts, assigning the various details to each writer according to the individual purpose of each in revealing Jesus, the Son of God. And the reserving of this irrefragable evidence for discovery in our day of questioning God's reality is so much more remarkable. It bespeaks the Spirit's continuing work of guiding us "into all truth."

# APPENDIX II

## THE PROBLEM OF PETER'S DENIALS

The utility of the principle of minute supplementation may be demonstrated in the solution that this harmony offers to the problem of Peter's denials. Discrepancy has been charged to this account because the related details are so diverse that they simply refuse to group themselves into just three denials without some very questionable manipulating of the texts. A surplus of details has proved embarrassing and the problem has long been deemed practically insoluble.

### JESUS' TWO WARNINGS CONTRASTED

The solution that this harmony has evolved is suggested first of all by noting the differences in the two warnings Jesus gave to Peter. The first, recorded by Luke and John, occurred in the Upper Room. John shows that this took place before Jesus' great farewell discourse, and indeed, seems to have prompted the opening words of that discourse. The second, recounted by Mark and Matthew, occurred much later. It was given when Jesus and the disciples were on the way to Gethsemane (see Sec. 139-142). Note then the difference in the wording of the two warnings. In the first warning, Jesus said:

". . . the cock will *not at all* crow this day till you have denied three times that you know me." (Italics indicate emphasis in Grk.) (John 13:38)

On the latter occasion he said:

". . . today, during the night, before the cock crows twice, you will deny me three times." (Mark 14:30)

From just a simple analysis of these words, it is evident that Jesus predicted Peter would both deny Him three times before the cock crowed *at all,* as well as three times before the cock crowed *twice.* The grammar itself demands this, for "not at all crow" and "before the cock crows twice" can hardly be equated. The evidence is that Jesus predicted six denials.

### PETER'S DENIALS CONTRASTED

**The First Three Denials**. By noting the first denials in

each account, it is evident that the one recorded by John occurred *first*. It had to, for it took place as Peter gained entrance to where the other denials were uttered. And his *second* denial was the second recorded by John, for here Jesus had just been taken bound from Annas to appear before Caiaphas. The others all occurred following the appearance before Caiaphas. This second denial was a response to the men around the court fire as Peter sat with them.

The *third* denial occurred also by the fire, this time in response to the query of the high priest's servant girl. Following this, Peter went out into the fore-court. But it was at this point, as Mark records (according to Textus Receptus),[1] that "a cock crowed" (Mark 14:68). (The genuineness of Textus Receptus here is confirmed by Mark's later reference to a "second" crowing, Mark 14:72). And, interestingly enough, this crowing occurred after only the first denial recorded by Mark. By allowing the Evangelists to minutely supplement each other, the first cycle of denials is seen to be precisely as Jesus had predicted: Peter denied Him three times before the cock crowed *at all*.

**The Second Three Denials.** The second series of three denials is then seen to be prompted by a variety of individuals. There is "another woman" (Matt. 26:71), a second query by the high priest's maid (Mark 14:69), "another man" (Luke 22:58), "another man" (Luke 22:59), and finally "a kinsman of the one whose ear Peter had cut off" (John 18:26). There is obviously some overlap in these accounts, but they are seen to draw out Peter's additional three denials *after* the first crowing of the cock. Following Peter's adamant curse and his final denial, Mark declares that the cock crowed "the second time." It was then that Peter's gaze met the Lord's from the court and he went out and wept bitterly, recalling Jesus' prediction concerning his denials. Surrounded by prodding accusers, Peter's denials seem to have "snowballed" and his adamancy to have increased. This is the picture that a minute supplementation of the combined accounts reveals, and the details fold together in strict conformity to the two warnings given Peter by the Lord.

SIGNIFICANT IMPLICATIONS

It is to be recognized that each of the individual Evangelists recorded and was evidently aware of only one warning by Jesus and only three denials by Peter. They each recorded accurately what they knew. And what they knew in the matter was not the same with any two of the writers. This demonstrates both the absence of collusion on the part of the human authors and the divine guidance of One Who knew all the facts to make the four accounts fit as one. Although Peter, of course, did know all the facts, it is doubtful that even he would have related the whole of the distasteful episode. What the writers did relate, under the Spirit's inspiration, fulfilled their individual purposes and preserved the absolute integrity of the accounts.

It might also be noted that this supplemented compilation bespeaks a structural symmetry that requires all four accounts for its perfection. This symmetry is not achieved if any one of the four accounts is omitted. But by allowing all four Evangelists to speak and by incorporating every detail, whether important or seemingly unimportant, the four-dimensional symmetry is preserved. In a sense this flawless symmetry constitutes something of a divine signature and authentication for the whole of the four Gospels.

# APPENDIX III

## THE GOSPELS' HISTORICITY CONFIRMED

A question that has aroused much attention in modern times concerns the historicity and reliability of the Gospel records. In many circles it is still a live issue today. This is the question as to whether the Gospel records can be relied on as true history. Might there not be a legendary element involved which represents more the interpretations of the early church than the precise nature of the case? This legendary hypothesis has taken many forms. It has been presented all the way from the viewpoint of postulating a wholly human Jesus Who arose from the dead only in the minds of the early church, to the view of the existentialists who feel that an *historical Jesus* is not really essential to the Christian faith.

It should be recognized that the very question of the Gospels' historicity constitutes a challenge to a basic proposition of the Christian faith. This is the proposition that the Christian faith with its theology of God grounds itself upon the objective foundation of the written Word of God.

The legendary hypothesis either challenges the *validity* of that foundation or it challenges the *need* of it. If the historical records are not reliable, the propositions they contain are certainly suspect, even to the point of questioning the reality of God Himself. That there is no logical stopping place short of this "death of God" concept has been duly demonstrated recently by those who insist on carrying the myth proposition to its logical conclusion.

This question then of the historicity of the Gospels is certainly crucial and demands a frank assessment. It may be a case of genuine and valid doubts, arising from sincere research of the texts themselves; or it may be the product of misconceptions and naive assumptions that simply need clarification. It is believed that this minute supplementation of the four Gospels in THE LIFE OF CHRIST IN STEREO so harmonizes the complete account as to dissolve nearly all of the seeming discrepancies and dispell all doubts as to the historicity of the records. To demonstrate this apologetic evidence, the charges against their historicity by a popular article in LIFE magazine will be examined. The article, entitled, "The Man Jesus," was

221

written by Robert Coughlan in which he pursues the thesis of
the graphic headline: "In detail and many important points,
the Gospels do not agree."[2]

## ARE THE GENEALOGIES CONFUSED?

The first charge advanced by Coughlan is that the genealogies of Jesus, given by Matthew and Luke, are confused
beyond explanation in the two lists of names traced back
through Joseph. He supposes that both Evangelists trace the
genealogy of Joseph. Some of the names are alike, although
most are different. The solution to this seeming discrepancy
is quite simple as shown in this combination, and it only
involves a change in the punctuation of one sentence to make
the solution apparent. The crucial passage in question is
Luke 3:23:

And Jesus himself began to be about thirty years of age,
being (as was supposed) the son of Joseph, which was
the son of Heli,

It is to be noted that there is nothing sacred about traditional punctuation, for it was not part of the original text.
With a change of two commas in punctuation and a proper
recognition of the emphatic words in the original text, the
verse is rendered thus:

Now Jesus, beginning His ministry at about thirty years
of age, being a son supposedly of Joseph, was Himself
descended from Heli.

Luke's point here is that Jesus was descended "from Heli"
through Mary, not through Joseph. This explains the differing
genealogies in Matthew and Luke. Matthew traces the genealogy of Joseph to establish Jesus' legal right to the throne. He
purposely does this through Joseph to Solomon and David, for
the kingly line had to come through Solomon, not Nathan the
progenitor of Mary. Luke, on the other hand, emphasizes the
true humanity of Jesus, and therefore, traces His physical
descent through Mary to Adam.

Thus, the seeming discrepancies of the genealogies are seen
to be non-existent and the purpose of each Gospel is fulfilled.

## ARE THERE DISCREPANCIES?

The second charge of the article in LIFE magazine is that Matthew and Luke are in disagreement because they trace a different sequence of events following Jesus' birth. Matthew describes the coming of the magi and the flight into Egypt; Luke, on the other hand, portrays the visit of the shepherds and others who worship the Christ child in Bethlehem and Jerusalem. Why these differing accounts?

This problem is also quite simply explained by noting the differing purposes of the writers. No one of the Gospels presumes to give a complete history of the Life of Christ or even of His public ministry. Each Evangelist selected events and materials consistent with his purpose in presenting a particular view of Jesus' life and ministry. But the selection of these materials by each author is seen to be divinely directed, for all the parts perfectly dovetail and complement each other when seen in the composite whole. And this stereo harmony displays the mutual interrelation of all the varied parts in such a way as to show that nothing is contradictory to the whole, and yet nothing is superfluous. To charge contradiction on the basis of silence is to invalidate much of the writings of history, if not the whole of literature.

The author of the article in LIFE, however, evinced a great fascination for and faith in this argument from silence, for he pursues the complaint by multiplying instances and charges where events are recorded by only one of the Gospels. A little reflection would readily suggest an entirely different conclusion, even for the skeptic. Contrary to the fallacious contention that contradictions are evident, this stereo combination of the four Gospels displays the amazing fact that the four accounts minutely complement and supplement each other, and this without the advantage of the authors' personal collusion. The implications of this conclusion are overwhelming, pointing to a guiding Superintendent, "within the shadows."

## ARE LUKE AND JOSEPHUS IN DISAGREEMENT?

A further case of disagreement has been claimed, not between the Gospel writers, but between Luke and the Jewish historian, Josephus. The matter concerns the "taxing" which Luke dates at the time of Jesus' birth. Josephus, however, appears to place it at least ten years later, after Archelaus had been deposed and Cyrenius had been sent as a Syrian magistrate.

It should first be noted that the term "taxing" (Luke 2:2) should better be rendered *census* or registration, which is the root meaning of the Greek word used (apographe). Though taxing generally followed, it was based on this census.

Secondly, it should be noted that Luke indicates that a series of enrollments was taken, and the one occurring at Jesus' birth was the *first* such enrollment taken by Cyrenius (Cf. Acts 5:37). Sir William Ramsay has demonstrated from the inscriptions that Cyrenius was twice in Syria, and he has also shown that periodic enrollments were taken every fourteen years. Thus, the *taxing* or enrollment referred to by Gamaliel in Acts 5:37 is precisely the same as that referred to by Josephus which is obviously not "the first" as recorded by Luke at the birth of Jesus. Almost as though Luke anticipated the problem, he supplied us with a reference to his knowledge of the second census (in Acts 5:37), if we would but hear him in both his inspired accounts.

It is to be regretted, however, that the author of LIFE'S article was so quickly satisfied with the basis of his challenge to the Gospels' historicity. Having cited the several difficulties already considered, he then averred that there are *many* such, too many to catalogue. And, on the basis of these unpursued difficulties, he then stated his doubts as to the accounts of Jesus' resurrection and other historical facts of the Gospels. He declared that if the Nativity and Resurrection "can be reduced to such dishevelment simply by comparing the Gospels, it is easy to imagine what difficulties might await a scholar trying to authenticate lesser events." It is indeed regrettable that his foreclosure on the Gospels' witness was given such coverage, for it was doubtless convincing, although shocking, to his mass of uninformed readers.

On the contrary, a truly honest comparison and combination of the Gospels has just the reverse effect, if all the details are accepted as given. And it is believed that this harmony of

THE LIFE OF CHRIST IN STEREO will demonstrate this fact and become a powerful antidote to these popular misconceptions. It will help to unscramble most of the so-called discrepancies and will commend the Gospels' veracity to any mind disposed to seek the truth and willing to give the Gospel records the same credence accorded other ancient documents of historical credibility.

Thus, when the individual Gospels are approached from the broad perspective of the whole and with a recognition of the general principles that apply to all literature, the alleged discrepancies are seen to be non-existent and figments of the imagination. The article by LIFE failed to cite one instance of an actual disagreement between any two Gospel records. The differences cited are only such as one would expect from four biographers of different backgrounds, writing at different times, in different countries, to different readers, and with different purposes in view. That there are differences in materials is not disputed; but differences do not constitute contradictions or even disagreements. Were all the same materials recorded by each of the four Gospels, and were they related with the same phraseology there would have been no purpose in preserving all four records. Indeed, the *absence* of differences would have been a more legitimate basis for suspicion. But the fact that four such records could be compiled under such varying conditions, without a single genuine discrepancy among the four, is hardly less than the literary miracle of the ages.

Thus, one of the values of this stereo combination is that the genuine historicity of the four Gospels is shown to be beyond question when all the grammatical and historical factors are minutely supplemented in the exact phraseology of the texts themselves. The stereo effect is an apologetic in itself.

# APPENDIX IV
# THE GOSPELS' FOUR-YEAR CHRONOLOGY

Among the startling discoveries that this combined harmony of the Gospels brings to light is that of a new and more exact chronology of the ministry of Christ. The process of minutely arranging all the materials in a sequentive order and allowing all the accounts to supplement each other requires that the texts be permitted to develop their own chronology. And in the process, the solution to many of the most perplexing questions in harmonistic studies is provided. The basic components of the problem and its solution will herein be summarized.

## THE TRADITIONAL THREE-YEAR CHRONOLOGY

The generally accepted chronology of Jesus' ministry is based on the references in John's Gospel to the Passover feasts. Three Passovers are noted in John 2:12, 6:4, and 11:55, and another is assumed from the reference in 5:1 to an unnamed feast. These four Passovers thus span a period of three years, from the first temple cleansing to Passion Week. Some authorities have disregarded John's notation in 6:4 and have postulated only a one or two-year ministry for Jesus, since the Synoptics mention only the one Passover of Passion Week. But nearly all the Gospel harmonies have posited a three-year chronology.

Accepting then the historicity and accuracy of John's documentations, it is quite clear that Jesus' ministry had to span two or three years at the least. But that it should be *limited* to three years is nowhere required by the texts. This limitation has merely been assumed from the silence on John's part with reference to a fifth Passover. The view assumes that John referred to every Passover of Jesus' ministry.

**John's purpose in mentioning Passovers.** It should be noted, however, that John's references to Passovers or other feasts were not for the purpose of suggesting a chronology of Jesus' ministry. These references are only incidental to his story and are given only as they relate to John's portrayal of the divine character of our Lord. He makes no mention of the important feast of Pentecost, for instance and mentions

Tabernacles only in connection with His third **year ministry**. A careful survey of Jesus' work from the first temple cleansing to the feeding of the 5000 indicates that that period involved a span of two years. And yet John did not specifically mention that second Passover (as we shall demonstrate). The obvious reason is that John was not relating the Passovers for chronological purposes. His Gospel was supplemental and was certainly not intended as a chronological outline of Jesus' ministry. Indeed, the ministry of Jesus might have been five years in length and not be inconsistent with the presentation of John.

**The problem of Jesus' final period of ministry.** One of the most questionable features of the traditional three-year chronology is that it compresses too many events into the last six months of His ministry. The usual approach is to tacitly assume that Jesus' departure from Galilee to attend the Feast of Tabernacles in John 7 is the same departure as that related by Luke in 9:51. No reconciliation is made with the fact that in John 7, Jesus went directly to Jerusalem within a few days, whereas in Luke 9 and following, the journey involved at least several months. The discrepancy of such an approach is glaring and inexcusable.

Various other attempts at harmonizing these passages have been made, all of which have proved quite futile, without remodeling the texts themselves. Adhering to the principle of the inviolability of the original texts, of which we have the almost exact facsimile in the original language today, there is every evidence that the two journeys simply are not identical. Recognizing this obvious fact, some have proposed to fit Luke's Travelogue (chaps 9:51-19:27) into a setting after the Feast of Dedication and before the raising of Lazarus which occurred in about late February. This would mean that within less than two months, He returned to the Galilean area and then, after some time, began His final journey to Jerusalem, involving the numerous events of the "Great Insertion" of chapters 9-19. Though such is not impossible, it is highly improbable. A more extended period seems essential to provide an adequate setting for this final traveling ministry.

**The logical alternative: A four-year ministry.** In utilizing the undistorted text, and allowing all these materials and events to fall into their natural sequence, the logical alternative suggested is that Jesus had a *four-year ministry*. It certainly is not out of keeping with His usual leisurely manner of confronting individuals to assume that His visit to the more than thirty-five cities after His final departure from Galilee occupied several months. His final canvas and search for penitent hearts was hardly a feverish whirlwind campaign. Assuming then a fourth year of ministry, and allowing for several short periods of silence in that year (which was true also of each of the preceding years), the inconsistencies disappear and none of the texts need be manipulated to harmonize. To show the general structure of such a scheme, a brief sketch of this four-year chronology will be described with various evidences that suggest such a chronology.

## THE DATE OF JESUS' MINISTRY

Luke designates the fifteenth year of Tiberius as the year that John the Baptist began his ministry (Luke 3:1). Since Roman history clearly states that Tiberius succeeded Augustus in August of A.D. 14, the fifteenth year of Tiberius would then be in the fall of A.D. 28. Although it has been generally believed that Luke's reference to the beginning of Tiberius' reign referred to the date that he began as a deputy of Augustus in A.D. 11, this view is hardly in keeping with the precise character of Luke's account. The date of his deputy-ship is quite inexact, while the date of his actual accession as Emperor is very definite. This was A.D. 14.[3] John's ministry then began in the fall of A.D. 28, and Jesus' ministry began the following spring of A.D. 29. And His public presentation to Israel took place during Passover that year at which time He cleansed the temple.

It should be noted that the assumed date at which Tiberius began his reign, A.D. 11, was probably propounded as a result of another misconception. The reasoning is as follows: Luke declares in Luke 3:23 that Jesus began His ministry at about the age of thirty. If we then recognize that Jesus was born in 5 B.C., before the death of Herod in 4 B.C., and add the thirty years of Luke 3:23, the date His ministry began seems to be late A.D. 26, and the date of John's, A.D. 25. If A.D. 25 was the fifteenth year of Tiberius, his reign would have begun in A.D. 11.

But Luke 3:23 does not give the exact age of Jesus. The expression *about thirty* (hosei) is only an approximation. In Luke 2:41, he does give Jesus' exact age in years when describing the event of His first Passover feast. His exact age was doubtless given on that occasion because it was precisely at the age of "twelve" (not "about twelve") that a Jewish boy became a "son of the Law" and began attending Passover. The designation "about thirty" for the beginning of Jesus' ministry, therefore, might readily signify *in his early thirties.* His precise age at this time seems to have been thirty-three (assuming 5 B.C. to be His birthdate).

## THE FIRST TWO YEARS OF JESUS' MINISTRY

From the time of His baptism and temptation to the feeding of the 5000 in Galilee, a period of a little over two years transpired involving three Passovers. The first is recorded by John in 2:13, and the third is noted in 6:4 at the time of His miraculous feeding of the 5000.

**The first year.** At what point the second Passover took place, however, is not specifically stated by any of the Evangelists. John's reference to a "feast of the Jews" in 5:1 has generally been understood to be the second Passover of this two-year period. A careful examination of the context, however, suggests that this almost assuredly had to be a later feast, occurring after the Sermon on the Mount which was spoken that summer. The feast of John 5:1 is rather identified with Tabernacles that fall, for the animosity between Jesus and the leaders seems to be more deep-seated and of a continuing nature at this point (5:18). The determination to "destroy" Him, asserted in Mark 3:6, was more initiatory there than the plot of John 5:16, 18; and even that decision occurred after the second Passover. Also, Jesus' emphasis on His power of resurrection in John 5 fits better after the first resurrection miracle that followed the Sermon on the Mount (Luke 7:15).

**The second Passover alluded to.** There is a reference, however, to the second Passover; but it is not given by John. Luke speaks of an early harvest event in Chapter 6, in which he gives an oblique reference to a second Passover, just after Jesus had called the Twelve for full-time discipleship (Sec. 36). On that occasion Jesus and His disciples were condemned for eating grain in the harvest field on a sabbath. This springtime event was obviously between the first and third Passovers, as evidenced in all three Synoptics. But further evidence of it being the second Passover is provided in a curious rendering of Luke 6:1, which has been all but lost in translations. The reason for its being lost was probably that it was altered by an early scribe who totally misunderstood its meaning. The phrase in question is, "the second First Sabbath," which is footnoted in the United Bible Society's new Greek text as having strong support in the Western and Byzantine Texts. The reading given in Sec. 36 of THE LIFE OF CHRIST IN STEREO is:

And it came to pass on the second First Sabbath that he was walking through the grain fields . . . .

What is the meaning of "the second First Sabbath?" A clue to its probable meaning is found in Leviticus 23:15-21, where directions for setting the date of Pentecost are given. Seven sabbaths were to be counted from the Feast of First-fruits or Passover. Consequently, these came to be known as "First Sabbath," "Second Sabbath" etc., down to the seventh. And, according to Julian Morgenstern, former President of Hebrew University, this practice continued in Galilee till the time of Christ or the Common Era. It is still observed by some groups in Palestine today. Thus, there was an annual date known as "First Sabbath," just after Passover. And Luke, the careful historian, records that this event in the grain fields took place on the "second First Sabbath" of Jesus' ministry. This, then, pin-points the occasion of the second Passover and indicates the completion of the first year of His public ministry.

**The second year.** The period between this Passover and the miraculous feeding of 5000 constituted His second year of ministry, called "The Year of Great Public Favor" (Sec. 36-56) Having chosen His twelve disciples, He then appointed them as apostles, taught them in the Sermon on the Mount and through numerous other experiences, and finally sent them out to preach at the end of that year. Mark gives nearly four chapters to this busy year (Mark 3-6). It was a year of sharp controversy with Israel's religious leaders. And it was at the conclusion of this second year that John the Baptist was beheaded by Herod.

## THE LAST TWO YEARS OF JESUS' MINISTRY

The feeding of the 5000 in Galilee took place coincident with the third Passover of Jesus' ministry (Sec. 55). This is quite generally accepted as indicated in John 6:4. But the period between this Passover and the final Passover has almost universally been taken to be a one-year span, primarily because no Passover feast is mentioned from John 6 to John 12. And this assumption has produced the three-year chronology, requiring that all the remaining materials be fitted into this period. Discrepancies have been recognized in this scheme, but they have been considered to be largely insoluble with. our present knowledge, and relatively unimportant.

The chronological arrangement presented in THE LIFE OF CHRIST IN STEREO, however, has brought to light some overwhelming evidence that this period involved *two* years rather than only one, and that Christ's whole ministry extended over a span of *four years* rather than three. This position seems to be more consistent with the text, and also more logical. The crucial evidence for this position will be herewith reviewed.

**The fallacy of assuming that John mentions all the Passovers.** It has already been demonstrated that John did not intend to outline Jesus' ministry by Passovers. He spoke of several Passovers, but only incidentally as they related to his presentation of the divine Person of our Lord. He mentioned the first, third, and last Passovers, but failed to speak of the second, as we have previously shown. That there was a second is clearly demonstrated in the Synoptics. Therefore, since John did not mention the second Passover, the fact that he does not mention another one prior to Passion Week is hardly evidence that there was none. If John 2-6 involved two years without mention of an intervening Passover, there is no reason that John 6-12 could not also span two years without requiring it to mention the intervening Passover.

**The fallacy of equating John 7-10 with Luke 9-19.** In

John 7, the Apostle declares that Jesus left Galilee to attend the Feast of Tabernacles in Jerusalem, evidently in October of A.D. 31 (Sec. 64). Since John does not again refer to Jesus in Galilee, it has been generally assumed that this was Jesus' last activity in Galilee prior to the cross. The contention is that He never returned to Galilee after the Feast of Dedication of December, A.D. 31. And since John records the raising of Lazarus directly after this feast episode, it has been thought that this resurrection miracle took place just a month or so later, about February, A.D. 32. By itself this plan fits nicely into the three-year chronology.

But the so-called parallel passage in Luke (9:51 ff.) introduces some insoluble problems for this arrangement. Luke's account of Jesus' final departure from Galilee is a long, detailed description of a journey which cannot be equated with His trip to Tabernacles in John 7. The trip in John 7 involved just a matter of days; Luke's account involved months, since he records that Jesus made scores of stops on the way. Thus these two journeys to Jerusalem simply cannot be equated.

**Fitting Luke 9:51 - 19:27 into the chronology.** To solve the problem some harmonists have placed Luke's Travelogue between the Feast of Dedication and the raising of Lazarus.[4] This is obviously the only alternative if the journeys are recognized as being distinct. But in the three-year chronology, there is hardly sufficient time to do justice to the mass of material involved in this period and to fit in the numerous stops that Jesus made in this journey as recorded by Luke.

To clarify the problem it would be well to briefly analyze the features and general itinerary of this final journey. After Jesus "set his face to go to Jerusalem" (Luke 9:51), He sent messengers to Samaria before Him to prepare His way. This venture was apparently without response, although a number of incidents occurred enroute. Following this, Jesus sent out seventy other disciples to at least thirty-five cities to which He intended to go. The purpose of this wide thrust was to make a final probe and to give a final solicitation to individuals who might yet respond. He declared at that time that, "The harvest truly is great," and He urged prayer that more laborers might be thrust out. This journey was hardly a whirlwind campaign that could be compressed into just a few weeks. Such a feverish swirl would be out of character with Jesus' leisurely manner of confronting individuals. Although He was busy and active, He was not disposed to being rushed by any circumstance (John 11:6).

Thus, it seems more consistent with the related facts to allow for another year to intervene between the Feast of Dedication of John 10, and the raising of Lazarus in John 11. (Doesn't the three-year chronology posit a year's lapse between John 5 and 6?) This allows ample time to accommodate the mass of events of Luke's Travelogue (9:51-19:27) without unaccountable time intervals of any extended length.

**Synoptic evidence of an additional Passover.** Two other events of the last half of Jesus' ministry are recorded which give further oblique references to an additional Passover. One is given by Matthew and one by Luke, both between the feeding of the 5000 and the final Passover.

Matthew records an event in which Jesus was dunned at Capernaum for the annual temple tax (Matt. 17:24; Sec. 76). This tribute was generally collected before Passover to allow the officers to take the proceeds to Jerusalem for the feast. Since Jesus had travelled in and out of Capernaum a number of times after the third Passover at the time of the feeding of the 5000, the implication of an additional Passover before Passion Week is hard to miss. If this tax inquiry related to the third Passover, why didn't they investigate Him earlier? The evidence seems to indicate that another Passover had occurred, probably about the time of the Transfiguration while Jesus and His disciples were travelling in the far north, out of Israel.

The second event is recorded by Luke in connection with which he also refers to that additional Passover by implication (Luke 13:1; Sec. 90). Luke's statement is: "Now at that time there were some present who told him of the Galileans whose blood Pilate had mingled with their sacrifices." Such a circumstance would involve one of the three major feasts, for only at such a time would Galileans journey to Jerusalem in numbers to make animal sacrifices. Furthermore, this massacre was an event that was related to Jesus as *news*. In other words, it occurred during a feast at which He was not present. And since

Jesus, Himself, attended the fall feasts of John 7-10, the event
has to be placed in the fourth year of Jesus' ministry, whether
Passover, Pentecost, or Tabernacles. This inevitably pushes the
last Passover to the end of the fourth year and makes it the
fifth Passover of His ministry.

In the four-year chronology this event fits nicely as part of
Luke's Travelogue, for in this scheme Jesus did not attend the
fourth-year feasts until the final Passover. Thus the massacre
event was related to Jesus as *news* and the additional Passover
is necessitated by implication.

## THE FOURTH YEAR ALLUDED TO BY PARABLE

Directly after the previous event, Jesus told a parable which
had definite chronological overtones (Luke 13:6-9; Sec. 90).
The parable pictures Israel as a barren fig tree, disappointing to
its keeper. Having twice emphasized the need for repentance
(Luke 13:3,5), Jesus noted the absence of it on the part of the
nation by telling this parable.

A certain man had a fig tree that had been planted in his
vineyard; and he came and sought fruit on it, and found
none. Then said he to the dresser of the vineyard, "Behold, for three years I keep coming, seeking fruit on
this fig tree and finding none. Cut it down; why have it
use up the ground?"
But he answering said to him, "Sir, let it alone this year
also, till I dig about it and fertilize it. Then if indeed it
bears fruit, all is well; but if not, you shall afterward cut
it down."

It is essential to recognize that the primary aim of Jesus'
parables was to enlighten, not to mystify. (The concealing
purpose related only to those hardened in their Messianic rejection, from whom He withheld Kingdom secrets). In His
stories He sought to emphasize one central truth, utilizing
details either to elaborate that truth or to give it realism. In
regards to evaluating details, A. M. Hunter has given sound
counsel:

Jesus, let us remember, intended His parables to be
meaningful for His hearers. If then you meet something
in a parable which almost cries out to be taken symboli-

cally, that is, allegorically, stop and ask yourself: Would this detail carry this symbolical significance for the men to whom Jesus spoke? If so, we may fairly take it so . . .[5]

It is apparent from the contextual evidence that Jesus was here speaking of Israel as the "fig tree" and of His own ministry as related to the nation. John the Baptist had announced that, "the axe is laid unto the root of the trees," and he called for "fruits meet for repentance," to avert supernatural judgment. In Jesus' ministry, He sought the fruit that should have been forthcoming, but found the nation barren of fruit, announcing, "except ye repent, ye shall all likewise perish." The central truth of the parable then relates to His fruitless search for repentance in Israel and the divine extension of His gracious ministry in a final solicitation for repentance.

It is certainly true that some of the details are given as mere "drapery" for realism, to enhance the persuasive power of the story. But, that other details "cry out" for interpretation as essential elements of the central truth is also evident. The setting of the story demands this. His hearers, both friends and enemies, knew the precise length of His ministry thus far, doubtless dating it from that first cleansing of the temple at Passover. For Him to have specified "three" years when it was actually two would certainly not have enhanced the persuasive power of the parable, but diminished it. Confusion would have been introduced which would have beclouded the central truth and made them question His mathematical ability. He was striking for decisions and would hardly have allowed such historic discrepancies to distract them. Furthermore, the immediately previous event of the "massacre of the Galileans" at Passover gives strong support to the literalness of the "three years" to which Jesus referred in the parable. And if the protasis, "three years," is to be taken literally, the apodasis, "this year also," must be understood similarly.

But Jesus' final "punch line" to this parable of The Barren Fig Tree was given to the disciples nearly a year later as they entered Jerusalem for Passion Week and He wept over the city's impenitence. Seeking fruit on a leaf-bearing fig tree the following Monday morning, He pronounced a curse upon the tree for its lack of fruit while pretentiously producing leaves.

The fig tree characteristically bore fruit when it produced leaves. The recording of this event by all three Synoptists was obviously not for the purpose of displaying Jesus' strain and anger, for He, Himself, used this event as an occasion to impress the disciples with their need of faith to move mountains. A fit of anger is no display of faith. Rather, the miracle is an acted parable, again portraying the nation, Israel, as a barren fig tree. Jesus' fine sense of analogy is seen as He pursues and applies that former parable, showing the continued impenitence of the nation throughout that additional year of divine mercy. The official rejection recorded here constituted the point of no retreat, after which the process of "drying up" began with the withdrawal of divine life. The tree was no longer to "cumber" the ground of Palestine, but would be cut down until a future day when a "holy seed" would arise from the stump (Isa. 6:13).

All these correlating parts lend support to the numerical significance of the "years" alluded to in the parable of Luke 13. Although presenting the truths in parabolic garb, Jesus strongly implied a four-year chronology for His ministry to Israel. And with the many other strands of corroborating evidences, the proposition that His ministry extended over a period of four years, rather than just three, is overwhelming. Though traditional views and insights are always weighty, they must give way to the irresistible force of the text, especially where such an overwhelming consistency of the text is revealed.

# EXPLANATORY FOOTNOTES

Corresponding to the alphabetical symbols within each section

Sec.

1a　Mark calls the entire Story "The Beginning." See also Luke's "began" in Acts 1:1. The Glad News was not ended with this Story.

2a　The Grk. pictures an attempt to pinch out a candle.

b　Since the aorist infinitive denotes an act, not a process, it is made clearer in English by this participle. "High estate" signifies "that which comes from wealth," literal meaning of the Grk. word for *authority.*

c　The writer, John, and others beheld the Transfiguration, (Sec. 73).

d　Born before Jesus, John the Baptist testified thus to His pre-existence (Sec. 18).

e　The Grk. expression pictures two persons at dinner, ancient style, reclining with feet away from the table, one leaning against the bosom of the other at his left; the symbolism pictures complete fellowship.

3a　The Grk. denotes a roll or scroll; so in the Jews' public records there was this "book" listing *Joseph's* descent from Israel's kings, information never contested by Jesus' enemies, as far as we know, though they had access to these records and supposed that Jesus was his son.

b　Uzziah was not Jehoram's direct son, for the sons of wicked Ahab are omitted; it was common usage to apply *begot* to a descendant.

c　If Joseph were Jesus' father, this would read, "Joseph, of whom was born Jesus." But Joseph's lineage is important, for his acceptance of Mary and her Son made Jesus legal heir to Israel's throne, *qualified* to be MESSIAH.

d　Mary, much younger than Joseph, was perhaps counted as the fourteenth.

4a　Partly from this some have supposed that Luke used Mark's Gospel and perhaps Matthew's among the many mentioned, but of this there is no proof. On the contrary, there is not one identical narrative sentence from them in Luke, *or in any two Gospels*, except one small instance, "And they laughed at him." (three Grk. words). Yet no copyright law forbade identical quoting. Even their quoting

237

4a    from Jesus shows only five exact correspondences, the longest being 24 words, the others much shorter. Furthermore, there are wide differences between all the Gospels in principal content, arrangement, style, and purpose; likewise they were evidently written from widely separated locations.

5a    He quotes from the last sentence of the Old Testament.

  b    The angel who appeared as told in Daniel 8:16 and 9:21.

6a    The promise to David: II Samuel 7:12-13.

7a    Her song echoes Hannah's rejoicing in I Samuel, and parts from Genesis, II Samuel, the Psalms, Job, Isaiah, and Micah; 17 instances in all. Evidently Mary knew her Bible.

  b    It was after five months of Elisabeth's pregnancy that Mary went to visit her; hence she left before John's birth, three months later.

8a    Here likewise are echoes from seven Old Testament books in some 17 quotations.

9a    Thus, Matthew's explanation agrees with Luke's in Sec. 6, fulfilling for us the directive in Deut. 19:15, "At the mouth of two . . . or three witnesses shall the matter be established." Matthew obtained his facts from Joseph's side of the family, Luke from Mary's; their agreement on the Virgin Birth is convincing.

  b    "JESUS" is the Grk. rendering of the Hebrew JEHOSHUA or JOSHUA, meaning *Jehovah is salvation.*

  c    Since duplications of meaning are necessarily omitted in a careful combining of the Gospels, Matthew's "and he called his name Jesus" (Received Text) yields to Luke's similar but fuller statement at the end of Sec. 10.

10a    There is no discrepancy here but rather an informative point of history. Luke does not say that the "taxing" was collected at this time, but rather that people were registered. See App. III.

  b    It is probable that only holders of inherited property had to go to their home town to register; possibly Joseph was owner of the house where the Wise Men later found the family. While he was in Nazareth he would have let it out to others, who could not be asked to move for his short stay.

  c    As earth is yet far from peaceful, the angels' chant can only describe the time when the Prince of Peace is to *reign.* The Received Text's "good will among men" is the only rendering that fits that prophetic picture.

11a  The Received Text, or "TR" appears to give the most consistent meaning; there is no point to Luke's mentioning her seven years married, if not to be added to the 84.

12a  The word *after* allows a substantial interval, limited only by the "two years old and under" of Sec. 13. So Joseph and Mary, found here in a house, have now *returned* from Nazareth and are residing in Bethlehem. For after the flight to Egypt which now occurs, we read of Joseph's plan to return to Judea, though kept from it by learning of Archelaus.

  b  The Grk. verb *kept asking* shows his agitation and the religious leaders' confusion.

  c  Thus plainly a supernatural manifestation.  This was its second appearance, perhaps months after the first.

13a  The words *a city called* would duplicate a meaning already expressed by Luke in Sec. 6, hence are omitted. Cf. note 9c.

14a  Luke here reveals his source of information up to this point, whether from Mary herself or through her relatives.

15a  Rejected in this book is the *joint reign* theory, which placed the call of John in A.D. 26; Jesus' ministry is dated instead from accepted Roman history. For Luke speaks here of Tiberius' 15th year as Caesar, and this would properly date from the death of Augustus in August, A.D. 14. The 15th year thus began in A.D. 28, placing Jesus' baptism in that same fall or winter and the first Passover of His ministry (Sec. 22) in the spring of A.D. 29. See Appendix IV.

  b  The Story fits together here consistently even though combining minutely the *complete* contributions of three writers—with no word but theirs used. Note that even a simple phrase such as Matthew's "In those days" has its needed place, making coherent connection between Luke's notable opening sentence and Mark's abrupt opening. Such provision, clearly unintended by the writers, occurs many times to give complete and marvelous unity to the interweaving.

  c  The term *tax collectors* is not here used, as it is misleading. The tax collector of our day bears no resemblance to the *publican* of the Gospels, who though a Jew, was employed by the Roman conquerors and often took advantage of his countrymen for his own enrichment.

15d  *Messiah* means the *Anointed One* (Grk, Christos, or *Christ*), who was longingly awaited for Israel's deliverance.

16a  This rendering departs from the traditional but inconsistent "Joseph, the son of Heli." Though never before proposed to our knowledge, this rendering is grammatically sound and clarifies the true intent of the passage. It only involves the addition of two commas in the Grk. (which had no punctuation in the original) and a proper recognition of the significance of the initial pronoun which stands in the place of emphasis. Using English punctuation for modern clarity, the literal rendering would be: "Now Himself was Jesus, beginning at about age thirty——being a son, as was supposed, of Joseph——descended from Heli, son of Matthat, . . ." His point is that Jesus descended, not from Joseph but from Heli through Mary. That Luke intended this meaning is suggested by the arrangement in the two oldest extant authorities, where Heli, not Joseph, heads the single-column listing of Jesus' human forbears back to Adam. [This rendering was presented to and well received by the Evangelical Theological Society, as well as by other competent Greek scholars——Ed. See App. III.]

  b  Thus, Jesus' humanity is linked with the whole human race, not alone with Israel as in His descent described by Matthew (Sec. 3) as Joseph's adopted son.

17a  The command marks this definitely as the last temptation. Luke used a different order in addressing Gentile readers, but did not specify that things occurred in his order; Matthew records Jesus' command at this point for Satan to depart (in the best Grk. texts).

18a  Their question concerning Elijah was based on Mal. 4:5-6; that concerning the Prophet, in Deut. 18:15, 18. By the latter they mistook John for the One he was to introduce.

19a  References to the time of day in John's Gospel are Roman reckoning. Egyptian water-clock hours counted from midnight and noon as ours today (although *a.m.* and *p.m.* come later). The *tenth hour* here would not be ten at night, so it was ten a.m. John mentions it to signify the length of this first interview with Jesus.

  b  How did the writer, John, know what happened here? Obviously because he was the unnamed one who with Andrew heard John the Baptist's exclamation. He thus brings himself into the Story without using the first personal pronoun, used at no time by John or any of these self-effacing writers, though John and Matthew participated in most of Jesus' ministry.

19c   *Cephas* is the Aramaic, and *Petros* the Greek, for "a stone."

20a   "The son of Joseph" only reflects the common supposition concerning Jesus mentioned by Luke in Sec. 16. When it was that Philip and others learned the truth, we are not told.

   b   With John the Baptist's "This is the Son of God" and now Nathanael's "You are the Son of God!" following the accounts of Jesus' unique birth and the Voice from heaven at His baptism, all four writers have emphasized early the basic theme JESUS THE SON OF GOD, observable throughout the Story and climaxed in its final paragraph.

21a   Thus interpreting the Grk. to mean literally, "What to me and for you?" This seems best to fit the context here and in Sec. 30 and 46. No disrespect, however, was intended in Jesus' use of it or the term *woman*.

   b   The Grk. *believed into* seems to connote more than belief *in*; hence our rendering *believed upon*, or in some cases, *trusted in*.

22a   The Grk. simply says "What sign . . .?" But a *miraculous* sign was what they wanted, and this implicit meaning is made clearer by using that word. The question shows that these Jewish leaders, well versed in the Old Testament, recognized His fulfillment of Malachi's prophecy, but their hearts could not accept it. For this reason, Jesus refused them a sign and uttered His riddle instead.

23a   Even though not labeled as such, this tells the *how* of the New Birth. You substitute *your* name for *whoever—that John Jones believing upon Him should not perish but should have everlasting life*.

   b   Whether the *unquote* belongs here or earlier in the passage is uncertain but immaterial, for the words are from God as the Author whether or not some are comments by John. But all would seem fitting as from Jesus, written by John as one present, giving Jesus' answer to Israel's leaders through Nicodemus. Since it was intended for all men as well, it fittingly occurs early in the Ministry and in John's record.

24a   In this case the quoted words clearly end here and the rest is from John the writer, agreeing with the Baptist's estimate of himself as inferior to this One from heaven, pointing out Jesus' colossal stature and the doom incurred in rejecting Him.

25a   This is Herod Antipas, a son of Herod the Great mentioned in Sec. 12-13.

  b   By pausing to disclose His identity to a morally low, Samaritan woman He carried out His own later directive (Sec. 93), "Go out into the highways and hedges . . . ." At Jerusalem those first *bidden* had refused His banquet.

  c   The disciples probably looked forward to the feast of Tabernacles (four months away) as the time to harvest a large following; but Jesus, thinking of the Samaritans on their way from the village, used the ripe grain in nearby fields to teach a lesson. Thus the month was evidently June of that first year.

26a   That is, He passed up Nazareth and went on to Cana, a few miles farther north. The miracle performed from there could have been performed from Nazareth, except that "a prophet has no honor in his home town."

27a   Enough time had now elapsed for word of the two miracles at Cana to have spread to Nazareth - but only to cause demand for a miracle there as well.

  b   The traditional punctuation in the texts has obscured the impact of this passage, by which He declared Himself as *Messiah, the Anointed One*, proving it by what Nazareth had heard about the boy's healing. But they were only the more incensed at Him.

  c   Cf. note 20a.

28a   It *was* at hand for Galilee, since the King was there and was being welcomed except by Nazareth (Sec. 27, first par.). It remained "at hand" for all Israel until eventually it was withheld, pending the future day when the nation will accept Him. Concerning the two names for the Kingdom, see note 44c.

29a   Implied in the Grk. by the kind of net spoken of.

31a   In pursuing the theme, "The Son of God," Luke reported the cry of the unclean demon (Sec. 30) and now quotes the confirming witness of "many" such intelligent beings from a realm where His identity was known.

32a   The singular rendering of *net* by Textus Receptus may be a scribal change from an original plural. The contextual evidence, however, favors it, in that it explains Peter's subsequent act of repentance.

  b   Many have equated this episode with the one in Sec. 29, but if we accept what the writers tell, it cannot be the same. That occasion

32b   (Mk. 1:16-18) preceded Jesus' first tour in Galilee (Mk. 1:39, Sec. 31) while this one in Luke 5 *follows* much of that tour (Lk. 4:44) which occupied some eight months or more.

33a   Because the fishermen joined the latter part of the tour, they saw this healing in one of the cities and the tremendous crowds that resulted. The leper, in going to Jerusalem to present himself to the priest, spread the news as he journeyed that 70 or 80 miles and returned. As until now the crowds had been local in origin, hereafter, they came "from every quarter."

34a   Here Jesus chose to present the heart of His mission and His identity as *the Son of God.* No better occasion could have been employed, for it was His first meeting with the nation's religious leaders, including those from Jerusalem. That they got the message is shown by their question, "Who can forgive sins but *God?*"

35a   Galileans often had two names, Jewish and Galilean. As a *publican* Matthew's work was that of a custom house official in an office by the Sea of Galilee where Jesus often passed by. Although the banquet he held in Jesus' honor is reported in the Gospels at this point, Matthew shows that it was actually held some months later, where we place it (Sec. 47).

36a   For explanation of this term, see App. IV. The first Sabbath shortly followed the Passover date in Galilee.

  b   This was a breach of Rabbinic law, not of the Scriptures.

37a   This consummated Jesus' first year of presentation and dialogue with the leaders, resulting in their initial consultations to destroy Him.

38a   Probably Mt. Tabor, so often resorted to by Jesus.

39a   These three beatitudes from Luke do not duplicate Matthew's, but logically fit as their introduction. Those whom Jesus was addressing had left their livelihood for Him and, doubtless, had already suffered privations to show the reality of their faith. Luke's report of the so-called Sermon fits with Matthew's account throughout. [Variations of the Sermon were doubtless spoken by our Lord on different occasions. Ed.]

  b   With the Jews, *hyperbole* was not uncommon in stressing an important point.

  c   Jesus here enjoins His disciples to imitate the Father by a perfection of love that is extended even to one's enemies. The motivation was not *to become* children, but because they were children of the Father.

39d The last two lines are so utterly appropriate that they deserve the benefit of any doubt. They were probably deleted in some early edition to conform to the rendering in Luke 11 (Sec. 82).

  e He reminds them that the true way is neither popular nor easy. Though He does not here expound the way of salvation, He does describe a characteristic of it.

  f A later statement forms an apt commentary here: "And *this* is the will of Him who sent me: that everyone who sees the Son *and believes upon Him* should have everlasting life . . ." (Jn. 6:40, Sec. 57).

40a Though the Kingdom was still being offered to Israel, the universality of the Glad News appears increasingly in the Story. The centurion was from the "west." The "sons" of the Kingdom were of Israel.

41a Israel's two great miracle-working prophets (Elijah and Elisha) performed resurrections.

42a This is the literal Grk. meaning and clarifies the picture, for at formal meals many Jews used the Roman manner of reclining, resting on the left elbow, feet extended away from the low table.

  b Anglicized plural of the Roman *denarius,* silver coin of the value of a day's wage.

  c In the Gospels, as well as the epistles, salvation is always by faith.

43a That is, as a refuge, although to no avail (probably Peter's home in Capernaum).

  b Satan, as the strong man, was to be finally bound and his usurped kingdom to be reclaimed by Christ who would deliver it back to the Father. (I Cor. 15:24)

  c It is significant that Joseph is not mentioned as living during Jesus' ministry. Only after Joseph's passing could Jesus have presented Himself as King of the Jews.

44a This whole subsection is parenthetical, telling what was said later that day. The next subsection resumes His parables spoken to the crowds.

  b The truths withheld were not concerning the way of salvation, but were secrets of the Kingdom, reserved for children of the Kingdom. Jesus never gave the way of salvation in parabolic language.

  c The Kingdom "of God" and "of Heaven" were interchangeable terms, Matthew alone using the latter for Jewish readers. When both occur in parallel accounts, both are quoted.

44d Doubtless, following His explanation (given earlier) of the parable of the four soils.

45a Not only is this exquisitely told, and a demonstration of His power as God's Son, but it also shows the heaven-directed accuracy of the writers. Thirty-one exact quotations form these 13 inimitable sentences, with nothing added in the interweaving and nothing omitted.

46a The Grk. *a certain man* seems appropriately rendered thus here and in John 11:49 (Sec. 106). Matthew speaks of two restored to sanity, but it is evident that one in particular was a violent and notable case. The companion may have been female. The tombs were doubtless caves.

b Why this? Because it meant no destruction to themselves and would incense the (Gentile) populace there against Jesus. Why then did He grant it? Doubtless, to emphasize the cost of discipleship in contrast to the former approach of calling men by acts of mercy (which approach to Israel was without response).

47a They looked *hopefully*, for "other small ships" had left there the evening before and very likely had been lost in the storm. So the seemingly irrelevant reference to them in Mark, supplemented by this from Lk. 8:40, shows that Jesus' stilling of the storm became public knowledge. It may explain Matthew's banquet in His honor, held in spite of a traditional fast.

48a The clause dates the banquet and its sequel just before the raising of Jairus' daughter; hence it followed the storm and the episode at Gadara, fitting thus into the order of events in Mark and Luke.

49a In three successive episodes the emphasis had been on "your *faith*," "only *believe*," and again "your *faith*."

50a Just when John sent his disciples, or when they found Jesus after journeying 100 miles or more (from Machaerus) we are not told. But it was in the summer of great crowds and many miracles, and forms a fitting climax to them by the nature of Jesus' reply. Note also that He did not criticize John, though He did not use His power to free him, as may have been expected. John was to precede Him to heaven, as he had preceded Him on earth; Jesus here referred to "the time of John" as having ended.

b Not literally, obviously, but as Gabriel said (Sec. 5), *in the spirit and power* of Elijah. For the receptive, John filled the office of Elijah in preparing them for Messiah.

**51a**   If John, the writer, had had modern punctuation available, it is probable he would have used "quotes" as here. For this reads like the advertising placard extolling the pool on behalf of its operators. It is understandable if it was stricken from an early edition of the Gospels by someone doubting the truth of the claim. Further, the invalid is not said to have been *at the pool* for 38 years; he may have been brought there but recently and so gave credence to the claim, caused by underground disturbances of the water. In any case, the point John made was not the supposed healing powers of the pool, but that Jesus here took occasion to give a "sign" to *Jerusalem.*

  **b**   The point is not that Jesus actually broke the Sabbath, but that He did so in the view of "the Jews." He rather showed Himself to be "Lord of the Sabbath," or creator and disposer of the Sabbath. They were Sabbath worshippers, having made the Sabbath their *god.*

  **c**   Jesus emphasized His submission to the Father as a true Son of Man, ever doing the Father's will and always operating in the Spirit's power.

**52a**   A comparison of Matt. 13:53 and Mark 4:35, indicates that the statement, "And Jesus withdrew from there," must be incorporated at this juncture rather than following the parables by the sea. Matthew here skips over the journey to Gadara and return (because he has already related it in Matt. 8-9), and immediately records the Nazareth affair. The placing of the withdrawal statement here is justified in that it forms a transition to the following story of the Nazareth visit as Matthew intended it to do, although the antecedent of "there" is obviously not the same in the combination.

**53a**   This preaching journey seems to have started from Nazareth, and so may have continued in southern Galilee. From there the six teams of disciples could go in all directions in Palestine. Note that the motive in Jesus' enormous labors was *compassion,* as told so definitely here.

  **b**   Matthew seems to group here as one discourse things uttered on various occasions. This applies to Matt. 10:17-23, used by us in the Olivet discourse (Sec. 132) where it interweaves perfectly, and Matt. 10:34-36, used with Luke's parallel report in Sec. 89. The remainder shows genuine unity. [It is essential to recognize that

53b Matthew's plan is thematic in contrast to the chronological plan of Mark. Ed.]

c These tours were continued from that fall until the following spring (Sec. 55).

54a Aithough Josephus (Ant. 18.5.2) attributes this arrest to Herod's fear of John's hold on the people, Mark's statement is not inconsistent with his. Herod's fear of a rebellion might well have come from their hearing of John's denunciation of his adultery. Josephus did not always tell the whole story.

b Not from fear of Herod, for He continued here and later in Herod's realm, Galilee and Perea. Instead it must have been in deep sorrow and prayer.

55a Most of this paragraph and many shorter parts of what follows come from the Gospel of John. Up to this point his voice has been separate from those of the other three evangelists, but here we come to an outstanding variation: *four* voices join in complete harmony down to the smallest detail. Further, what they tell here is one of the most widely-known and significant events in all of Jesus' dealings with Israel. If these claims were untrue, there were hundreds still living when the Gospels were written who could have disputed what is told here, but no enemy of Christ came forward with any such proof. That fact and the way the four accounts fit together *proves* the Gospels' accuracy *and the historicity of John's Gospel.* This will be demonstrated also in a number of later portions where John's voice will mingle with the others more frequently and with the same complete unity and clarity.

b This must have been His way of observing the Passover, as otherwise there was no point in John's mentioning the imminence of that feast. And it appears that *Jesus attended no Passover at Jerusalem after the one where He was rejected*, until the Passover of the Crucifixion.

56a It was a strong windstorm, not necessarily with clouds; also it was the time of the Passover full moon.

b The Grk. reads simply "I AM," with "It is" left unspoken but evidently His meaning. In the light of a later utterance (see note 68a) He thus identified Himself with the divine Voice of Ex. 3:14.

c The Gennesaret ministry was resumed following the discourse of the next day (Sec. 57), as shown in the first sentence of Sec. 58.

57a  Enterprising fishermen had, no doubt, responded to the people's plight, transporting them across the sea.

b  The "seal," doubtless referring to the Voice from heaven at His baptism, and the Holy Spirit in the form of a dove.

c  John's reference to "the Jews" usually signifies "the scribes and Pharisees."

d  Obviously a symbolism; i.e., Christ's perfect (but broken) life on earth and His sacrificial death are the true believer's spiritual food, as pictured in the elements of the memorial bread and cup.

58a  Mark adds this comment on the first century problem of "clean" vs. "unclean" meats.

59a  Here a new chapter opens not only in our arrangement but in the character of Jesus' labors, a transition from dealing primarily with Israel to His going to various regions of the Gentiles. His rejection by Capernaum (Sec. 57) had been a heavy blow, followed (Sec. 58) by the questioning of a large delegation from Jerusalem sent to undermine His influence.

60a  But evidently not the same mountain as in earlier episodes.

61a  This is clearly a separate instance from that of Sec. 55, both cases being reported in both Matthew and Mark. And it is not a mere redundancy, for it shows the response of the *Gentile* world in the size of the crowds, their eagerness and desire, and the rewards received by the many healings and now this food. Note that the restored demoniac (Sec. 46) may have started it all!

62a  This may likely refer to the 69 sevens (or "weeks") of Dan. 9:25, which were to mark the interval until Messiah. (See Sir Robert Anderson's THE COMING PRINCE, pp. 51 ff.)

b  He meant that there was no need to worry about bread, but to avoid the Pharisees' traditionalism and the Sadduccees' skepticism.

63a  Bethsaida had rejected Him (cf. Sec. 79); hence this command to stay away.

64a  With His tours in Sidonia and the Decapolis occupying the late spring and summer of this third year of ministry, it was now early fall. Great crowds would go to Jerusalem for this October Thanksgiving "festival"; so the stepbrothers' challenge was a natural one. (Concerning the placing of John 7-10 here, see App. IV).

65a  The "one work" spoken of was probably His healing the invalid man at the pool, Sec. 51.

65b Some knew of the intent to kill Him, but not all (see preceding paragraph).

66a More than 30 years having passed, those who knew of His birth in Bethlehem had either died, were not present, or remained silent.

67a This passage speaks for itself as an appropriate and authentic account, although omitted in the earliest extant texts. The answer to the problem may be that it was deleted in the post-apostolic period for fear of its being used as an excuse for sin.

68a That is, *the Messiah*, the Holy One, indeed the "I AM" who spoke in the burning bush of Ex. 3:14. The Grk. reads, *if you believe not that I AM* ("HE" being an English addition).

b They were to know it by His resurrection, and even (like the centurion) by His conduct on the cross.

c Their emphatic "We" distinguished them from Him whom they presumed was the son of Joseph and thus conceived out of wedlock.

d Because of His dealings with Samaritans (Sec. 25).

e He had probably aged greatly in His labors and sorrows, and the questioners may not have seen Him on His earlier visits there.

69a Not the same day but at some time between Tabernacles and Dedication (Sec. 70). Note that the disciples were with Jesus in Jerusalem.

b An allusion to His statement in Sec. 23, next to the last paragraph.

70a Stoning to death was the Jews' punishment for blasphemy (Lev. 24:16).

b The language suggests a rather substantial stay, described by one who was there.

71a This withdrawal from Perea was not from rejection but for a time of secluded rest in the north. Furthermore, there were confidential matters to be discussed. After fulfilling these purposes He came back to Perea (end of Sec. 77).

b In Sec. 57, Peter as spokesman for the disciples said, "You are the Holy One of God," but now he made the full declaration for which Jesus had waited.

c The Grk. *Petra* distinguishes this from Simon Peter personally, who was a "Little Rock." [Note Eph. 2:20, where the foundation is seen to be "the apostles and prophets, Jesus Christ himself being the chief corner stone."]

71d The proper rendering of the future perfect indicative verb; i.e.,

71d  assuming Peter's actions are to be in accord with heaven.

71e  Having been rejected by the nation as their Messiah, He was preparing to fulfill His role as the *Suffering Servant* (Isa. 53), moving toward the cross.

72a  Obviously, this journey was to be the last. Its beginning is told in Sec. 78, the *only* journey remaining as the Story is here arranged.

  b  Doubtless a reference to the vision of Christ in His glory on the mount which directly followed.

73a  Elijah had talked with Jesus but had not himself as yet returned as foretold in Mal. 4:5-6. Jesus explained that that coming is yet future, though John came in his "spirit and power."

  b  This could be a reference to I Kings 19:10.

74a  Doubtless taunting their inability to restore this boy.

  b  He spoke perhaps of Mt. Hermon, which was still in sight, where the Transfiguration must have occurred.

  c  A rebuke to their "professionalism" and lack of prayer to seek God's power.

75a  The private character of their withdrawal journey is thus shown.

76a  This tax for the temple, payable preceding Passover, was naturally overdue, for Jesus had not been here, His adopted home town, since the Passover more than a year earlier, when Capernaum rejected Him. So the collectors hastened to collect, for He was no longer a citizen of distinction, and might soon leave (as He did).

77a  This and the similar hyperbole in Sec. 39, are both reported by Matthew; it is not a parallel or a duplication, but belongs in both contexts.

  b  Evidently the child in their midst was one of others nearby. Their status in the Kingdom in their age of innocence is here beautifully portrayed.

  c  A reference to Deut. 19:15.

  d  More than $10,000,000 (as compared to 100 days' wages below).

78a  So He begins the final journey foretold in Sec. 72, with Perea the starting point of an indirect tour of great extent, as presently appears.

  b  A Jewish way of saying, "remain home till my father dies."

79a  The 70 heralds were sent two by two to *not less than 35 localities*, perhaps more, to be visited on foot by Jesus on this tour. We are not told what directions were taken, nor are the localities named, except that the journey was to lead at last to Jerusalem; its

79a importance was chiefly in the character of Jesus' teachings. This great journey well accounts for the time remaining till the Passover of A.D. 33. It also included two visits at Bethany (Sec. 81,105) and an unstipulated interval at Ephraim (Sec. 106).

b They were *not* told to avoid "Gentile neighborhoods and any city of Samaritans" now (Sec. 53), for in view of Israel's refusal the invitation was now open to all.

c Perhaps a symbolic reference to enemies of the truth, reminding us of John the Baptist's calling some of his hearers "You offspring of vipers."

80a The Grk. reads, "And taking it up, Jesus said." The setting is not given, but the telling of this incident here is significant. Jesus was Himself the *Samaritan* (called so in Jerusalem, cf. note 68d), Who *ministered* to Israel's wounds instead of passing by on the other side. This great final tour was a supreme expression of His compassion, being undertaken in the spirit of the servant in the fig tree parable. (Sec. 90)

81a Not "they" but "He" went into this village, and the word "they" harks back to the 70 heralds of Sec. 79. Probably Jesus rested at the home of Mary, Martha, and Lazarus while the heralds were on their errand, though this visit was delayed in the telling to give precedence to other matters. Whether these friends lived at Bethany at this time is not told, but is probable.

82a Followers other than the Twelve were often called disciples; so here was a man not present in the instance of Sec. 39. Further, the differences in the model prayer are not errors in reporting. It was not fitting now to add "For thine is the Kingdom . . .", for the Kingdom offered had been rejected and must now remain in the background.

b With different listeners and contexts, He repeats this important teaching given earlier (Sec. 39); it is, therefore, not a duplication but is needed for completeness.

83a The same principle applies here as in note 82b. (Cf., Sec. 43)

b Asserting His true relationship to "the strong man," Satan, and his "house." He would take his "house" after He bound the "strong man," doubtless prophetic.

c This saying concerned non-believers in contrast to the reverse saying in Sec. 77, that concerned sincere believers.

84a Hebrew idiom regarded any fragment of a day as a *Nuktlemeron* or a "day and night" (Farrar).

b Again see note 82b. (Cf. Sec. 39)

85a Cf. Sec. 80, another answer to a lawyer; also Sec. 126.

86a The great gathering of crowds here was partly precipitated by His challenging the religious leaders (Secs. 84-86).

b Again see note 82b. (Cf. Sec. 53)

90a Cf. note 62a.

b For chronological significance of this parable, see App. IV.

92a This was not meant literally, of course, for it was some months until the journey's end. It was a riddle to be given Herod, meaning that even Herod could not change His purpose to die at Jerusalem.

94a Hyperbole is here used for exaggerated contrast to emphasize the priority of one's love for Christ over all else.

95a Again note 82b applies (Cf. Sec. 77).

98a By our using Lk. 16:16-18 elsewhere (Secs. 50, 39, 104, respectively), this paragraph forms a unity with what follows.

b Jesus alludes to His own rising (and perhaps that of Lazarus) from the dead. (Cf. note 2e)

101a Or "within you." ("You" is used in the generic sense) Although the Kingdom will be revealed in an outward manifestation in the Messianic reign, it is essentially spiritual, beginning in the heart.

b This parabolic saying has special meaning for the closing days of this age, showing the coming of the Kingdom after a time of carnage in Palestine.

104a Jesus specified *fornication* (here and in Sec. 39) as being the only legitimate ground for divorce in the eyes of God, it being so devastating as to spiritually kill the union.

106a The words "when I come" are strongly implied since Martha has spoken of "the resurrection at the last day."

b His deity and humanity are pictured together, as so often in the Gospels.

107a This was the last authentic prophecy in Israel (except for the things yet to be uttered by our Lord, Israel's last true High Priest).

108a Probably the ruler of the synogogue in some town on their journey.

b Jesus acknowledged and emphasized the ruler's unknowing confession of His Oneness with God.

108c Not just a reference to a low gate in the city wall, for the Grk. indicates an actual needle for sewing. [Luke specifies a surgical needle. Jesus' later statement signifies it was "impossible," not merely difficult; Ed.]

110a Amazingly true, for this was at least the seventh explicit reference to His coming death (previously in Secs. 69, 72, 73, 92, and twice in 75).

111a The rebuke to them was direct, but a gentle one, as also in Sec. 78.

113a Not only by descent but by the faith and works of Abraham. Zaccheus' change of heart was what mattered, not his past.

114a A picture of Israel's attitude as shown a few days later, Secs. 153, 154.

115a Matthew's account is partly used here as well as in Sec. 112, for he recorded the two cases together. Luke reported only the first case (on the approach to Jericho) and Mark this one (on their leaving Jericho). The similarity suggests that Bartimeus heard what happened to the other blind man and used the same approach, meeting a similar response. No evangelist gives all the details of any occurrence; combining the accounts gives a clearer picture.

116a The Synoptists place this supper in a thematic context to contrast Mary with Judas; John definitely establishes the time of the supper as being on Saturday evening. His entry into Jerusalem occurred on Sunday.

b Meaning of course not the literal day by "the day of my burial." And just as the woman in Sec. 42 anointed Him as Prophet, so Mary unknowingly anointed Him as *Priest*, the One who by His death would *mediate* between God and men. (Also, since He was anointed by the Spirit of God at His baptism, there still remains to be accomplished only His anointing *by Israel as King*, when their eyes are opened to His identity.)

117a Note that *32 parts* were fitted together to include every element of all four writers' narratives in these two paragraphs; yet the result reads as if one hand could have written it, and any supposed discrepancy is shown to be non-existent.

b His entry as Messiah was "Triumphal" in the enthusiasm of His followers from Galilee and other country districts, but to the populace of Jerusalem, He was only an object of curiosity. His true Triumphal entry is yet future and this was only a prophetic foreview.

118a A "tree" was a well-known Jewish symbol for national authority, and a fig tree is pictured even today on one of Israel's coins. The fig tree characteristically bore fruit when it produced leaves.

   b Although this *seems* similar to Sec. 22, the details are distinctly different; it was fitting that He should fulfill Mal. 3:1-3 symbolically at both the beginning and close of His labors as the "Messenger of the Covenant."

119a The disciples were evidently unaware of the fulfillment of the fig tree parable (Sec. 90), and Jesus did not choose to elaborate, but pointed to other lessons instead. The seeming discrepancy as to the time of this question is only because Matthew did not trouble to mention (21:20) that another night had intervened. Mark's account is more specific.

   b This hyperbole was similar to one in common Jewish use concerning the seemingly impossible.

120a His authority to cleanse the temple, no doubt, the administering of which belonged to the Sanhedrin.

121a This sentence negates the *silent Wednesday* theory (as does also a statement in Sec. 133). While the evangelists give no strict dating of most discourses in this week, they show that the Olivet discourse was on Wednesday.

122a Another clear allusion to the fig tree parable (Sec. 90). The vineyard of the Lord of hosts was Israel as a people (Is. 5:7); the fig tree planted in that vineyard was their nation of that day, and especially its leaders, who readily recognized that they were also the vineyardists in the present parable.

123a A veiled forecast of the destruction of Jerusalem in A.D. 70.

124a This was a cunning challenge. A "no" would embroil Him with the civil authorities, a "yes," with the ecclesiastical, who held that such payment dishonored the rule of Jehovah. But Jesus used it to teach a significant lesson, while rebuking their hypocrisy.

125a The Sadducees intended their question to discredit both Jesus and the concept of a life hereafter. Jesus referred them to Ex. 3:6, to show that Abraham still lived though dead.

126a Here Jesus quoted the Jews' favorite scripture for rejecting Him as God's Son. [In the passage quoted, Deut. 6:4, the Hebrew term used for "one" is *echad* rather than *yakeed*, signifying a *oneness* with diversity within, as husband and wife are one. Gen. 2:24, Ed.]

127a The obvious answer was that such a Son had to be more than a mere man; the Lord gave David's confirmation of His deity which they so wanted to disprove.

b A confirmation of note 121a.

128a For the third time now He states this principle (previously in Secs. 93 and 103), emphasizing its importance. He also exemplified it in His life.

b Another forecast of the destruction of Jerusalem, A.D. 70, which many of those He was addressing would experience.

c As a small minority of the nation testified in Sec. 117.

129a Her deed is told not only for its own sake but for contrast with the picture in Sec. 128.

130a Jesus does not ignore the Greeks, but shows how their approach to Him would be on the basis of His work on the cross.

b They recognized that His being "lifted up" meant to die by crucifixion, but could not reconcile this with His being the Messiah. As it was too soon to answer in detail, He only asked them to believe.

131a A reference to Isa. 6:1-10. John says the One whom Isaiah saw was the same One whom they rejected.

b This was His last public utterance to Israel, declaring the Father's authority behind His message.

132a Though this may have seemed an incredible prediction, it was literally fulfilled. He also said (Sec. 117) that the *stones would cry out*, and this they still do in testimony to His Sonship; for not one is left upon another today, except part of the foundation, the wailing wall.

b The instruction given concerns the faithful of the "end-time" period just prior to the King's return to earth, of which the disciples had asked. The persecution, fleeing from city to city, and world-wide proclamation of the King's return must be seen in this context where Jesus put it.

c The sign for which they asked was to be that spoken of by Daniel which he placed three and one-half years before the end (Dan. 8:11-13; 9:27; 11:31). The obvious implication is that the temple will be rebuilt before that desecration occurs.

d Could this regathering "from one end of the heavens to the other" refer to man's invading space? If so, the supernatural character of this One is again emphasized, for such a possibility was scientific

132d foolishness until the present generation.

e By "generation" Jesus may have referred to the ethnic race of Israel which would inevitably continue until all God's prophecies were fulfilled. Another possibility is that Jesus referred to that particular "generation" of the end-time who, in spite of the great Jewish purge, would persist to behold the coming of the Kingdom just mentioned.

f There are similarities in this parable to the one in Sec. 114, but the differences are far greater.

g This judgment will be a judgment of those living just prior to the King's return, determining who will enter with Him into His Millennial Kingdom. Their judgment will be based on their treatment of His brethren (the 144,000 of Rev. 7), and their response to their message of salvation in the King's return. It is not a "works" salvation, but a response of faith.

133a A generally accepted reckoning has been to count these two days on the same basis as the previously mentioned six days (see note 116a), i.e., from Thursday evening. It thus placed the foregoing Olivet discourse late on Tuesday, and left Wednesday unaccounted for, hence called "silent Wednesday." But notice how *Jesus* counted them: after two days the Passover *and the betrayal and crucifixion.* These were on *Friday* (according to Luke 24:21 and other time indications in the record, cf. note 121a). Also, it is probable that that day began with Sec. 128.

b Matthew and Mark recount at this point the anointing of Jesus in Bethany, but do not say that this was when it occurred, whereas John gives a definite dating (Sec. 116) of what was plainly the same event. Judas' offer, however, belongs here, probably in the early hours of Thursday.

134a The day of Unleavened Bread was reckoned as involving eight days, thus beginning the same time as Passover.

b Ordinarily only women carried water.

135a That is, before the supper now beginning.

b That is, gladly render any helpful or even menial service to each other.

c Cf. note 68a.

136a Jesus' reply to Judas had perhaps been inaudible to the others; also more than one dipped in the wide dish with the Lord.

136b Not inconsistent with Sec. 133, for Satan can enter and re-enter.

c His leaving was, of course, to notify the chief priests where Jesus could be found, thus setting off the chain of events leading to the cross.

d Sec. 68, second subsection.

139a Peter was pondering Jesus' statement at end of Sec. 136.

b Confirming and enlarging upon His promise in Sec. 109.

140a Here referring to Peter's question in Sec. 139.

b The Grk. *Paracletos* means *One called alongside.*

c Still expecting his Messiah to appear in an immediate Messianic age, he receives an indirect answer, but not a rebuke.

d It reads as if the disciples had a secretary recording every word, who wrote down even this detail. But it is evident that, after they rose and picked up their belongings, Jesus resumed speaking and they gathered about Him till the prayer and the closing hymn.

e In Sec. 135, second subsection.

f Peter had asked, but now there was no need to.

g Speaking of His resurrection.

142a In Sec. 53, also 79.

144a His function was to locate and identify Jesus at night, a necessary service to expedite the proceedings before next sundown.

b Cf. note 68a.

c Undoubtedly John Mark who provides the detail.

145a As a retired general is still called "General", Annas was still referred to as high priest.

146a Again John avoids the first personal pronoun.

b Secs. 146-148 are composed of 77 parts from *four* writers' differing accounts, including their every detail, yet form a vivid and convincing narrative that reads like the work of one hand.

147a That is, all of the Sanhedrin then present.

b Recognized by the High Priest as a reference to Dan. 7:13-14.

c Nicodemus and Joseph of Arimathea were probably absent from this illegal, nocturnal trial.

148a The probability is that this clause was deleted in some early edition of Mark because of its seeming inconsistency with Jesus' prediction. Combining the four accounts shows that it belongs in the record, forming an appropriate link to solve what has long been a puzzling "discrepancy."

148b Counting the first denial in Sec. 146, the combined accounts thus reveal a total of six denials, three before each of two cock-crowings, as seen in Jesus' two warnings to Peter, Secs. 139, 142. (See Appendix II).

149a A greater number than those who met after midnight in Sec. 147.

150a Described further in Acts 1:18.

151a An indication of their meticulous concern for "hand ritual" in contradistinction to their purposeful intent to unjustly condemn and slay Messiah.

  b He was to die by being "lifted up" (i.e., crucifixion), not by the Jewish method of execution which was stoning.

  c The words for "now" and "from here" are in the place of emphasis in the Grk. The implication is that there *is coming a time* when His Kingdom will be centered physically in the earthly sphere.

152a Probably the purple clothing and crimson cloak which appear later in the narrative, though removed for the scourging.

153a An effort to release Jesus by threatening the alternate release of one who was dangerous to society (Acts 3:13-14).

  b An attempt to release Him by appeasing their sadistic nature.

154a The word for "preparation" and "Friday" is the same, *paraskeue.*

  b Thus He was clothed with *both* colors, of which Mark mentions one and Matthew the other; one or both garments were probably supplied by Herod (Sec. 152).

155a Cf. Romans 16:13.

  b Another reference to the fig tree nation and the fate it was to suffer.

  c The "third hour" mentioned here (and later the "sixth" and "ninth" hours) represents Jewish sundial time.

  d Slight differences between the accounts are due to the different languages of the inscription, one account based on one, the other on another.

156a In mockery of His agony, as He writhed in pain, as also pictured in Psalm 22:7-8. (Indeed most of that Psalm, written ten centuries earlier, is a prefiguring of His crucifixion.)

  b A clear example of salvation by faith, completely apart from works or rituals.

  c Probably in Jerusalem rather than in Galilee.

157a This could not be a solar eclipse, for it was the time of the *full* moon.

**157b** A different Grk. word from the "vinegar" of Sec. 155. The wine was there for the soldiers' refreshment and did not contain the stupefying myrrh.

   c Spoken to the centurion.

**158a** A supernatural occurrence, for this was a thickly woven curtain more than 30 feet tall. (Cf. Hebrews 6:19-20)

   b His realization now advanced beyond his earlier exclamation, which had harked back to Pilate's final statement, Sec. 154. He saw Him now as a supernatural Being.

   c By comparing with two names in Sec. 52, it is possible that this was the mother of Jesus.

   d A special or "high" Sabbath because conjoined with the Passover festival.

   e The plural "you" is emphatic in the Grk.

**159a** A fulfillment harking back to Isaiah 53:9.

   b By apothecary weight about 100 lbs.

**160a** Thus to the Jews "after three days" and "the third day" meant the same. By their reckoning, Friday, the Crucifixion day, was the "first" day, Saturday the second, and Sunday the third.

   b The stone was round like a huge millstone or cart wheel and was set upright against the cave in an inclined groove. The Roman seal wedged the stone in place.

**161a** Matthew's puzzling first statement (28:1) is in his typical abbreviated style by which he omits the purchase of the spices by the women. This omission has caused some to judge that Jesus rose on Saturday evening, in spite of the other Gospels' testimony otherwise. But his "late on the Sabbath" is modified by the clause "as it began to dawn toward the first day of the week." What the verse says is only that *the women went to the tomb the morning following its sealing*, that morning being specified by Matthew as the one that followed the Sabbath.

   b Evidently the earthquake was well before dawn, for the guards recovered and departed before the Magdalene's arrival.

   c This "spurious" passage of Mark thus confirms John's account. As to the evident authenticity of this and other statements in Mark 16:9-20, see note 167a.

   d Her "we know not" does not suggest that other women were with her. As a woman addressing two men, who likewise did not

161d "know", she respectfully included her hearers with herself. Note also that at the meeting with Jesus she was still alone. The other women's part in the matter was after sunrise.

    e John, though so actively involved, still avoids using the first personal pronoun, a strong confirmation of Johannine authorship.

    f The grave-clothes lay as the body had withdrawn through and out of them (Westcott), as He also later went through doors.

    g Probably a reference to Psalm 16:10, Peter's text in his Pentecost sermon (Acts 2:27).

    h The verses naming Mary Magdalene with the other women (Matt. 28:1, Mark 16:1, Luke 24:10) are *summary* statements, two of these writers, Matthew and Luke omitting to specify that the Magdalene's part was separate. Mark, however, after thus summarizing, particularized by explaining that her part was separate and earlier. This was later made more understandable to readers by John's detailed account. This listing of the women who arrived after sunrise omits Mary Magdalene, since her part in the story of the morning has been completed (Luke 24:10).

    i The angels being six feet apart, at the head and feet of the burial place, only one could be seen from the entrance. Upon the women's entering they both stood.

    j So, the women were with Jesus and the disciples on the return from Caesarea Philippi (Sec. 72), the only time He spoke thus in Galilee.

    k Peter was given special mention because of the denials and to prepare him for a special visit.

    l Among His last words to the disciples (Sec. 142, and cf. note 140g).

    m After saying to Mary, "Touch me not, . . ." He had possibly ascended to the Father and returned. The short time interval and long "distance" were, of course, no problem for the glorified Lord.

    n Their continuing unbelief concerning Jesus' resurrection points up the great improbability that they could have built the Christian movement on "hallucinations" or wishful thinking. Nothing short of a personal witness of His resurrection could have changed the direction of their despondent thinking.

    o Thus, twisting the explanation of the guards that they were rendered senseless for a time. But the chief priests failed to explain how, if they were asleep, they knew that *the disciples* took the body.

162a Doubtless, including some of the 59 quotations from the Old Testament which occur in this Story.

 b It was typical of Jesus that, because of the apostles' unbelief, He appeared first not to them but to a woman (one formerly demon-possessed), then to other women and to two people from the countryside, before appearing to Peter and the Twelve.

163a Suggesting their fear of the future purge.

 b Proving beyond question this was no mere vision.

 c Jesus here emphasized the need of the Holy Spirit's discernment for the exercising of this authority.

164a This was following Sunday evening by Jewish reckoning (eight days inclusive).

165a The leadership of Peter is again highlighted.

 b Peter had claimed a greater love than the others in saying that although all forsook Him, he never would (Sec. 142). Peter's response to Jesus asserted a warm, natural affection, based on emotions, whereas Jesus inquired as to his deep spiritual esteem, based on a reasoned commitment to Him. Love for Christ was essential to service for Christ.

166a Probably Mt. Tabor (note 32a). The hearers of this Great Commission are probably the "500 brethren" of I Corinthians 15:6.

 b The guarantee of His presence here is not geographical, "end of the world," but temporal, "end of the age" (although the other is certainly true also). He would be ever with them throughout the age as they discipled the "nations".

167a A cogent reason for the authenticity of this passage in Mark is the coherent conclusion it provides for the Story. In the preceding section, Jesus was in Galilee; yet His ascension was from the Mount of Olives at Jerusalem. Here in Mark we have the needed link. The disciples had returned and were at dinner in Jerusalem, when He appeared unannounced (as He did also in Sec. 163). He spoke these farewell words as found in Mark and Luke, then led the way out to near Bethany for His departure. The incorporation of this "spurious" passage in Mark from Textus Receptus is so fitting and credible as to constitute a strong confirmation of its authenticity.

 b In His final words, He gave a sweeping statement of the essential elements of the gospel relating to its objective source and its

167b subjective power in individuals. Having completed the objective work, He would now send forth the Holy Spirit to work in and through individuals. For His further instruction, see Acts 1:5-8.

It is also to be noted that the last three sections of the Story constitute a unified conclusion, utilizing the concluding materials of all four Gospels. This was also true of the introduction which was unified by incorporating the details of all four. This is a capstone evidence of the superintendence of a divine Author Who guided the four human writers to infallibly record the facts as they knew them, in their own style, and yet with the accuracy and imprimature of the Spirit of God Himself.

## FOOTNOTES TO THE APPENDICES

[1] Or the "Received Text," dating to Erasmus and built on the later MSS of the Byzantine Texts, rather than the earlier now available.

[2] Robert Coughlan, "Who Was the Man Jesus?" LIFE, Vol. 57, No. 26 (December 25, 1964), pp. 90-91.

[3] George Ogg, CHRONOLOGY OF THE PUBLIC MINISTRY OF JESUS (Cambridge: Cambridge University Press, 1940), pp 203-277.

[4] Wm. A. Stevens and Ernest D. Burton, A HARMONY OF THE GOSPELS (New York: The International Committee of Young Men's Christian Associations, 1905), pp. 128-134.

[5] Archibald M. Hunter, "Interpreting the Parables," INTERPRETATION, Vol. XIV, 1960, p. 443. See also Hunter's work, INTERPRETING THE PARABLES (Phil.: The Westminster Press, 1960), p. 82.

# A SUGGESTED OUTLINE
## FOR A COURSE ON THE LIFE OF CHRIST*

**THE INTRODUCTION OF JESUS AS MESSIAH**

## Lesson 1 — The Four Gospels' Introduction of Christ.

1- Mark's divine title. (Sec. 1)
2- John's introduction of the Son of God. (Sec. 2)
3- Matthew's introduction of the Son of David and of Abraham. (Sec. 3, 9)
4- Luke's certification of the story. Jesus' physical lineage. (Sec. 4,16)

## Lesson 2 — The Birth and Preparation of Jesus

1- The birth of John the Forerunner. (5, 8)
2- The announcements by the angel. (6)
3- The birth of Jesus and the shepherds' visit. (10)
4- The worship of Simeon and Anna. (11)
5- The visit of the wise men and the fury of Herod. (12)
6- The flight and sojourn in Egypt. (13)
7- Jesus attends Passover at age 12. (14)

## Lesson 3 — The Baptism and Temptation of Jesus.

1- John the Baptist seeks to prepare the nation. (15)
2- Jesus is baptised and anointed for service. (16)
3- Jesus is tested and approved as the Son of Man. (17)

**THE FIRST YEAR OF JESUS' MINISTRY**

## Lesson 4 — Jesus' Early Ministry In Jerusalem.

1- Introduced by John, He calls His first disciples. (18-20)
2- A preliminary miracle: water turned to wine. (21)
3- His judgment begins in cleansing the temple. (22)
4- A religious man, Nicodemus, is brought to the Kingdom. (23)
5- An immoral woman of Samaria is brought to the Kingdom. (25)

---

*For class instruction purposes:
1) Unify each lesson around the central theme. Some lessons may be further divided into two separate lessons.
2) From each event, generally speaking, one should seek the historical lesson taught, the doctrinal truth involved, and the abiding principle for current application. Christian theology is rooted in history and must be related to present-day living.

263

## Lesson 5 — Jesus' Early Ministry In Galilee.

1- He emphasizes faith in healing an officer's son. (26)
2- He is rejected by His home town of Nazareth. (27)
3- Moving to Capernaum, He enlists full time disciples. (28-29; 32)
4- Multitudinous healings including Peter's mother-in-law. (31)
5- A leper is healed for a testimony to the priests. (33)
6- Jesus displays His credentials to the leaders by forgiving sins. (34)

### THE SECOND YEAR OF JESUS' MINISTRY

## Lesson 6 — Jesus' Authority as Lord of the Sabbath.

1- Eating in the fields on the Sabbath. (36)
2- Restoring health on the Sabbath. (37)
3- The initial consultation to destroy Him. (37)
4- His ministry of mercy to outcasts and needy. (38)

## Lesson 7 — Jesus' Clarification of True Righteousness (The Sermon On the Mount).

1- He describes true children of the kingdom. (39a)
2- He notes the eternal character of the Law. (39b)
3- He stresses the internal character of the Law. (39c)

## Lesson 8 — Jesus Distinguishes True and Superficial Religion.

1- Almsgiving — the right and wrong motives. (39d)
2- Praying — the right and wrong approaches to God. (39e)
3- Fasting — the right and wrong concepts. (39f)
4- Daily living — the true way of life for a child of God. (39g)

## Lesson 9 — Jesus' Display of Messianic Powers.

1- He rewards the great faith of a Roman Centurion. (40)
2- He raises a widow's son from the dead. (41)
3- His miracles are attributed to demonry. (42-43)
4- He commands the winds and the sea. (45)
5- He commands a legion from the demon world. (46)
6- He declares the evident intransigence of Israel's leaders. (47)
7- He raises a girl from the dead. (48)
8- He reassures John the Baptist by His miracles. (50)

## Lesson 10 – Jesus' New Program Introduced by Parables.

1- Two parables on the planting of the kingdom. (44a)
2- Three parables on the growth of the kingdom. (44b)
3- Two parables on the value of the kingdom. (44c)
4- Two parables on responsibility in the kingdom. (44d)

## Lesson 11 – Jesus' Equality With the Father.

1- He alerts the leaders by healing at Bethesda. (51a)
2- His works are equal with those of the Father. (51b)
3- All judgment is given unto the Son. (51c)
4- As the Son of Man He does the Father's will. (51d)
5- He confirms His divine claims by four faithful witnesses. (51e)
6- In Galilee, He is again rejected at Nazareth. (52)

## Lesson 12 – Crucial Events at the Mid-point of His Ministry.

1- A wide solicitation is made to the lost sheep of Israel. (53)
2- John the Baptist is slain by Herod. (54)
3- Across the Sea Jesus feeds the 5000. (55)
4- Jesus walks on the raging Sea to reassure the Twelve. (56)

**THE THIRD YEAR OF JESUS' MINISTRY**

## Lesson 13 – Jesus' Rejection By His Home Town of Capernaum.

1- He reveals Himself as the "Bread" from heaven. (57a)
2- His denial of physical bread brings a mass desertion. (57b)
3- He denounces their religious hypocrisy. (58)
4- He turns to minister in Gentile areas. (59-63)

## Lesson 14 – Jesus' Ministry At The Feast of Tabernacles.

1- He is challenged by his unbelieving brothers. (64)
2- Jerusalem is confused as to His true identity. (65-66)
3- He shows mercy to a sinful woman but judgment to the Pharisees. (67)
4- He declares Himself the Light of the world and the I AM. (68)

**Lesson 15 — Jesus' New Fold For His Sheep.**

1- A blind man is healed and then excommunicated from Israel. (69a)
2- The healed man is given spiritual sight by Jesus. (69b)
3- Jesus declares Himself as "The Door" to life. (69c)
4- Jesus declares Himself as "The Good Shepherd." (69d)
5- Jesus declares the security of His sheep. (70)
6- He has a fruitful ministry in Perea. (70)

**THE FOURTH YEAR OF JESUS' MINISTRY**

**Lesson 16 — Jesus' Announcement of His Death and Resurrection.**

1- He reveals His plan to build the church. (71)
2- He reveals His coming death and resurrection. (72, 75)
3- He reveals His Glory in Transfiguration. (73)
4- He reveals the disciples' great need of God's power. (74)
5- He teases the unbelieving with a temple tax pittance. (76)

**Lesson 17 — Jesus' Invitation To Disciplined Service.**

1- He requires that personal ambitions be forsaken. (78)
2- Seventy disciples canvas Israel two by two. (79a)
3- The privileged cities of Galilee are condemned. (79b)
4- The Good Samaritan exemplifies service for God. (80)
5- Prayer is a Father-son relationship. (82)
6- To reject Christ is to invite demon control. (83, 90)

**Lesson 18 — Jesus' Denial of Further Signs to the Nation.**

1- Only the sign of Jonah to be given Israel. (84)
2- Their religion of hypocrisy denounced. (85, 86, 91)
3- The god of covetousness warned against. (87)
4- The need for servants to watch, work, and war. (88-89)
5- God's additional year of grace to Israel. (90)

**Lesson 19 — Jesus' Emphasis On Stringent Discipleship.**

1- Discipleship involves an active response. (92)
2- Discipleship involves humility and self-sacrifice. (93)
3- Discipleship involves renouncing all for Christ. (94)
4- Discipleship involves a concern for the lost. (95-96)
5- Discipleship involves stewardship and servanthood. (97-99)
6- Discipleship involves good family relations. (104
7- The need to be thankful, watchful, and prayerful. (100-103)

## Lesson 20 – Jesus' Final Solicitation On the Way to Jerusalem.

1- He challenges Jerusalem with His greatest miracle. (106-107)
2- He stresses the negative need to forsake personal idols. (108)
3- He states the principles in God's reward program. (109)
4- He receives the down-and-out and the up-and-out. (112-113; 115)
5- He stresses their need for faithfulness during His absence. (114)

**THE FINAL WEEK AND CONSUMMATION**

## Lesson 21 – Jesus' Final Word to the Jewish Leaders.

1- He enters Jerusalem in fulfillment of prophecy. (116-117)
2- He asserts Priestly authority in cleansing the temple. (118-120)
3- He condemns the leaders as anti-god and anti-Israel. (121-122)
4- He turns their questions into challenges. (124-127)
5- He condemns the leaders as henchmen of hell. (128)

## Lesson 22 – Jesus' Final Word to the Nation.

1- He symbolizes the nation in cursing the fig tree. (118, cf. 90)
2- He signifies His death will draw all classes of men. (130-131)
3- He predicts destruction of Jerusalem and the temple. (132a)
4- A time of unparalleled persecution will precede His 2nd coming. (132b)
5- His Second Coming will be in power and great glory. (132c)
6- The faithful will be characterized by active waiting. (132d)

## Lesson 23 – The Final Passover and the Lord's Supper.

1- The conspiracy of Judas. (133)
2- Jesus exemplifies humility in the foot-washing. (135)
3- The departure of Judas to commence his betrayal. (136)
4- The institution of the Lord's Supper. (137)
5- The first warning of Peter's denials. (138-139)

## Lesson 24 – Jesus' Final Word to His Own In the Upper Room.

1- His absence will be followed by an early return. (140a)
2- The Father will send the Holy Spirit. (140b)
3- They are united to Christ as a branch to a vine. (140c)
4- The new relationship will bring persecution, but also power. (140d)
5- Jesus prays to the Father. (141)

Lesson 25 — Jesus' Trial and Crucifixion.

1- His prayer in Gethsemane. (143)
2- His betrayal and arrest. (144)
3- His trial before the religious leaders. (145, 147, 149)
4- His denial by Peter. (146, 148)
5- His trial before the civil leaders. (151, 152, 153, 154)
6- His crucifixion on Golgotha. (155-158)
7- His burial and the seal. (159-160)

Lesson 26 — Jesus' Resurrection and Appearances To His Own.

1- He appears to the women near the tomb. (161)
2- He appears to the disciples near Emmaus. (162)
3- He appears to the ten disciples Sunday evening. (163)
4- He appears the following Sunday. (164)
5- He appears to the disciples at Galilee. (165)
6- He commissions the disciples for service. (166)
7- He ascends to heaven from the Mount of Olives. (167)

# INDEX OF SCRIPTURES

# INDEX OF SUBJECTS